Stillroom Cookery

Also by GRACE FIRTH

A NATURAL YEAR
LIVING THE NATURAL LIFE

Stillroom Cookery

The Art of Preserving Foods
Naturally, with Recipes, Menus
and Metric Measures

Grace Firth

Illustrations by Lynn Dudak

EPM Publications, Inc.

McLean, Virginia

Design by Gerard A. Valerio

Illustrations by Lynn Dudak

Library of Congress Cataloging in Publication Data

Firth, Grace.
  Stillroom cookery.

  Bibliography: p.
  Includes index.
  1. Cookery. 2. Food — Preservation. I. Title.
TX652.F49 641.4 76-28240
ISBN 0-914440-13-6

For Martin Firth,
Marie Firth,
Penny Firth,
that young people will understand
old ways as they reach for tomorrow.

Contents

Acknowledgments

I wish to extend my sincerest thanks to Virginia O'Neill and
Eleanor Prince of Calvert County, Maryland; Crimora Waite
and her splendid Culpeper, Virginia Library staff; Ruth Smith
and Ellen Anderson. I thank each and the many other friends who
have helped me with ideas and suggestions. I extend special apprecia-
tion to Jeffrey V. Odom of the National Bureau of Standards. Most of all I
thank Lewis, my husband, who encouraged me and tested all of my trials
and errors.

A Note about the Use of Metric

The recipes in this book, given in both customary and metric measurements, are seen as a bridge to the inevitable adoption of full metric cooking in the United States. To my knowledge STILLROOM COOKERY is the first general cookbook that converts traditional ways of cooking into the metric system.

This book is an ideal vehicle for introducing change because stillroom cookery was never an exact science. In years past cooks stirred "butter the size of a goose egg" into muffins and "a teacupful of top milk" into sauce. Converting old-fashioned directions into present day measurements is necessarily imprecise, and converting present recipes into metric units also leads to imprecision because the cups and spoons that we have been using do not readily convert into exact metric factors.

In STILLROOM COOKERY, I present the recipes in "reasonable or round conversion;" the metric measurements are rounded out. Thus, cooks can become familiar with ordinary metric units such as the 250 milliliter "metricup" while using early American recipes. Ratios of measurement are unchanged. The National Bureau of Standards, Department of Commerce, has worked out general guidelines similar to those used in Canada and these guides are incorporated in STILLROOM COOKERY. An appendix includes a brief description of the major metric units of measurement as they pertain to cooking and a complete temperature conversion chart.

G.F.

Stillroom Cookery

CHAPTER I

Doorways to the Stillroom

Stillroom cookery, the art of fermenting food to save it from spoiling, evolved naturally. Man first preserved food by drying, later he discovered that cooking and smoking also retarded decomposition. Foods immersed in pots of fat or honey were known as potted and the process preserved meats and cheeses for leaner days. Finally, salt or brine-fermented foods became popular and were called pickled. As recently as our grandparents' time all of these methods were used to give variety to pantry produce.

Pickled, potted, brewed or dried, foods were given wondrous flavors within the walls of ancient stillrooms; additionally, the act of preserving foods gave a family roots. Fermenting foods established an allegiance with the earth and gave people faith in tomorrow.

The stillroom in an early American home was a woman's secret stage, a sheltered bower where she could feel free to cohabit with friendly fungi and create enticing cheeses, breads, beers, pickles, sausages and schnapps. The stillroom of most nineteenth century homes was an unheated alcove of stone or heavy log built just outside the kitchen and attached to the house or constructed as a part of the detached summer kitchen. Earthen or stone-floored, the cool, dusky chamber served as a varmint-free work area where a woman could brew, make dyes, cure and hang meat, "destyl" medicines, pot cheese, pickle geriatric hens or design perfumes to captivate local swains. Philosophers mused that the secrets of all nature lay hidden in the stillrooms of New England and I can attest that an inner life was present in my own family's cellar in Missouri. Once when our cat had kittens on a barrel head, the cask blew, and foam, fur, kittens and fizz flooded the place as the mother cat flew into a purple rage. The earth's secret ferment certainly could not contain itself in that berry brew.

I came from a long line of fermenters; my grandfather could brew beer

3

from a corn cob and Grandma lost her finger tip to a tin-headed beer maker. I remember that a grandaunt had a two story stillroom, a whole bevy of kids and that she baked daily. Although I bake weekly and use a package of dry yeast, my aunt set a slushy sponge of ferment, flour and sugar to rise each night. The following day she saved out a cup of sponge to leaven the next batch of bread, then added salt, sugar, shortening, warm milk and stiffened the dough with flour. Her bread was "set to rise" over hot water in the stillroom except during the winter when everything and everybody clustered around the kitchen range. My aunt's generous goodies spilled over the county but she used words sparingly. When I asked her how she managed to bake four or five loaves every day plus tins of sweet hearth cakes and four kuchen at a time, she said simply, "Order."

In addition to the daily dough, my aunt sealed pots and spheres of cheese; she "put by" shelves of bottled beverages and firkins of wine, wide-mouthed crocks of potted meats; and stalactites of her sack meat and sausages swung from the rafters. My grandaunt's stillroom also housed a variety of pickled and dried pleasures together with medicinal and cosmetic curios.

Fermented fruits and vegetables were her answer to adolescents. "Youngsters gotta chew on something or someone to sharpen their teeth for society. A pickle bites back. When my kids get uppity with me, I tell 'em, 'Go get a pickle.'"

As America became more urban and manufacturing services spread, the stillroom gave way to the pantry and cellar. Pantries with their bins and barrels or basements crowded with bacteria encouraged our grand-parents to cure or ferment any surplus food that appeared on their doorsteps. Today, with modern refrigeration and convenience foods, many people have missed out on the things their forebears could have taught them to make. And how many of them have alienated themselves from the wonderful world of nature because so much of modern living is not real? Spinach in gritless cubes, parents striving for perfection in everything and always the escape tube with its Disney endings.

Sociologists tell us that man has four basic needs: security, response, recognition and new experience. They claim that neglecting any one of these basic needs leads to personal or social disorganization. Coaxing clabber into cheese may not save society, but it does forge a tiny link in the chain of personal contentment. Every cheese is a new experience; recognition and response are by-products of good food, . . . and certainly

there is security in knowing that if someone drops by, there is a treat on hand in a snack of homemade cheese, toast and tea.

Working with the natural processes of fermentation offers endless new experiences. I have experimented using directions planted by my grandparents in the crevices of my memory and found that fermenting your own food is pure fun. If you have an abundance of produce, and you have canned, frozen and given away all that you can, or if you just want to try something new to add zest and variety to ordinary fare, fermentation is the way to go.

You need no fancy equipment and probably no more space than what may otherwise be going to waste. I utilize a corner of our basement, a crawl space and the vegetable drawer at the bottom of our refrigerator for my stillroom. Out of these simple quarters has come a bounty of homemade breads, wines, beers and other brews, cured meats and fish, sauces, cheese and a variety of fermented milk products. In the following pages I will tell you not only how to copy my successes but also how to avoid some of my failures. My stillroom goodies are complemented by recipes that my family and I have enjoyed. I have selected items that can be fermented or processed in an ordinary kitchen using everyday utensils and the recipes are presented with metric as well as traditional measurements. Ingredients are listed at the point of use so that a scan will tell you if the dish meets your needs.

As you cross the threshold into the new world of fermented products, as in any new experience, you should think positive. This is especially important in dealing with milk products. Discard from your mind that demon concept, sour milk. Think clean-flavored cottage cheese instead, tangy feta or nutty cheddar; think of a blue-veined curd cavorting in a crisp salad, and be at ease.

A friend once asked, "Why do you make cottage cheese? It's so cheap to buy." "Fingertip convenience," was my answer. I usually keep a bit of milk clabbering, have my cloths and strings on a hook, my routine down pat and with a few minutes of attention every couple of days, I have an ever-ready source of fresh cheese that I slip into casseroles, salads, or sandwiches. Any leftover curd goes into refrigerator jars for ripening into middle-aged happiness or a full and splendid maturity. The last time someone questioned me about the smells attending the curing of my cheese, I hurried home (a bit wounded, I must admit) to the stillroom corner of the refrigerator and took inventory: There were the smoky paraffin-encased cheese, the waxy cheesecloth bags of double cream (Brie type) and the veined phony bleu that I make from skim milk. Outside the icebox, high on a shelf, the grating cheeses were drying, and I fingered their gritty flesh. In my mind the sweet milk odor of fresh curd draining over the sink, from whence all these cheeses came, wafted across my memory, and I wondered how anyone could not love everything about these wondrous cheeses.

Abruptly, my tantalized senses whirled and succumbing, I snatched a tight-lidded jar of fine, strong Limburger, poured a beer and sat back to evaluate. I thought of the actual time that I had put into making the smelly cheeses. No more than one hour to create, salt, inoculate, turn, resalt and "set to cure;" plus four months in the crisper, before eating or sealing. Thus assured, I spooned the last of the Limburger into a cup of fermenting curd to act as an inoculator and start the action on yet another batch of stillroom delight.

Most cooks have probably had some experience with the fermentation of yeast doughs. I grew up with kneading dough as a way of life. It wasn't until I became a teacher at a boarding school, however, and was called to substitute for the baker whenever he was hungover that I really learned much about yeast. I learned a lot from that lonely man with overcast eyes. He seemed endlessly to be seeking love and respect and at times it appeared that he actually needed to feel shame — an excuse to redeem himself with his glorious pastries.

That baker taught me that yeast transforms sugar into alcohol and carbon dioxide, which in turn puffs up dough because the gluten in wheat flour stretches like rubber. He taught me to knead with a firm yet gentle touch, that it was necessary to measure everything and that different flours require different amounts of moisture. He insisted that bread must rise three times. He taught me that old, refrigerated dough rolls out better than new for pizza or strudel; that with breadmaking there is hope, that without hope life is certain torture. My philosophical baker friend also taught me not to trust a man with overcast eyes; he made off with 40 gallons of my finest berry wine that was aging in the storeroom behind the flour.

My own family's introduction to home-fermented fizz drinks was a literal blast. We replaced the basement window and decided henceforth to read the directions more carefully. Now, after a half-a-lifetime of pleasant brewing, blending and drinking my discoveries, I can wholeheartedly recommend experimenting with ales, beers, stouts, wines, cider, and fizzy soft drinks in your own home stillroom corner. We use a wedge of basement space but I have brewed in my barracks room, in an apartment and behind the stove in a remote homestead cabin.

Ingredients vary but basically all fermented drinks are made out of liquid, flavoring, sugar and yeast. The yeasts eat the sugar and give off carbon dioxide and alcohol to create fizz and pow. Soft drinks are sealed immediately after mixing, thus the fermentation is stopped and both alcohol and fizz is minimal. The yeasts of beer are allowed to eat sugar and produce pow; but beer is capped before all of the sugars are devoured, thus beer has fizz and only a moderate amount of alcohol. Wine runs out the string; the gluttonous yeasts gobble sugar until they manufacture sufficient alcohol to kill their yeasty comrades and themselves.

Although true-blue oenologists would hardly consider my offbeat efforts as real wines, they are colorful and alcoholic, and some are great. I brew small batches of any edible flower or fruit, mix the ingredients, ferment at room temperature for about two weeks, strain, settle, bottle and cap lightly (or use a fermentation lock) to allow the wine to finish working in peace. When all primary fermentation stops, I seal with cork and paraffin. As in any stillroom cookery, after you have mastered the

basics you can experiment, but it is best to begin by using rules and extracts. Cleanliness and caution (to guard against flying glass) are vital concerns of brewing. Also vital, insofar as the Treasury Department is concerned, is a wine permit.

Beers, cordials and mock brandies are simple to make and great brewers of friendship. Because we were all busy and rarely visited one another, the women of our block decided to gather weekly at each others' houses for a three-to-five get together. We held fast to two rules: no talk about our children and no gossip. What hearty good chatter our 'Ladies Drinking Society' enjoyed. Although we often took nothing at all to drink, one time I led the ladies down into our musty cellar where I had lit candles and arranged kegs for seats. The seven of us opened, tasted and discussed mischievous as well as mundane wines and we had a ball! Actually we were still in the cellar when our husbands came home and they insisted on a scientific evaluation of our choices of the best brew. (The Blackberry Port and a Foxy Burgundy won.)

We had a wonderful neighborhood and I like to believe that fermentation helped to knit us together and lighten the lonely weight of suburbia. ... Bogus peach brandy over chipped ice at poolside. ... A bombasity beer on the back steps (from a neighboring brewmeister who mixed in twice as much sugar as prescribed and sugar determines alcohol content in fermented brew). ... Fourth of July with children racing around, laughter, music, fried chicken, potato salad and quarts and quarts of homemade rootbeer. ... Quiet foursomes, a clean, light beer, contented conversations. ... A sudden meeting and a robust drink to the health of the earth. ...

One hardly needs any reassurance about making his own brews because failures can nearly always be used as vinegar. Good vinegar can be made from most alcoholic liquids; the vagabond fungus MYCODERMA ACETI infiltrates and instead of appearing in a candlelit glass, the brew ends up in marinades or pickles. I would never discard a bad batch of brew. With a little ingenuity and a handful of herbs you can originate *"vinaigres bons et biaux!"* I especially like to flavor vinegar with herbs, decant them into jars and have their every-ready aromatic bite available for salad. I keep a jug of malt vinegar (a tawny, slightly bitter brew) in the cupboard for marinades ever since I discovered that moosemeat becomes tenderhearted after a night in the jug. For table use tarragon or dill vinegar give a lift to beans or greens and my grandfather swore by a swig of elderbloom vinegar to cure his kidneys of the "twists."

I love to cook anything but I guess my soul is in the sauce. Sauce — what cumulus clouds of delight the word conjures up. I use vinegars, wines and beers; I tease my sauces with spices and herbs; I use brown meat stock, sour cream, bouillon, chicken broth, eggs, butter, drippings, tomatoes, apples and try anything, from glazes such as Roast Reindeer in Lyonnaise to cold sauces, Russian Supreme to Spinster's Sauce. Sauces put trills in my heart and make me itch to get back to my kitchen and stillroom chambers. I confess a sauce nearly did me in once. Top of a mountain, a friend and I fishing, hiking, climbing, a few Dolly Varden trout, a pint of wild mushrooms and rice, Ahhhh! While the man that I was trying to impress went to gather tea, I turned to make a devilish Sauce Aux Champignons. Butter, chopped onion, sliced mushrooms, flour, pepper, salt, rice water and, just as my comrade was returning over the hill, a half-cup of white wine. Ugh! The wine turned out to be gin, the trout were muddy tasting and the rice clung like paste.

For years my husband, Lewis, and I have produced some crazy but wonderful sausages, corn cures and jerked joy meats from caribou, deer, goat, bear as well as from domestic animals. If you have limited freezer space but lots of imagination and a cool corner for hanging, you should try curing. Lewis and I have determined that a 875 pound steer will average about 450 pounds of beef (a little more than 50%.) After we have frozen the choice pieces of beef, together with soup bones and hamburger, we put down about ¼ of the meat into brine-cured products and sausage. We pickle and corn about 60 pounds and make 50 pounds into beef sausage.

Pork is a different story. A hog having a live weight of about 250 pounds will dress out to about 195 pounds carcass weight (a little less than 80%.) A good portion of our pork is converted into bacon, ham, head cheese, scrapple, lard and sausage, with a relatively small part fresh frozen. We always save some trimmings for dried and semi-cured sausages, and we grind pork fat into all cured sausages because it is moist.

Lewis does not raise pigs on our small acreage in the Blue Ridge; our retreat is a weekend place and hogs require daily care. For pork we usually prearrange a date at the slaughter house, attend a livestock auction sale, bid for a tender-looking pig, have it trucked to the slaughter house and pick up the fresh and frozen/packaged meat a week later.

Why do we bother with sausage making and salt curing when frozen hamburger is so versatile? Because they give us instant food, new taste treats and carefree preserving. A corned beef moreover seems to stretch farther than a roast; the flavor permeates dishes and sandwiches more readily so that less of corned beef than fresh is needed to feed a family.

Curing meat—game, beef, pork or kid—is as simple as rubbing a roast with salt, allowing it to stand for a specific number of days, washing and hanging the meat to dry and smoking the cured product before wrapping and storing.

Sausage making is equally easy. We usually ask a meat cutter to grind our meat and then follow a recipe for the amounts of salt, spices or spirits to be kneaded-in. A homemade stuffer (milk container, can and tape contraption), home-sewn muslin sleeves for casings, a screen, pet and pest-free curing box, a backyard or patio cardboard smoker; and you're in the sausage business. And what a glad and joyful business stillroom curing of meat can be! No cereal, coloring or additives—just good solid food!

One caution, if you don't wish to end up with pounds of over-salty cured meat (or fish, because curing seafood is quite as much fun as putting down meat), is STOP THE ACTION by sealing or eating each batch when it is prime.

Stopping the action at the proper time and stabilizing your product at the peak of its transformation is the key to success in all stillroom cookery, for fermentation is an ongoing process. A fermenting product continues to change until acid, ammonia or rot sets in. Unchecked, wine turns sour, pickles disintegrate, dough becomes catatonic, cheeses hide behind beards, frustrated meats get ulcers and mushrooms weep.

Catching, cleaning, cooking and curing fish were routine tasks in early days when many communities were built adjacent to the water, and though fishing for table food is limited today, the fish are the same. They enjoy an early worm, a noonday snooze, supper at dusk or a snack before bedtime. Like my forebears, I rise to the bait if anyone mentions wetting a line, but I believe that the most important part of fishing is the cooking. I have tried nearly every method I have heard of; like a true-blue fisherman, I am perpetually eager to explore anything new. Frying a small fry, baking a biggie, Lew's Fish Bone Soup, fish pickled or pied— all contribute to the excitement of "going fishing." Crabs, clams, oysters and turtles add magic to the menu; lobster and shrimp lend elegance and flair. The netherworld of water bestows grand gifts of food on land-bound lives.

According to my grandmother, a girl didn't reach maidenhood until she could kill, pluck, draw and cook chicken, so I plucked and cleaned chickens like mad thinking it would shorten my tour of adolescence. Nature took its own sweet time, and I prepared hundreds of hapless hens before I woke to the fact that butchering a chicken and catching a beau were in different ball parks. Years later, however, I learned that the route to a man's heart passed through a chicken-filled stomach. Since man first tasted chicken, these meaty fowl and their eggs have reigned as benevolent monarchs of the table. Eggs and chicken, stuffed, baked or deviled, have supported stillroom cooks through lean days and sumptuous spreads.

Other stillroom staples that the overburdened earth faithfully supplies are garden vegetables and sweets, grains and beans. We will take them less and less for granted as the world's population increases and conventional energy supplies decrease. Our planet will have to produce about 4% more food each year if all peoples are to be fed. Unfortunately, potential energy sources necessary to multiply food production are limited. Energy is the weak link. The manufacture of equipment to till the fields, the production of fertilizers and pesticides, the harvesting, processing and distribution of foods, as well as home food preparation and disposal of wastes all strain against energy chains. One of the many suggested solutions is help for people who desire to relocate in small rural settings where they can grow much of their own food with natural fertilizers and pest control methods. More home-growing would retard the increasing need for energy-consuming farm and marketing equipment.

Authorities indicate that energy restraints and the maximum utilization of available land will limit the production of uneconomical grain fed animals, and a lower per person consumption of meat will result. They call for more extensive experimentation and research into hybrid and specialty bred plants; the development of more efficient nitrogen producing bacteria; more reliance upon natural food preservation methods rather than refrigeration; and more dependence upon home gardening, especially the production and usage of protein rich foods.

Emphasis on vegetables and grains is a complete turnabout from today's reliance on meat. Food scientists stress that non-meat protein, that which is found in beans, soy and wheat gluten must be regularly substituted for a part of our meat intake in tomorrow's menus if man is to live within the earth's available energy resources. By combining such foods as beans with grains, protein equal in quality to that of meat can be provided.

Mimicking stillroom techniques of using meat as a flavoring agent for garden-produced soups and stews, meat may be used in the near future predominately as an adjunct to vegetables and grain-based meals. Soups and stews cooked in energy-saving pressure cookers and "low and slow" pots are already staging a comeback.

Preserving garden produce in the home by fermenting, canning and drying not only reduces the energy consumption involved in the packaging and distribution of locally-grown foods, but it saves marginal products. Commercial canners must abide by regulations and preserve only A-Number-1-Perfect produce; a home canner is able to utilize all vegetables from her garden whether on the table, in the pickling crock or in the fruit jar. When a person coaxes a seed into life, the relationship becomes personal and few fruits are wasted.

When you work in concert with nature, whether gardening or using her kitchen helpers, the friendly fungi, yeasts and bacteria, you soon learn that all things that live render joy. You will discover why stillroom cookery is such an ever-changing, promising, creative adventure. It opens new doors for people who wish to be a part of nature because, like the living process of fermentation itself, the roots of stillroom cooking come out of the past and hold firmly to the pulse of the earth.

II

Cheese and Savory Stillroom Milk Products

Natural cheesemaking is a lighthearted stillroom chore that consists of curdling milk and processing the solids into bricks or soft curds. I take solace in the knowledge that cheeses rarely spoil, and as in unplanned parenthood, many accidental curds turn out to be 'just right.'

Today's supermarket dairy cases flaunt such extravagant colors and flavors that it is difficult to believe that natural cheese is made by simply fermenting and curdling milk, draining off the whey (liquid), pressing, salting and aging the curd. There are four ingredients in cheese: 1. milk; 2. a starter, eager-beaver bacteria that impart acid; 3. a coagulant or thickening agent; 4. salt. Plus, in some products, a few microbes and molds.

Cheesemaking milk may be whole, whole milk enriched with cream, skim or instant powdered. After milk has been curdled, separated and drained, the curds, solids, may be eaten fresh as unripened cottage cheese, or they may be ripened for a sharper taste and longer keeping. Ripened cheese may be hard, such as Cheddar which is made from curd that has been salted, pressed into a cake to expel moisture and sealed in wax for a secondary fermentation; or ripened cheese may be soft, such as Camembert which is not pressed nor aged so long.

As with other stillroom tasks, rules of cleanliness and temperature apply to cheesemaking. Promiscuous procaryotes lurk everywhere to taint careless clabber and, as I have discovered, hot curd turns into pencil erasers. Washing and sterilizing all cheesemaking utensils and containers safeguards against wayward bacteria. By following the rules of the road, however, making cheese in your own kitchen can become an "easy-osey" as my kin would say.

Although milk in the United States is pasteurized when sold the process warrants directions for those who have their own milk animals.

To pasteurize, heat water in the lower part of a double boiler to about 130°F (55°C), place the upper part containing the milk on top of the lower part and heat the double boiler rapidly until the milk reaches 145°F (62°C). Hold the milk at this temperature for 30 minutes. Stir milk while heating. Remove the pan of milk and place it into a pan of cold water to cool the milk as quickly as possible. When the milk temperature has been lowered to room temperature it may be poured into boiled and cool, sterilized bottles for processing into cheese.

Most cheeses are made from milk and both a starter and a coagulant but some cheeses are made from milk and a starter only, others are made from milk and a coagulant only. Spontaneous cheeses use neither a starter nor a coagulant; the milk is allowed to ferment and clabber naturally.

Starters such as commercially produced lactic culture, sour milk, buttermilk, sour cream and yogurt are used to get the cheesemaking enzymes started in order to give cheese 'bite'. In anticipation of making cheese I sometimes sour a small amount of milk for a starter by holding it covered at room temperature for 3 or 4 days. I have found that ½ cup (125 ml) of sour milk will inoculate ½ gallon (2 liters) of milk. Equal amounts of buttermilk, sour cream or yogurt will start cheesemaking enzymes working, and covered starters may be saved in the icebox for two weeks. I usually save ½ cup (125 ml) of clabber from one batch of cheese to the next rather than go the 'from scratch' route each time.

Coagulants speed up clabbering and thus impede the growth of off-tasting bacteria in cheesemaking milk. Rennet, and sometimes dried or fresh nettle tops, cleavers and Jerusalem artichoke flowers are used to curdle milk. Rennet is the most predictable coagulant and will form clabber faster than substitutes. However, I have made a strong tea by boiling a handful of the vegetable coagulants in 2 cups (500 ml) water. After cooling I have used ½ cup (125 ml) of curdling tea to ½ gallon (2 liters) of milk and it worked fine. Spontaneous clabbering of milk was sometimes employed in the old stillrooms but natural fermentation is tricky and I have ended up with cheese that tasted like herring roe.

There are many combinations for coagulating and/or starting cheese, and like your own offspring, each is unique.

Salt not only improves the flavor of cheese but it also cuts down on acid and helps to keep cheese fresh longer. Large quantities of salt stop the action of fermentation.

The action in cheesemaking develops in three stages: 1. Starters added to milk eat the sugars of milk and turn them into lactic acid. 2.

Furry fungi feed on the lactic acid and give cheese its bitter flavor. The action of fungi must be stopped, however, or fermenting curd will "shoot to juice." 3. Secondary fermentation is induced which slows down the lactic acid gluttons and thus gives cheese time to mature.

As with other fermented products of the stillroom, the enzyme action must be stopped at the proper time otherwise cheeses will continue to 'work' until they deteriorate. Bacteria and yeasts need warmth, moisture, food and air to survive; take away any one, and their action is retarded or stopped. Cheeses may be preserved by cold temperatures, salting, drying or immersion in paraffin. Commercial manufacturers vacuum-seal some cheeses or preserve them with chemicals, but whatever process is used, stopping fermentation at the peak of flavor is necessary for good cheese.

In most of the following cheesemaking recipes I work with ½ gallon (2 liters) of liquid which yields about ½ pound (225 g) of cheese, or if the liquid is fortified with additional dry milk solids the yield is closer to ¾ pound (350 g) of cheese.

On the next several pages directions for making small batches of cheese will be followed by recipes for using homemade or commercial cheese. I use homemade cheese if I have it, if not, I buy cheese.

Cottage Cheese

Although there are numerous variations, there are basically two types: Small Curd, High Acid Cottage Cheese, made without a coagulant, and Large Curd, Low Acid Cottage Cheese, made with a coagulant.

Small Curd, High Acid Cottage Cheese

Preparation time: About 48 hours curdling, 1 hour to process.

In the upper part of a double boiler reconstitute skim milk by dissolving 3½ cups (875 ml) of instant nonfat dry milk in 7 cups (1.75 liters) of warm water, about 85°F (30°C). Stir well. Inoculate with ½ cup (125 ml) of sour milk or other lactic acid starter, mix briefly, cover and hold at room temperature for 48 hours or until it curdles. If cold set pan of milk in warm water. Do not stir the inoculated milk.

After about 48 hours, test whether the milk is ready for processing by pulling the curd away from the side of the pan and if it is firm and breaks smoothly, the curd is ready to cut. Using tenderness, cut the curd all the

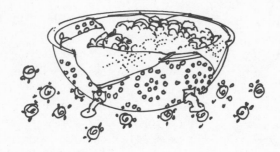

way through into about ¼ inch (0.5 cm) cubes, then put the curd pan on the top of a double boiler that has been partly filled with lukewarm water. Heat the double boiler slowly until curd heats to about 110°F (45°C) stirring gently with a slotted spoon or with your hand and holding the curd at that temperature for about 10 minutes. The liquid curd will feel nice and hot, like good dishwater. Increase heat to about 120°F (50°C) and hold about 10 minutes. This water is hot to the touch, but like a hot, hot bath in which your bottom gets red, you get used to the heat after a minute or two. Test the curd for firmness by pinching a piece together and if it springs back, it is done. Remove pan from the heat, line a colander in the sink with a wet, double thickness of cheesecloth and drain the curd into the cloth. I sometimes save the whey and use it to cook vegetables or as liquid in bread. Gather the corners of the cloth to form a bag and rinse the bag of curd up and down in cold water to cool it and wash away excess acid. Hang the cheese until it stops draining, about 20 minutes. Remove from bag into a bowl, break apart with a fork and if desired, ½ teaspoon (2 ml) salt, butter, cream or sour cream may be mixed in.

Large Curd, Low Acid Cottage Cheese

Preparation time: About 12 hours curdling time plus 1 hour to process.

This cheese is made in the same way as Small Curd, except that you also use a coagulant. When using rennet to coagulate milk follow directions on the package. I dissolve ½ tablet of rennet in a little water and add it to the milk with the starter as directed in the Small Curd Cottage Cheese recipe. Let the milk stand undisturbed at room temperature for about 12 hours or until curdled. Cut curd a little larger, ½ inch (1 cm) and heat, stir, test, drain, wash and finish as with small curd.

Cottage Cheese may be eaten plain or flavored with grated onion or chives, horseradish and mayonnaise, caraway seeds, chopped olives or parsley, celery, bits of cucumber, green pepper, minced clams or shrimp, nuts of every kind, dates, honey, apple butter or applesauce or any stewed fruit, or served with preserves.

Lewis calls for cottage cheese when he cannot manipulate the scales by body English to read his 'proper weight.' Diet food or staple, large and small curd cottage cheese may be used in many dishes to add flair and nutrition to meals.

CHEESE GOULASHKA

This has been my family's favorite fast filler-upper.

Preparation time: 15 minutes. *Serves:* 5.

	U.S. CUSTOMARY	METRIC
Boil, salt and drain	4 cups noodles or about 8 oz. dry	1 liter noodles (225 g dry)
Melt in big skillet	½ cup butter	125 ml butter
Add to skillet, mix and cover	the noodles	noodles
	2 cups raw cabbage, shredded	250 ml cabbage
	2 tablespoons paprika	30 ml paprika
	1 cup cottage cheese	250 ml cheese
	salt and pepper	salt, pepper

Steam for 5 minutes and eat at once. Children love the crunchy cabbage with its oodles of noodles and cheese.

COTTAGE CHEESE PANCAKES

A Sunday night supper when served with applesauce.

Preparation time: 15 minutes. *Serves:* 4.

	U.S. CUSTOMARY	METRIC
In bowl mash	1 cup cottage cheese	250 ml cheese
Stir in and mix well	2 eggs	2 eggs
	1 cup flour	250 ml flour
	3 tablespoons corn meal	45 ml meal
	¼ teaspoon salt	1 ml salt

Spoon patties into a lightly greased skillet and fry. Turn once and serve with applesauce or sour cream.

BACON OLIVE LASAGNE

Preparation time: 1 hour. *Serves:* 5.

	U.S. CUSTOMARY	METRIC
Boil, drain, set aside	8 oz. noodles	225 g noodles
In saucepan boil	2 cups tomatoes	250 ml tomatoes
	2 tablespoons catsup	30 ml catsup
	1 clove garlic minced	garlic
	1 teaspoon each, salt, sugar, oregano, chili powder	5 ml salt, sugar, oregano, chili powder
	¼ teaspoon pepper	1 ml pepper
Fry, drain excess fat, stir into sauce	¼ pound chopped bacon	125 g bacon
	1 large onion, chopped	1 onion
	2 tablespoons green pepper, chopped	30 ml gr. pepper
In greased casserole layer	½ of the noodles	noodles
	½ of the sauce	sauce
	1 cup pitted ripe olives, save few for topping	250 ml olives
	1 cup cottage cheese	250 ml cheese
	½ of the noodles	noodles
	½ of the sauce	sauce
Top with	cottage cheese bits, chopped olives	cheese and olives

Bake at 350°F (175°C) for 25 minutes. Turn off oven. Pour over casserole 3 tablespoons (45 ml) Marsala or other sweet wine, return to oven for 5 minutes, cool briefly and serve with a huge green salad tossed with wine vinegar, olive oil, basil and pine nuts. A thimbleful of Marsala and Porcupines, apples poked and baked with almonds completes this robust salute to our Latin forebears.

Cottage Cheese Dressing for Baked Potatoes

Use cottage cheese to dress baked potatoes for those who are on a low fat diet by mashing cottage cheese with a few spoons of skim milk and adding chives or chopped green onions and a little salt and pepper.

Cottage Cheese Salads and Sandwiches

Conjuring up compatible salad companions of cottage cheese leads to heady thoughts of watercress, shredded cabbage, nasturtium flowers, figs, eggs, mushrooms and raw spinach, preserved ginger, citrus marmalade, pickled tongue, braised fennel, little marrows, sauteed chicken livers, mint leaves, chervil, cooked okra, quartered artichokes or their hearts simmered in butter, brussel sprouts, lean ham, caviar or anchovies. Cottage cheese and avocado sandwiches are scrumptious and cottage cheese on crackers sprinkled over with dill sprigs is a delight. But the most unusual cottage cheese innovation is Evelyn Metzger's Eyeball Salad. Simply mix equal parts of cottage cheese and seedless white grapes. Great!

COTTAGE CHEESE PIE

An old favorite that may be made with skim milk if desired.

Preparation time: 1 hour. *Serves:* 5.

	U.S. CUSTOMARY	METRIC
In bowl mash	1 cup cottage cheese	250 ml cheese
Add and stir well	2½ tablespoons flour	40 ml flour
	1 cup sugar	250 ml sugar
	1 teaspoon vanilla	5 ml vanilla
	½ teaspoon salt	2 ml salt
	2 egg yolks	2 egg yolks
	2 cups milk	500 ml milk
Beat and fold in	2 egg whites	2 egg whites
Pour into	1 unbaked pie shell or pastry-lined cake pan	1 pie shell unbaked

Bake at 450°F (230°C) for 15 minutes, then at 300°F (150°C) for 30 minutes. When a knife inserted into the custard comes out clean, it's done.

Slip and Bonny Clabber were "turned" or thickened milk products that rural Americans relished during hot weather. Holding these homely dishes so as to retain the consistency of baked custard was accomplished by putting the bowl of Bonny Clabber in the coolest part of the stillroom and sending it to the table the moment it was to be served. Eaten with cream, sugar and grated nutmeg, both dishes were considered the choicest of desserts.

My grandmother used to make Bonny Clabber by adding ½ rennet tablet dissolved in a little water to a pan of whole milk which she put into the warming oven above the range. When it was curdled but not tough, she drained the delicate clabber and served it in plain glass custard cups. For years I ate a cup of clabber after saying my prayers at bedtime because she was trying to make me fat. It didn't work. But I still associate nighttime prayers with clabbered milk and vice versa.

Skim Milk Clabber

I make and cook with Skim Milk Clabber using it as an alternate for sour milk, buttermilk and in some instances sour cream.

Preparation time: 9 hours. *Makes:* 1 quart (1 liter) approximately.

In a large pan dissolve 3½ cups (875 ml) of instant nonfat dry milk in 7 cups (1.75 liters) of warm water, 85°F (30°C) and add ½ cup (125 ml) of buttermilk or sour milk. Mix briefly, cover and allow to stand undisturbed in a warm place for about 8 hours. A pilot-warmed oven is ideal. After 8 hours of inoculation, turn on the oven, heat to 400°F (200°C) and allow the clabber to form at that temperature for 30 minutes. Turn off oven and let set for the whey to separate. Remove from oven, drain off whey by pouring the custard-like clabber into a wet, double thickness cheesecloth that has been draped across a colander in the sink. Do not drain dry or wash clabber. Store in icebox to be used in cooking; it will keep for about a week.

Stillroom cooks often kept a crock of clabber handy for leavening quick breads. Baking soda was mixed into the flour and when clabber was added, gas lightened the viscous mixture. ½ teaspoon (2 ml) of soda was suggested for each cup of clabber.

SODA CRACKERS

More substantial than commercial crackers, these old-timers are nice to keep in a jar with a tight lid. Children love them with peanut butter.

Preparation time: 1 hour. *Makes about*: 1 pound (500 g).

	U.S. CUSTOMARY	METRIC
In bowl mix	3 cups flour	750 ml flour
well	½ teaspoon baking soda	3 ml soda
	2 tablespoons sugar	30 ml sugar
Add	1 tablespoon oil	15 ml oil
	1 cup skim milk clabber	250 ml clabber

Mix and beat vigorously. Divide into two parts, roll paper thin on a floured surface. Salt if desired by brushing on a bit of milk and salting with a shaker. Transfer to a greased cookie tin, prick all over with a fork, roll lightly and cut with a pizza cutter into 1½ inch squares (4 cm). Bake at 350°F (175°C) for 8 minutes or until lightly brown.

IRISH SCONES

Preparation time: 30 minutes. *Makes:* 12 scones.

	U.S. CUSTOMARY	METRIC
In bowl	3 cups flour	750 ml flour
mix well	1 teaspoon salt	5 ml salt
	½ teaspoon baking soda	2 ml soda
With hands mix	4 tablespoons soft butter	60 ml butter
Gradually add	1 cup skim milk clabber	250 ml clabber

Turn dough onto a lightly floured surface and knead briefly. Shape into a ball, roll out into an 8 inch (20 cm) circle and cut into 12 pie-wedge triangles. Brush with butter, bake at 400°F (200°C) for 14 minutes or until lightly brown. Sure 'n your lad from the old sod will pinch your shamrock and give you a wee kiss if you bake him scones and set with a pot of piping hot stew.

SOMERSAULT PIE

This is a good one. The pie turns a somersault during baking.

Preparation time: 1½ hours. *Makes:* 1 pie.

	U.S. CUSTOMARY	METRIC
In bowl make	1 cup sugar	250 ml sugar
a dough by	4 tablespoons soft butter	60 ml butter
mixing	1 egg	1 egg
	½ cup skim milk clabber	125 ml clabber
	1¼ cup flour mixed with	300 ml flour
	½ teaspoon baking soda	2 ml soda
Spread dough on	1 unbaked pie shell	1 pie shell
In the empty	1 tablespoon flour	15 ml flour
bowl mix	½ cup sugar	125 ml sugar
	1 teaspoon cloves	5 ml cloves
	½ teaspoon cinnamon	3 ml cinnamon
	1 egg, beaten	1 egg
	½ cup molasses	125 ml molasses
	½ cup water or clabber	125 ml water

Pour over dough that is spread on the unbaked pie shell. Bake at 450°F (230°C) for 15 minutes, lower temperature to 350°F (175°C) and bake for 40 additional minutes. Cool, cover with whipped cream and serve.

CLABBER SHERBET (PINEAPPLE OR BANANA)

Preparation time: 2 hours. *Makes:* 1 refrigerator tray.

	U.S. CUSTOMARY	METRIC
In bowl mix, then turn into tray and freeze to a mush	2 cups skim milk clabber or buttermilk	500 ml clabber
	⅔ cup sugar	170 ml sugar
	½ teaspoon salt	2 ml salt
	1 cup crushed pineapple	250 ml pineapple
	2 teaspoons vanilla	10 ml vanilla

Remove from freezer tray, whisk mushy sherbet until frothy.

Fold in and return to tray	1 egg white beaten stiff	1 egg white

Freeze to desired consistency but not icy hard.

BANANA CLABBER SHERBET

Substitute for pineapple	1 cup mashed banana	250 ml banana
	1 teaspoon lemon juice	5 ml lemon
Add	⅓ cup sugar	80 ml sugar

Freeze to a solid state but not as hard as ice cubes.

BUTTERMILK PIE

Preparation time: 1 hour, 30 minutes. *Makes:* 1 pie.

	U.S. CUSTOMARY	METRIC
In pan melt	¾ cup butter	175 ml butter
Stir in	2 eggs	2 eggs
Mix, add and beat well	1 cup sugar	250 ml sugar
	1 tablespoon flour	15 ml flour
Fold in	2 tablespoons vanilla	30 ml vanilla
	1 cup skim milk clabber or buttermilk	250 ml clabber
Pour into	1 unbaked pie crust	1 pie crust

Bake at 350°F (175°C) for 50 minutes. Check for doneness by inserting knife into the custard and if the knife comes out clean, remove pie from oven. This is a delicious treat.

GERMAN CHRISTMAS COOKIES

May be made in November and kept in a covered canister because they get better as they age and make the whole house smell Christmassy.

Preparation time: 2 hours. *Makes:* 250 cookies.

	U.S. CUSTOMARY	METRIC
In pan warm	1 quart corn syrup 1 cup sugar 2 cups butter	1 liter syrup 250 ml sugar 500 ml butter
Pour into a large bowl and add	1 tablespoon each, cloves, salt and cinnamon 1 teaspoon each, nutmeg, ginger, allspice 1½ teaspoon baking soda dissolved in 1 tablespoon hot water	15 ml each, salt, clove, cinnamon 5 ml each, nutmeg, ginger, allspice 7 ml soda dissolved in 15 ml hot water
Mix in	2 eggs ½ cup skim milk clabber 1 orange peeling, finely chopped or slivered 4 tablespoons anise seed	2 eggs 125 ml clabber 1 peeling 60 ml anise
Gradually add	10 cups flour	2.5 liters flour

Work dough with hands adding more flour to make very stiff. Divide into quarters and roll out on a floured surface to about ¼ inch (0.5 cm) thick. Cut with a 2 inch (5 cm) circle cookie cutter. I stamp each cookie with a quatrefoil, a medieval symbol of good luck. Bake at 350°F (175°C) for 12 minutes or until nicely done.

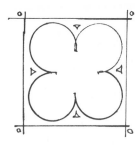

Mock Sour Cream

By substituting whole milk for the reconstituted skim milk in the Skim Milk Clabber recipe, adding 4 tablespoons (60 ml) of sour cream and allowing the finished clabber to set at room temperature for 4 days, mock sour cream, although not as rich as the real thing, can be made and is fine for cooking.

SOUR CREAM PIE
Filled with fresh raspberries or strawberries, this pie is unbelievably easy and good.
Preparation time: 1 hour, 15 minutes. *Makes:* 1 pie.

	U.S. CUSTOMARY	METRIC
Line pie pan with	1 unbaked pie shell	1 pie shell
Fill with	2 cups drained berries	500 ml berries
Mix in bowl	1 cup sour cream	250 ml sour cream
	1 tablespoon flour	15 ml flour
	½ cup brown sugar	125 ml brown sugar
	1 egg slightly beaten	1 egg

Pour over berries. Bake at 350°F (175°C) for 45 minutes or when golden brown, remove, cool and eat.

SOUR CREAM MACARONI CUCUMBER SALAD

A tasty covered dish for summer picnics.

Preparation time: 30 minutes, plus 30 minutes to stand. *Makes:* a bowlful.

	U.S. CUSTOMARY	METRIC
Boil, drain, wash in cold water, set aside	1 package 8 oz. macaroni	225 g macaroni
In bowl chop fine and mix	1 cucumber	1 cucumber
	1 green pepper	1 green pepper
	1 carrot	1 carrot
	2 stalks celery	2 celery
	4 sweet pickles	4 pickles
	1 onion, small	1 onion
Add	the cooked macaroni	macaroni
	2 cubed tomatoes	2 tomatoes
In a dish mix and pour over salad	2 tablespoons vinegar	30 ml vinegar
	1 teaspoon salt	5 ml salt
	¼ teaspoon each, garlic powder, basil, pepper, dill seed	1 ml each, garlic, basil, pepper, dill seed
	1 cup sour cream	250 ml sour cream

Toss lightly, garnish with sliced olives and radish roses, cover, let stand in refrigerator for 30 minutes before serving.

Cream Cheese

A simple cheese with a hundred names and uses.

Time required: Overnight plus 2 hours. *Makes:* 1 cup (250 ml) or ½ pound (225 g).

Empty ½ gallon (2 liters) of whole milk into a pan and mix in ½ cup (125 ml) sour milk or lactic starter. Heat slowly to 85°F (30°C) by putting the pan over a double boiler of hot water. Hold at that temperature for 30 minutes. Cover and set in oven overnight. The following morning warm again to 85°F (30°C), add ½ rennet tablet dissolved in a little water, stir briefly and allow to set clabber undisturbed. When a firm curd forms, that is, the solids pull away from the side of the pan and the curd breaks sharply, dip off most of the whey with a cup and pour the clabber into a large pan that has been filled with an equal volume of hot water 180°F (80°C). Stir gently, breaking curd as you do, test with a thermometer and as soon as the curd and water solution reaches 130°F (55°C) pour through a wet, double thickness of cheesecloth draped in a colander in the sink. Pull up the four corners of the cloth to form a bag, hang and allow the whey to drain. Do not wash. When the bag of curd feels like thick oatmeal, about 20 minutes, empty into a bowl and with a fork mix in ¼ teaspoon (1 ml) plain salt. Form into a cube and eat or refrigerate.

Homemade cream cheese is excellent as a spread for bread, in dips, casseroles, sandwiches, omelets, desserts or as a substitute Ricotta in Italian food.

MUSCAT CHEESECAKE

My grandmother made this very delicious cheesecake when our cow, Lucky Strike, came fresh.

Preparation time: 1½ hours. *Makes:* 1 cheesecake.

	U.S. CUSTOMARY	METRIC
In a bowl mix	½ cup sugar	125 ml sugar
	3 tablespoons flour	45 ml flour
	¼ teaspoon salt	1 ml salt
Soften, mash in	1 pound cream cheese	500 g cream cheese
Add and beat	¾ cup cream	175 ml cream
until smooth	3 egg yolks	3 egg yolks
and creamy	1 teaspoon vanilla	5 ml vanilla
Make separately	1 pie crust, unbaked	1 pie crust

Beat egg whites and fold into the above filling. Line an oblong cake tin, 11 × 7 ×1½ inches (28 × 17 × 4 cm) with rich pie dough. Sprinkle the bottom with a layer of muscat raisins and pour the cheese mixture over them. Bake at 450°F (230°C) for 15 minutes, then at 325°F (160°C) for 10 minutes longer. When a knife inserted into the custard comes out clean, remove from oven, cool and dust with powdered sugar.

Schmierkase

Schmierkase is made very much like cottage cheese. My grandmother was touchy about her Schmierkase and was quick to correct anyone undiscerning enough to call it cottage cheese. Somehow she believed that Schmierkase was of a higher class than the other curd. I use the two cheeses interchangeably.

Preparation time: 4 days.

For Schmierkase dissolve 3½ cups (875 ml) of nonfat dry milk solids in 7 cups (1.75 liters) of lukewarm water and inoculate with ½ cup (125 ml) sour milk or lactic starter. Cover and hold at room temperature for 48 hours or until coagulated. Do not stir. When the curd is firm but not hard and brittle, tip the pan against its cover and drain off excess whey and pour the clabber into a pan of warm water, 120°F (50°C), which is hot to the touch but not unbearable. Stir with fingers to break curd into particles the size desired in the finished cheese. Allow to set, fire off, for 10 minutes. Pour the warmed curd into a wet cheesecloth draped over a colander in the sink, pull up the corners to form a bag and pour a teakettle of warm water, 120°F (50°C) over it. Repeat twice. For a low acid cheese wash the curd by dipping the bag up and down in cold water. Hang to drip for one hour then serve with sour cream or refrigerate.

SCHMIERKASE STUFFING
A handy potato substitute, may be baked or fried over low fire.
Preparation time: 45 minutes. *Makes:* 5 servings.

	U.S. CUSTOMARY	METRIC
In bowl break apart	8 slices old bread	8 slices bread
Stir in	1 or 2 eggs	1 or 2 eggs
	1 onion finely chopped	1 onion
	1 cup milk	250 ml milk
	1 teaspoon salt	5 ml salt
	½ teaspoon sage	3 ml sage
	¼ teaspoon pepper	1 ml pepper
	3 tablespoons oil	45 ml oil
	1 cup schmierkase	250 ml schmierkase
If desired	nuts or caraway seeds	nuts/caraway

Bake in an uncovered greased casserole at 350°F (175°C) for 30 minutes.

Bourek

We called our kitten Bourek ever since the day she jumped into the schmierkase crock and Grandma, unaware, made Bourek out of the cheese. With or without the kitten, these are tasty cheese filled pastries.

Preparation time: 50 minutes. *Makes:* 3 dozen.

Roll out Light Bread dough or pie dough paper thin and cut into 2 inch (5 cm) squares. Put a teaspoon of schmierkase, a cupful of which has been mixed with one egg and a pinch of pennyroyal or other mint, on each and fold the dough over diagonally to form a triangle. Moisten edges to seal and fry in a skim of oil until brown.

Spinach Schmierkase

Preparation time: 30 minutes. *Serves:* 4.

In a generously buttered oven dish, layer briefly precooked, drained and chopped spinach with spoonfuls of schmierkase. Here and there daub butter, salt, pepper and season faintly with garlic. Bake at 350°F (175°C) for about 20 minutes and before taking the dish to the table slice a hard-boiled egg in a circle on the top and put a billow of sour cream in the center. Sprinkle with paprika and serve piping hot.

Schmierkase Potatoes

Preparation time: 20 minutes. *Serves:* 5.

Fry a couple of slices of finely chopped bacon with a clove of chopped garlic, remove from the skillet and fry 5 or 6 sliced potatoes in the grease with salt and pepper. Cover and cook until the potatoes are done, add a cup of schmierkase, turn the potatoes once or twice so that the cheese will snuggle into them, cover, turn off fire and let them steam a minute before dishing them up and sprinkling on the cooked bits of bacon.

Bel Paese Beauty

A kindhearted little cheese that is nearly foolproof.

Preparation time: 10 weeks. *Makes:* about ½ pound (225 g).

Put ½ gallon (2 liters) fresh whole milk in a pan, add a small amount of lactic starter or 4 tablespoons (60 ml) sour milk and over a double boiler heat to 110°F (45°C) which is hot to the touch. Mix in ½ rennet tablet dissolved in a little water and set pan of milk in a warm place without agitating it. When firm enough to cut, about 8 hours or when the curd will hold its shape and break sharply when gently pulled away from the side of the pan, cut all the way through into ⅜ inch (1 cm) cubes. Be careful not to mash but cut as fast as possible so as to expel the whey quickly. Dip with a sieve, draining as you dip, and transfer the curd to a wet cheesecloth-lined 1 pound (500 g) coffee tin that has had nail holes poked in the bottom. I make my cheese press by cutting off the top of a coffee can with a can opener, saving it, emptying out the coffee and poking holes in the bottom of the can with an ice pick. Holes should be poked from the inside for a smooth inner surface. I sterilize both the can and its metal top in boiling water. After the curd is in the cloth-lined coffee tin, the lid is inserted as a follower in order to keep the cheese as warm as possible. I cover the coffee can with a towel and set it on a cup in a cake tin to facilitate draining. Drain 8 hours and turn the cheese 3 times during the draining by lifting the cheesecloth-encased cake from the can, turning it over and replacing it upside down. Remove cheese from the can after 8 hours. At this point I cut a 6 inch (15 cm) square of cheesecloth to fold over the cheese which makes handling easier during the salting. Salt Bel Paese Beauty by immersing in a strong brine, 4 tablespoons (60 ml) salt dissolved in 1 cup (250 ml) water. Hold in brine at 55°F (13°C) overnight. Drain and save brine. Dry cheese at room temperature for 2 days turning often, then sprinkle with 1 teaspoon (5 ml) salt and store uncovered in the fresh meat compartment of your refrigerator. Temperature should be around 40°F (5°C) or colder. Hold in cooler for 3 weeks, wash the cheese in the saved brine 2 times each week to keep the slime coating thin and the rind firm and clean. After 3 weeks clean the cheese thoroughly in brine, dry and wrap in foil to cure 3 to 6 weeks in the vegetable drawer, where the temperature should be around 48°F (9°C). Bel Paese Beauty may be eaten at this time, or if you keep it longer, the cheese should be dipped in paraffin and sealed in foil. Keep refrigerated.

If you see that your cheese is deteriorating at any time during its curing period due to temperature, salt or ferment irregularities, remove mold and use as a cooking cheese or in casseroles.

CHEESE LOAF

The Barter Island Eskimo cook who gave me this recipe said, "Use any opened cheese that's going south." (Her Arctic people believed that the devil lived in the south and that foods that were beginning to pale were about to give themselves up to Beelzebub.) The Indian school where my Barter Island friend cooked received shipments of government surplus cheese, some of which were "going south" when they arrived in Alaska. Our cook threw nothing away so we ate cheese in many ways.

Preparation time: 30 minutes. *Serves:* 4.

	U.S. CUSTOMARY	METRIC
In large bowl	4 eggs	4 eggs
beat	½ cup water	125 ml water
Mix in	2 tablespoons sugar	30 ml sugar
	¼ teaspoon nutmeg	1 ml nutmeg
	¼ teaspoon mace	1 ml mace
	½ teaspoon salt	2 ml salt
	dash of cloves	cloves

Butter 4 slices of bread and crumble them into the mixture. Stir and allow to soak. Add 1 pound cubed or slivered cheese that is beginning to "go south", or cottage cheese, mix well and press into small, well buttered pie tins. Bake at 375°F (190°C) for 20 minutes, remove from pan immediately; if they cool in the pan, removing them is a terrible task. Serve with potato salad, sliced tomatoes, buttered broccoli and an open-faced blackberry pie topped with ice cream.

Camembert Counterfeit

A surface-ripened cheese that is inoculated with a culture taken from commercial cheese.

Preparation time: 2 months, 3 weeks, 2 days and 8 hours.

Put ½ gallon (2 liters) whole milk into a flat bottom pan over a double boiler, add ½ cup (125 ml) lactic starter or sour milk, warm until the milk is about 85°F (30°C) and add ½ rennet tablet dissolved in a little water. Set aside. When curd has firmed, 8 hours or so, cut into fingernail-size pieces and with a slotted spoon carefully transfer the curds to a wet cheesecloth-lined 1 pound (500 g) can that has holes poked in the bottom. A cheese press is made by cutting off the top of a coffee can and poking holes in the bottom from the inside with an ice pick. Set the coffee can of draining curd on a cup in a cake pan so that the liquid can drain freely. Cover with a cloth and leave at room temperature for 2 days. Remove the settled cheese by pulling the cloth and holding the tin upside down. Gently remove the cloth and rub the cheese surface with 1 teaspoon (5 ml) of commercial Camembert cheese, the rind mixed with its creamy insides, and sprinkle 1 teaspoon (5 ml) of plain salt on the top of the surface inoculated cheese. Gradually dry the small cheese by setting it in a wide-mouthed jar on the door inside the icebox. The temperature of the door area should be about 50°F (10°C) and humidity about 80%. Drop slices of apple around the cheese to help give humidity. Cover jar lightly. Cure for 3 weeks on the door, turning the cheese over from time to time and replacing the slices of apples. Move the cheese in the jar to the vegetable holding area where the temperature

will be closer to 48°F (9°C), turn cheese frequently and hold in the
crisper for 2 months. I make new cuts of apple again, and lay them close
for humidity. The surface of Camembert Counterfeit will grow pale and
a trace of yellowish freckles will appear, but sprinkle with salt if the mold
becomes too pronounced. After time in cure is up, rub cheese with a
cloth dipped in wine and wrap cheese tightly in parchment (I use
discarded commercial Camembert coverings or wax paper) and then in
foil to exclude air. Keep refrigerated until you broach your proud curd
with good friends. This shy cheese goes especially well with a fine white
wine such as elder blow.

Oven Fried Chicken with Cheese

A first rate dish that is especially good with goat's milk.

Preparation time: 1 hour, 30 minutes. *Serves:* 5.

Salt, pepper and dredge with flour 1 cut up chicken and lay in a well
oiled flat, low-sided baking pan. Bake at 350°F (175°C) for 45 minutes
turning the chicken once. Pour 2 cups (500 ml) of whole milk or goat's
milk over it and return to oven for 30 minutes. About 15 minutes before
serving break bits of cheese, Camembert Counterfeit or other distinctly
flavored cheese, over the custard coated chicken and return pan to the
oven. Serve with French fried onion rings, buttered turnips, raw
cauliflower knuckles with lemon and oil and a hot rough bread.

Blue Cheese

Preparation time: 3 months, 2 weeks. *Makes:* ½ pound (225 g).

To make Blue, put ½ gallon (2 liters) fresh whole milk into a double
boiler, warm to 85°F (30°C), add ½ cup (125 ml) lactic starter or sour milk
and ½ rennet tablet dissolved in a little water. When curd is firm, that is,
when it pulls away in a solid mass from the pan side and breaks sharply,
cut to express the whey. With a slotted spoon or strainer dip curd into a
wet cheesecloth that has been draped over the colander in the sink.
When drained but not dry, about 20 minutes, pour cheese into a bowl
and mix in 2 teaspoons (10 ml) of crumbled commercial blue cheese and 1
teaspoon (5 ml) of plain salt with a fork. Transfer the inoculated cheese to
a cloth-lined coffee tin with holes in the bottom, cover with the tin coffee
can lid, press down with your fingers just a bit and cover can with a towel
to keep it cozy. Turn cheese upside down 3 times during its 24 hour stay

in the can by gently pulling the cake out of the can by its cloth and inverting it. When firm, rub the cake of cheese with 1 teaspoon (5 ml) dry salt, wrap lightly in cheesecloth and store on the door inside the icebox where the temperature is about 50°F (10°C). Cover the cheese with sliced apples to keep it moist during salting. After a week poke a dozen holes in the cheese with a knitting needle in order that the blue mold will grow on the inside. Wrap in cheesecloth and cure for 3 months in a lightly covered wide-mouthed jar on the door of the refrigerator. Be sure to keep slices of apples in the jar for humidity. At the end of 3 months the cheese is scraped of excess mold, wrapped in foil and tucked into the fresh meat chamber, where the temperature is around 40°F (5°C). It can be eaten now or sealed in paraffin for later use.

Blue Strudel

Try this if you have strudel in your noodle and leftover dough.

Preparation time: 45 minutes.

Mix, half and half, Blue Cheese and Cottage Cheese, mash, blend in an egg, a little salt, pepper, chopped dill and spread over buttered strudel dough or Light Bread dough stretched tissue paper thin. Allow to dry a few minutes. Roll up loosely as you would roll a jelly roll, seal edges and carefully transfer to a buttered cookie tin. Bake at 450°F (230°C) for 20 minutes or until a little brown. Serve with sour cream.

False Feta

False Feta, a pickled virgin cheese, is made from whole or skim milk and those who know about such things say that it rivals the real thing made from ewe's milk.

Preparation time: Cheese may be ready to eat in a week.

Pour ½ gallon (2 liters) fresh whole milk or reconstituted dry skim milk into a double boiler, heat to body temperature, add ½ tablet of rennet that has been dissolved in a little water and hold at that temperature until firm. Cut curd to release the whey. Pour the cut curd into a colander in the sink that has been draped with a wet double-thickness of cheesecloth. Drain well and spoon curds into a cheesecloth-lined, 1 pound (500 g) coffee can that has holes in the bottom. Elevate can on a cup to facilitate draining. Press gently on the cheese with the tin lid of the coffee can, cover with a towel and let stand at room temperature overnight. When the cheese firms to a single block, 12 to 18 hours, remove from cheese press and salt surface liberally with about 1 teaspoon (5 ml) plain salt. Place on a cloth-covered rack. Later the same day turn the cheese over and salt a second time with 1 teaspoon (5 ml) plain salt. The following morning cut cheese into 1 inch (2.5 cm) slices and sprinkle with 1 teaspoon (5 ml) dry salt. Allow Feta to stand at room temperature for 24 hours and pack into a jar that has salt sprinkled in the bottom. Sprinkle top of cheese lightly with salt, cover and keep refrigerated. Feta may be eaten in 4 or 5 days as a nibble with melon, fresh figs or with a light and pleasant white wine such as Pasture Daisy. Or Feta slices may be immersed in a holding brine and kept in a cool, dark place such as on the lower shelf of your wine rack in the basement or on the stillroom floor. To make a holding brine, boil equal quantities of water and plain salt for 25 minutes in a covered pan. Cool, pour over the cheese and cover tightly. Feta may be washed in cold water if it becomes too salty.

A friend fries dry Feta by simply slicing and frying in hot oil. I have heard of others dipping Feta into egg and then into breadcrumbs before frying. I have tried neither because we like it just as it comes from the jar.

Limburger

A surface ripened cheese with a strong character and aroma.

Preparation time: 4 months. *Makes:* ½ to ¾ pound (225-340 g).

Warm 7 cups of water to 85°F (30°C), pour into a double boiler and stir in 3½ cups (875 ml) of instant nonfat dry milk, ½ cup (125 ml) of sour milk or lactic starter and ½ rennet tablet dissolved in a little water; keep warm and do not stir until curd is formed. When curd is firm and readily pulls away from the side of the pan, cut into ½ inch (1 cm) cubes and drain off whey by pouring into a wet cheesecloth-lined colander set in the sink. Wash curd in a weak brine by gathering the corners of the cloth and raising and lowering it in a bowl of water with a handful of salt added. This will help to lower the acidity of the cheese. Pour curd into a cheesecloth-lined 1 pound (500 g) coffee tin with holes punched in the bottom and cover with a tin coffee can lid. When the cheese is firm enough to retain its shape, about 2 days, remove and rub each surface of the cheese with a teaspoon of commercial limburger rind that has been mashed with a little milk. Salt liberally by patting on 1 teaspoon (5 ml) plain salt on the cheese daily for 4 days. Cure in a cool place, 60°F (15°C). I use the crawl space under the house for this and put the cheese in a screen-topped canister that allows it to breathe yet keeps varmints out. Limburger-in-the-making sometimes turns yellowish red and forms a slime but do not be discouraged. After 4 days, wrap cheese loosely in the parchment that has been removed from a commercial limburger or in wax paper and cure at about 60°F (15°C) for 2 weeks. You will be tempted to chuck the whole cheese thing during these two weeks, critters will be tempted to dig under the house and your spouse will repeatedly empty trash cans in an effort to find the odoriferous truant. On the other hand you will miss the interesting comments when, after the cure in the can is up, you wrap the cheese tightly in an outer layer of foil and place it on the door of the refrigerator for a 3 month cure.

It is important to label and date your cheese. I have mistakenly opened Limburger for a fastidious guest and nearly ruined a friendship.

Brick

Midway between Limburger and Cheddar in strength, Brick Cheese is American through and through. From its elastic accommodation, to its steadfastness against crumbling, to its soft heart: Brick is American.

Preparation time: 3 months, 3 weeks. *Makes:* ½ pound (225 g).

Pour ½ gallon (2 liters) whole milk into the top of a double boiler and warm to body heat. Add lactic starter or ½ cup (125 ml) sour milk and ½ rennet tablet that has been dissolved in a little water. Maintain temperature until a firm curd develops. Cut curd into small cubes and stir gently for 30 minutes while raising the curd temperature to 115°F (47°C), hot as a hot bath. Hold at this temperature until the curd is springy and it does not mush between your fingers when you pinch a piece gently. Do not wash, but with a slotted spoon dip the curd directly into a cheesecloth-lined 1 pound (500 g) coffee tin with holes punched in the bottom. Drain by putting the can on a teacup in a cake tin and cover with both the metal coffee can top and tea towels to keep the curd from losing its heat. For Brick and other of the harder cheeses I poke holes in the metal coffee can lid after it has been cut from the can because hard cheeses should be turned upside down every half hour to facilitate proper draining. Turn the whole coffee can cheese press upside down 5 times at 30 minute intervals. The cheese will slide to the bottom on each turn. At the end of the turning period, weight the curd with a brick, about 5 pounds (2 kg), and drain under pressure overnight. Keep the press covered. Because a brick will not fit inside a coffee tin, I place a large-mouthed glass on top of the coffee-can-lid follower and balance the brick on the glass. Lewis says that my stillroom cheesemaking equipment looks like a Rube Goldberg contraption, but it works.

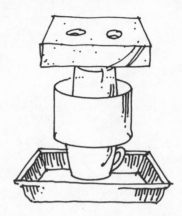

The following morning remove the cheese and rub all surfaces with 1 teaspoon (5 ml) of plain salt. Repeat daily for 3 days while you hold the brick of cheese uncovered at room temperature. Cure cheese at a temperature of 60°F (15°C); I put cheese in my screen-topped canister that is in the crawl space for 2 weeks, and lay sliced apples around the curd for humidity. A cheesemaking colleague lays his cheese on a wine-dampened cloth for humidity. Reddish bacteria may grow on the surface so wash the cheese every 3 days in salt water, 4 tablespoons (60 ml) salt to a cup (250 ml) water, in order to discourage the bad guys. After 2 weeks in the canister, shift the cheese to the door inside the icebox and hold there a day or two until dry. If any slime develops wash with brine, dry and dip in paraffin for keeping. Wrap Brick Cheese in parchment or brown wrapping paper, then in foil and cure for 3 months in the vegetable drawer of the refrigerator, at 48°F (9°C). Brick may be eaten fresh or cooked, it melts readily and gives a twang to food.

OVEN OMELET

Preparation time: 45 minutes. *Serves:* 4.

	U.S. CUSTOMARY	METRIC
Turn on oven to 350°F (175°C).		
Put in large skillet and set in oven to melt	1 tablespoon butter 1 cup milk ½ cup brick cheese, slivered	15 ml butter 250 ml milk 125 ml cheese

In bowl beat	5 eggs	5 eggs
until light	1 teaspoon salt	5 ml salt
	¼ teaspoon cayenne	1 ml cayenne

When cheese melts remove from oven, pour into the eggs, then back into the skillet. Bake 30 minutes.

Dried Cheese

Using cheese that has finished its stay in the canister but a Brick that is not fully cured, I rub the cheese with salt, 1 teaspoon (5 ml), and hang it in a cheesecloth from my pantry ceiling. I salt the cheese every week for a month and when hard I dip the cheese in paraffin and store it in the icebox vegetable crisper until needed. Dried cheese keeps a couple of months after it has been opened and I send the cube to the table with a paring knife for scraping over spaghetti.

Cheddar Cheese

A wan-colored cousin to a commercial Cheddar, but sharply flavored.

Preparation time: 6 months. *Makes:* ½ pound (225 g).

Warm 3 cups (750 ml) water to 85°F (30°C), pour into the top of a double boiler, stir in 2 cups (500 ml) of instant nonfat dry milk together with 1 quart (1 liter) of fresh whole milk and add ½ cup (125 ml) sour milk or lactic starter. Maintain temperature and stir on and off for about 1 hour. Thoroughly mix in ½ rennet tablet dissolved in a little water and allow milk to set, covered and undisturbed until a firm curd develops, usually overnight. When the curd firms, that is, it can be pulled away from the side of the pan and breaks smoothly, cut into ¼ inch (0.5 cm) cubes and agitate with fingers or a slotted spoon. Heat the curd in a double boiler very gradually to fever warmth, 100°F (40°C); the heating should take about 30 minutes. Remove from fire and drain by holding pan lid across the top and gently pouring off the whey. Cheese curd will be packed about 6 inches (15 cm) deep on one side of the pan. Tilt the pan on a knife handle so that the residual whey will drain away from the stacked curd and drain for 15 minutes. Remove curd with a cup, make a pile 6 inches (15 cm) high on the sink counter and turn frequently to express whey. When no more liquid runs out, chop the curd to the size of rice and mix in 1 teaspoon (5 ml) plain salt. Cover with a towel and allow to weep. When the salt is fully dissolved, transfer to a cheesecloth-

draped 1 pound (500 g) coffee can with holes in the bottom, insert follower (the tin coffee can top) then a large-mouthed glass and press with 4 bricks overnight. I set the coffee can cheese press on a cup in a cake tin, insert the glass on the metal follower and balance the bricks on top of the glass. The next day remove cheese, rub all surfaces with 1 teaspoon (5 ml) salt and return the cheese to the press. Again press overnight with 20 pounds (10 kg), the weight of 4 bricks. The next morning remove the cheese, rub with 1 teaspoon (5 ml) salt, dry for 4 days at 60°F (15°C) and dip in paraffin to seal. Cure the sealed Cheddar Cheese in the vegetable crisper for 6 months and eat with a light heart. This cheese, though pale in color because I use no coloring agent, will please the taste buds of any gourmet.

Serving Cheese

Cheese is served immediately following the main course and before the dessert in many formal dinners; each cheese is served on a separate plate. Some people serve cheese with butter earlier in the meal to give the diner a choice of butter with cheese or vice versa. At one very elegant dinner I remember cheese was served on small boards at each end of the table and everyone cut his own wedge. A nibble of cheese clears the taste buds making them ready for sweets, my Grandmother told me but Grandaddy ate cheese with dessert contending that well-aged cheese complements sweetness like a blush does a pretty girl; he would always look at me and I would blush. How I hated to blush and now I don't know how to do it. Time is a strange teacher.

Party Snacks

Thanks to the Russian custom Zakuski, hors d'oeuvres have infiltrated nearly every American life-style. Snacks nibbled with a drink before luncheon or dinner are as much in fashion in this century as East Indian Sweetmeats, tea and gut-shriveling brandy were in the last. Though not prima donnas of the platter, cheeses are the backbone of our meal before the meal. Cheeses try to please but unfortunately, cheeses cubed on a plate or sliced in rounds sometimes just lie there in need of a front man. Cheeses seem to need a P.R. organization.

Decorations such as tufts of watercress, chickweed, chervil, pennyroyal, fennel or a pinch of frosty young kale laced between rows of rigid cheese will lure nibblers and add a refreshment of their own.

Wedges of tame fruits and vegetables: pears, pomegranate and turnips, as well as wild friends: Indian cucumbers, Jerusalem artichokes and frittered milkweed pods lend a certain flair to a cheese dish.

And don't forget flowers: carnations, cattails, chrysanthemums, elder, meadowsweet, honeysuckle, violets, roses, day lilies and thistle blow.

Mix and match cheese with red and green pepper crescents, pickled beets, dilly beans, fennel root, preserved cherries and peppery cheerful eggs. At one party I was aghast to watch six eggs literally slither down a very skinny man's throat as he hovered over the dish. Whether deviled or straight, hard-boiled eggs always go well with cheese snacks.

Brioches play up cheese personalities; dark breads and hot whites please cheese. Wedges of toast are true-Blue friends and surprisingly, a bite of sweet such as a gargantuan Danish coffee cake satisfies, and complements cheese comrades.

Try a dish of Brick cubes snuggling with frogs legs, or cornets of Brick with pickled mushrooms. Crab, shrimp, clams, bacon, and sausage all stretch when nicely wedded with cream cheese, and they do not lose their first class status either. Giblets cooked in wine sauce and young, crisp fried okra are nice finger food with Bel Paese. Oysters smoked in your own fireplace grace a cheese plate as the smoke fragrance reaches out to entice. Tiny baked potatoes with a chivey fluff of sour cream mellow a bite of Blue. A patty dish of cumin next to Cheddar makes it think it's Munster, and it assumes a regal air.

Of course there is Limburger with green onions, but you must be outside for that — poolside is great.

There are no limits on fondue variations, ramekins and tarts, that blossom with Bel Paese.

And Feta, heaven lies hidden in its simple goodness.

Simplicity, the key, the riddle's answer.. . . Beauty is a riddle; life, joy, hope are riddles. Taste is a riddle. A simple cheese with good friends answers the riddle of happiness.

CHAPTER III

Raised Doughs and Yeasty Treats

Breadmaking has been a traditional stillroom task. From small, hearth-baked cakes made from coarsely ground grains to sophisticated loaves raised with yeast, bread has been the joy and mainstay of American meals.

The ingredients of bread: yeast, flour, liquid, sugar, salt and shortening rarely change, although techniques and embellishments vary. As in other areas of stillroom cookery, breadmaking deals with natural phenomena and though nature is an easygoing mistress, she tends to enjoy capricious streaks. By their very naturalness, flours and yeasts are sometimes not standardized so the baker must exercise his own creative powers to compensate for their tricks. There can be as much as 20% difference in the moisture content of flour and some yeasts contain a lot more vim than others.

Before the days of dependable baking powder, stillroom cooks employed yeasts to give variety and leavening to breads and desserts. Stillrooms incubated fancy yeasts, pure strains coveted for winemaking; executive-type yeasts skimmed from beers; as well as laborers, home-grown worker yeasts to be used for daily baking. Yeasts and fermentation were two of the most important aspects of early American cooking.

For years I have been curious about making yeast 'from scratch' and after trying my hand at various concoctions I came up with a workable ferment — workable if you're not in a hurry.

To make yeast add four boiled and mashed potatoes to two quarts of water containing a handful of dried hops (drug store). Boil fifteen minutes and add six tablespoons of flour that have been mixed in a cup of cold water with one cup of sugar and one tablespoon of salt. Stir, scald and set aside. When almost cold add one cup of old yeast skimmed from the top of brewing beer and thin the liquid with one-half quart of warm water. Stir, pour an equal amount of the liquid yeast into three quart jars, cover and use at the rate of one-half cup for each batch of bread. This yeast will stay active in a cool place for about two months and longer if stored on the floor of the stillroom.

Yeast plants devour the sugars in bread dough and give off carbon dioxide which expands causing rising, or bubbles of gas to form in the loaf. Yeast also softens the gluten of flour making it elastic and more digestible. Most important, however, yeasts produce the fresh-baked-bread fragrance that enchants the senses and mellows the heart.

I use packaged active dry yeast for my baking needs and dissolve it in cozy warm water, about 110°F (45°C), for a few minutes before using in order to insure that it is a healthy, vigorous strain. For quicker action a pinch of sugar and/or two packages of yeast may be utilized.

All-purpose flour is generally best for breadmaking because it contains a blend of hard, high-gluten wheats, as opposed to soft, low-gluten wheat flour preferred for baking cakes. When flour is kneaded with liquid, fibers of gluten stretch to hold the yeast bubbles and baking sets the gluten framework so that the loaf retains its shape. When you buy flour for breadmaking make sure the flour is all-purpose or plain. I unknowingly once bought 25 pounds of self-rising flour and it took two batches of salty, leaden bread for me to catch on and read the label.

Liquid, such as water, milk, vegetable cooking water, eggs or old beer, mixes with the flour to form a dough. Milk or eggs tend to make a softer, malleable loaf, water makes a crusty, drier bread and vegetable water seems to bring out an earthy flavor.

Sugar (white, brown, honey or molasses) flavors bread and furnishes food for the yeast. It also helps loaves to brown nicely.

Salt seems to whiten the bread and strengthen the wheat flavor. Studies show that salt slows the rate of yeast formation and acts as a time capsule for slow-rising breads.

Shortening or oil tenderizes baked goods, keeps them soft and retards drying. Shortening rubbed on the top of rising dough moisturizes and tends to lighten heavy dough.

Eggs and malt liquids add color, tenderize and moisten the crumb.

Flours made from beans or grains other than white-flour-processed wheat rarely contain sufficient gluten to allow a loaf to 'stand high'. For this reason rye, oat, corn, whole wheat and bean loaves are usually fine grained, moist, and heavy compared to white bread. Combined with all-purpose flour (one part to three or four parts white) they make a slightly heavier but more flavorful loaf.

In mixing breadmaking ingredients I usually activate the yeast in a large bowl then stir in liquids, salt, sugar, shortening and lastly add flour. I am partial to cooking oil (corn, peanut, or whatever your choice) and am a true patron of kneading. I believe that kneading bread is psychologically good for the kneader and physiologically excellent for the loaf.

When the flour and liquid are well mixed and the dough no longer sticks to the sides of the bowl I flour my hands, turn the dough out on a floured surface and work it briskly with my palms. Pressing down with both hands, but mainly using the base of the palms and thumb muscles, I push on the dough stretching away from me that which is under my right hand. I then fold the right hand's dough back over the depression made by the left hand and when bringing the neck of dough back, I turn the whole wad of dough counterclockwise a half circle. Repeat the pushing down with both heels of the hands, stretching out with the right, folding back the right hand neck of dough and turning the whole thing with both hands.

The dough will be sticky at first and you will be tempted to knead in more and more flour, but you must be cautious that only a thin film of flour is on the board after the initial stickiness disappears.

Development of gluten is achieved by firm kneading for about 10 minutes and when "dough is done" a sheen or low glow emanates from its surface. The dead gray of newly mixed dough is not visible. It's like riding a bicycle, once you have mastered the technique, you never forget. A baker senses the lightness and knows when his dough is ready to "set to rise."

Unless specifically stated I allow bread to rise three times: twice in the bowl and once in the pans. Each rising should be in a cozy, warm place, about 80°F (26°C), that is, as warm as a summer day. I grease the top of rising dough and cover the container with a tea towel. For a faster rise I put the bowl of dough over a pan of hot water or set it on the radiator or stove pilot. In hot weather rising dough should be kept in the cooler part of the room.

The first rising usually takes longer to double its original bulk than later risings. When double, test by gently pressing your finger against the dough and if the depression does not pop up, the bread dough is ready to punch down. Punching inward, folding the dough over or kneading the dough gently usually takes less than a minute. The purpose is to let out some of the gas so that fermentation can continue without stretching the gluten too far and injuring the dough. Remember to get all your aggressions out of your system on the first kneading because subsequent handling should be gentle. The second rising helps to give a fine even grain to bread.

After the dough has risen in the bowl a second time it should be punched down, divided and molded into loaves that will half fill the pans selected. The top of each loaf should be greased to keep the surface elastic, the dough should be allowed to rise in the pan under a tea towel and when double, baked.

Pan size determines length of time for rising and baking. I like my 'small' pans, 7 × 4 × 2 inches (18 × 10 × 5 cm), they make a 1 pound loaf (500 g), bake quickly and give a good crust. Medium pans, 8 × 4 × 2½ inches (20 × 10 × 6 cm), give a 1½ pound loaf (725 g) and are great if you have a gang to feed. Large pans, 9 × 5 × 2½ inches (22 × 12 × 6 cm), make a 2 pound loaf (1 kg) which generally takes a longer time to bake and at a lower temperature than small bread.

Preheat the oven to the temperature required and place pans on shelves so that heat can circulate around each pan. To test if a loaf of bread is done tap it lightly with your fingernail; if it sounds hollow, it's done. I cool my loaves by removing from the pan and setting each loaf crosswise on the top of the empty pan.

When I baked bread in a mining camp in the mountains where I was chief cook and bottle washer for a summer, I halved all leavening after my first and second batches of bread exploded. An enormous 'swoosh' nearly heaved the oven off its little cast iron legs as my bread gave up its spirit and flattened itself across the pans. The second time it happened, the men said that the stove sported bowed legs thereafter. Altitude increases the power of yeast; to compensate use one half the amount of yeast called for and test the rising by pressing the edge of the dough even before it doubles in bulk.

Breads that were made in early American stillrooms are simple to create in today's kitchens and they are especially pleasureful family fare because round-the-table discussions about our forefathers and the reasons behind their actions develop an understanding of ourselves. On the next several pages a few updated recipes for pioneer breads are offered, followed by more traditional as well as fancy breadstuffs.

BACHELOR'S LOAF

A rich, single-rising bread recipe that makes good rolls, too.

Preparation time: 2 hours, 30 minutes. *Makes:* 2 loaves.

	U.S. CUSTOMARY	METRIC
In a bowl dissolve, let stand 5 minutes	1 package dry yeast ½ cup warm water 1 teaspoon sugar	1 pkg. yeast 125 ml water 5 ml sugar
Warm and add	1 cup milk 2 tablespoons butter 1 teaspoon salt	250 ml milk 30 ml butter 5 ml salt
Alternately stir in	3 eggs 4 cups flour	3 eggs 1 liter flour
On surface knead in	1¾ cups flour	425 ml flour

When the dough stiffens turn out onto a floured surface, beat and knead until the surface glows and the dough becomes elastic. Form into 2 loaves, place into pans, grease tops, cover with a tea towel and allow to rise for 2 hours in a warm place. Bake at 450°F (230°C) for 20 minutes.

Old Maids

These pleasant though hefty and hearty 'lady buns' are made from part of the Bachelor's Loaf dough. Roll a part of the dough to about ½ inch (1 cm) thick and cut into rounds with a coffee cup. Sprinkle corn meal on the board and press each cake into the meal to give an interesting gritty surface. The Old Maids are allowed to rise for an hour then fried over a low flame in a lightly greased griddle. Turn once. These bread-cakes are straw-colored, ringed with brown and in taste resemble English muffins or old fashioned hoecakes. By the way, if your oven is out of order or if you're camping, these slowly fried Old Maids are a perfect substitute for store-bought bread. Eaten hot with butter or smothered in yellow tomato preserves, these softhearted Old Maids hit the mark.

POWHATANS

Preparation time: 2 hours, 30 minutes. *Makes:* 2 dozen rolls.

	U.S. CUSTOMARY	METRIC
In a bowl dissolve	1 package dry yeast 1 cup warm water	1 pkg. yeast 250 ml water
Mix in	1 teaspoon salt 1 tablespoon sugar 4 cups flour 3 eggs (reserve 1 white) 4 tablespoons oil	5 ml salt 15 ml sugar 1 liter flour 3 eggs 60 ml oil
Pour onto flat surface	½ cup flour	125 ml flour

Turn dough onto floured surface and knead to form a firm dough. I work this dough about 10 minutes or until it captures a sheen. Replace in bowl, grease top, cover and set to rise for 1 hour. When double in bulk empty dough onto a floured surface and cut off sections about the size of a hot dog. Roll them between your greased palms until each rope is about 12 inches (30 cm) in length. Moisten and pinch ends together to form a hoop, then holding the two sides of the circle twist the hoop twice to form a cruller-shaped roll. Press each end firmly together to hold shape. Allow Powhatans to rise a second time on a greased cookie sheet for about 1 hour and brush each roll with egg white before baking at 450°F (230°C) for 15 minutes. Golden and glazed these bread  crullers are great with a supper of tamali pie, pickled Jerusalem artichokes on a wedge of lettuce and blackberry kuchen.

BABY JEAN ROLLS

Make these rough rolls if you feel in need of exercise.

Preparation time: 40 minutes. *Makes:* 3 dozen.

	U.S. CUSTOMARY	METRIC
Dissolve in	2 packages dry yeast	2 pkg. yeast
bowl	2 cups warm water	500 ml water
Add and mix	2 tablespoons sugar	30 ml sugar
well	2 teaspoons salt	10 ml salt
	4 tablespoons oil	60 ml oil
	6 cups flour	1.5 liters flour

When too tight to mix with a spoon pour onto floured surface and knead, beat and pound until the dough blisters and shines. This dough takes an incredible amount of abuse and muscle to bring out the 'sheen'. When finished beating pull off walnut-sized chunks, roll into a ball with your hands, hammer with your fist to flatten, transfer to a greased tin, prick all over with a fork and bake at 450°F (230°C) for 15 minutes.

Baby Jeans are like old-fashioned Beaten Biscuits that southern cooks used to beat with an axe on a biscuit block (usually the stump of an oak) and like Beaten Biscuits, they are an excellent release for frustrations. Fresh-baked Baby Jeans are like the Sea Biscuits that you buy. In our pre-pizza days (the days when our youngsters preferred peanut butter to pizza) I would beat out some Baby Jeans for the kids and roll some of the dough on a pizza tin. Although it puffs a bit in baking, Baby Jean dough works well for a snappy pizza.

MASHED POTATO BREAD

Preparation time: 3 hours, 30 minutes. *Makes:* 4 loaves or 2 loaves and 2 dozen biscuits.

	U.S. CUSTOMARY	METRIC
Peel, boil,	3 medium potatoes, or	3 potatoes
drain and mash	leftover mashed spuds	
Dissolve in	1 package dry yeast	1 pkg. yeast
large bowl	1 cup warm water	250 ml water
	1 teaspoon sugar	5 ml sugar
Add and work	1 teaspoon salt	5 ml salt
well with spoon	4 teaspoons oil	20 ml oil
	mashed potatoes	potatoes
	3 eggs	3 eggs
	8 cups flour	2 liters flour

Add no other liquid but mix well, pour onto floured board and knead vigorously. The dough will not gleam "like a baby's spanked behind" as proper dough should do, according to my grandmother, but will be rather soft and flabby. Cover and let rise in a warm spot for 1½ hours. Push down, form into loaves, butter tops and let them rise in the pan for 1 hour. Bake at 450°F (230°C) for 20 minutes. I usually bake 2 loaves of Potato Bread and form 2 inch (5 cm) round biscuits from the rest of the dough. Place the biscuits rather closely together in a pan, butter tops, let rise for 1 hour and bake at 450°F (230°C) for 15 minutes.

Potato Bread Dumplings

This dough makes nice dumplings if you have stock or soup on the stove. Using kitchen shears snip lanky dumplings, the size of your thumb, into boiling broth making sure to dip the scissors in the boiling liquid between each snip. Boil dumplings uncovered for 10 minutes. Serve at once in soup or remove from liquid with a slotted spoon and serve as a potato substitute. Dollops of sour cream and a sprinkle of chopped winter onion tops go well on Potato Dumplings, or if you have to hold them before serving, put them into a pan with a little butter and a handful of toasted breadcrumbs; the slickity and crunch go great together.

RUSKS

An old-timey sweetish tea cake that nearly everyone loves.

Preparation time: 20 minutes to mix, an overnight stay, plus 2 hours to complete and bake. *Makes:* 5 dozen rolls.

	U.S. CUSTOMARY	METRIC
Things to do the night before:		
In a bowl dissolve	1 package of dry yeast	1 pkg. yeast
	1 cup warm water	250 ml water
Beat together and add	4 eggs	4 eggs
	2 cups warm milk	500 ml milk
	6 cups flour	1.5 liters flour

Mix with a spoon to make a sponge, cover well (I wrap it in a blanket) and put in a warm place overnight.

The following morning:

Work into the dough	½ cup soft butter	125 ml butter
	1 cup sugar	250 ml sugar
	1 teaspoon salt	5 ml salt
	4 cups flour	1 liter flour

Pour dough out onto a floured surface and knead briskly. (At this point I sometimes sneak a wad of Rusk dough, roll thinly into a rectangle, butter, sugar and scatter coconut, raisins, cinnamon or chopped nuts, roll up as for a jelly roll, slice into 1 inch (2 cm) pieces, roll each piece flat into 3 inch (8 cm) rounds, place on a buttered cookie sheet and bake at 450°F (230°C) for 10 minutes. Instant breakfast!) However, real Rusks should be allowed ro rise in the bowl a second time, then shaped with the palms into patty pans, egg-shaped biscuits, and allowed to rise on greased cookie tins until double and very light. Wet the Rusk tops with sugar mixed with cream and bake at 400°F (200°C) for 15 minutes. I have discovered that Rusk dough may be refrigerated and baked another day. Remove from the icebox 2 hours before shaping into biscuits, rise in the pan, and bake as regular Rusks. I have also discovered that these old-fashioned biscuits have great man appeal at cocktail parties. I must warn, however, that there is always one clown who smears his Rusk with Liederkrantz.

CORN DODGERS

Corn Dodgers and Ash Cakes were basic breads in many southern diets, and although I have been told and shown how to make both breads, my skills fail me. If someone wishes to try their luck, this recipe was given to me by a delightful woman whom I met under an oak tree when we were both trying to beat the squirrels to the acorns. Her Dodgers were very good.

Preparation time: 1 hour. *Makes:* 2 dozen biscuits.

	U.S. CUSTOMARY	METRIC
Mix into a	4 cups white corn meal	1 liter meal
dough	1 cup (scant) cold water	250 ml water
	1 teaspoon salt	5 ml salt

Work well with hands, press into oblong cakes, place in a greased iron skillet or griddle. Bake until edges are brown and crusty in a moderate oven, 350°F (175°C), for about 40 minutes. Even though Dodgers contain no sugar, they are sweet.

Ash Cakes

Ash Cakes are made similarly but the palm-sized 'pones' of dough are laid on the swept-clean hearth, just in front of the fire of an open fireplace. When the tops of the pones are slightly dried they are draped with grape or collard leaves, covered with wood ashes and allowed to bake until firm, about 15 or 20 minutes. Ashes are shaken off the breads before they are served!

CORN BUBS

A more conventional yeast corn bread that may be formed into loaves as well as Bubs (buns).

Preparation time: 4 hours, 30 minutes. *Makes:* 1 dozen Bubs, plus 2 loaves.

	U.S. CUSTOMARY	METRIC
Dissolve in	1 package dry yeast	1 pkg. yeast
large bowl	1 cup warm water	250 ml water
Mix in to	1½ cups warm milk	375 ml milk
make a	3 tablespoons sugar	45 ml sugar
soft dough	1 tablespoon salt	15 ml salt
	3 tablespoons oil	45 ml oil
	4 cups flour	1 liter flour
	1 cup yellow corn meal	250 ml meal
Pour onto	2 cups flour	500 ml flour
kneading flat		

Empty dough onto floured surface, knead until smooth and place in a bowl, grease top, cover and set to rise in a warm place for 2 hours. Punch down and let rise a second time in the bowl. When nearly double the second time, punch down, grease hands and shape dough into balls, arranging them close together in a round cake pan. Form two small loaves of bread from the rest of the dough and place in greased bread tins. Cover, allow to rise until double. Bake at 400°F (200°C) for about 25 minutes and brush Bubs with butter when they come from the oven.

SWEET POTATO BISCUITS

I use this recipe for one pan of biscuits and a loaf of sweet potato bread, which makes grand toast. I have used this recipe substituting winter squash, pumpkin and turnips, all well drained and mashed, for the sweet potatoes and each vegetable lends its own personality to the bread. This is a good way to use up a couple of cups of leftover vegetables.

Preparation time: 30 minutes to mix, the overnight stay, plus 1 hour (or 2½ hours) to rise and bake. *Makes:* 30 bright orange biscuits, or one pan of 15 biscuits and 1 loaf of bread.

	U.S. CUSTOMARY	METRIC
Peel, boil, drain and mash	5 large sweet potatoes	5 sw. potatoes
In a bowl dissolve	1 package dry yeast	1 pkg. yeast
	½ cup warm water	125 ml water
Mix in	2 eggs	2 eggs
	1 teaspoon salt	5 ml salt
	mashed sweet potatoes	potatoes
	1 cup flour	250 ml flour

Stir until well blended, cover and let rise in warm place overnight. The following morning:

Work in	4 tablespoons oil	60 ml oil
	3 cups flour	750 ml flour

Pour onto a well floured surface, knead in flour until firm and elastic, mold into small biscuits, place closely on a greased cake pan, allow to rise until double, about 1 hour, and bake at 450°F (230°C) for 20 minutes. For a lighter biscuit or for loaves of bread, after kneading in flour let dough rise in the bowl until double before shaping into biscuits or loaves, then let rise in the pan and bake.

Sweet Potato Biscuits or bread are especially good on frosty November nights when served with chicken in wine sauce, asparagus tip salad, rice, buttered corn and chocolate cupcakes.

RYE BREAD

After bombing every rye bread recipe that reached my kitchen I finally found one that gave rye the lightness yet full gusto that I remember as a child.
Preparation time: about 6 hours. *Makes:* 5 small loaves.

	U.S. CUSTOMARY	METRIC
In a large bowl	1 package dry yeast	1 pkg. yeast
dissolve	2 cups warm water	500 ml water
	1 teaspoon sugar	5 ml sugar
When activated stir	1 cup warm coffee	250 ml coffee
in and mix until	1 cup warm milk	250 ml milk
well integrated	4 tablespoons honey	60 ml honey
	4 teaspoons salt	20 ml salt
	6 tablespoons oil	90 ml oil
Blend in	4 cups rye flour	1 liter rye flour
	4 cups white flour	1 liter white flour

As the dough becomes stiff pour onto a well floured surface and knead in about 2 additional cups (500 ml) white flour to make a pliable but soft dough. Knead vigorously for at least 5 minutes. Return dough to the bowl, grease top, cover and allow it to rise at room temperature for 2 hours or until double in volume. I sometimes divide rye bread dough into three separate bowls, add ½ cup (125 ml) raisins and a sprinkle of cinnamon to one bowl, knead in 2 tablespoons (30 ml) caraway seeds to the second wad of dough and allow one part of the rye dough to be plain. After the dough has doubled in volume, punch down, grease top, cover and let rise a second time in a comfortable place. When nearly double, about 1½ hours, form into loaves, place into greased pans and allow to rise in the pan until double. Bake at 400°F (200°C) for about 30 minutes. Remove, brush with butter for a deep color, cool and eat.

WHEAT BREAD

Preparation time: 3 hours. *Makes:* 2 loaves.

	U.S. CUSTOMARY	METRIC
Dissolve in	1 package dry yeast	1 pkg. yeast
bowl	½ cup warm water	125 ml water
Warm and add	1 cup milk	250 ml milk
	⅓ cup molasses	80 ml molasses
Mix well	1½ teaspoons salt	7 ml salt
	3 tablespoons oil	45 ml oil
Alternately	2 cups flour	500 ml flour
stir in	1 egg	1 egg
	2 cups whole wheat flour	500 ml whole wheat
Heap on knead-ing flat	1 cup flour	250 ml flour

Pour dough onto the floured surface and knead until light and elastic to the touch. Place in bowl, grease top, cover and let rise until double in volume, about 1½ hours. Push down, allow to rise a second time in the bowl for about 1 hour. Fold down, shape into 2 loaves, place into greased pans, cover and rise in the pans until double, about 1 hour. Bake at 400°F (200°C) for 30 minutes or until crusty brown.

Beans, precooked then baked with a small pork shoulder, tomatoes and molasses; a fresh fruit salad with a banana mashed in lemon juice and mayonnaise as dressing; plus hot buttered Wheat Bread makes a modest yet splendidly hearty supper.

RAISIN OATMEAL BREAD

Supergood with or without raisins.

Preparation time: 3 hours, 30 minutes. *Makes:* 4 small loaves.

	U.S. CUSTOMARY	METRIC
Boil, cool and set aside	1 cup quick oats	250 ml oats
	2 cups water	500 ml water
In a bowl dissolve	2 packages dry yeast	2 pkgs. yeast
	½ cup warm water	125 ml water
	4 tablespoons sugar	60 ml sugar
Mix into yeast, stand 10 min.	½ cup flour	125 ml flour
Add, mix well and pour onto a floured surface	the oatmeal	oatmeal
	1 tablespoon salt	15 ml salt
	2 tablespoons oil	30 ml oil
	5 cups flour	1.25 liters flour
	¾ cup raisins	175 ml raisins

Dough will be glucky and stick to your hands, but flour them and knead with determination for 5 minutes, cover and let rise in a bowl until double, about 1½ hours. Knead down, shape into loaves, place into 4 greased pans, brush with oil, cover and let rise in the pans until double, about 1 hour. Bake at 450°F (230°C) for 30 minutes or until freckled with brown.

Serve Raisin Oatmeal Bread slightly warm with a supper of potato soup, winter cabbage salad and apple brown betty. This child-appealing bread is especially nutritious plastered with honey or toasted for breakfast the following morning.

RUM ROLLS

Preparation time: 4 hours, 30 minutes. *Makes:* 30 rolls.

	U.S. CUSTOMARY	METRIC
In a large	1 cup warm milk	250 ml milk
bowl mix	1 package dry yeast	1 pkg. yeast
Stir in	½ cup sugar	125 ml sugar
	4 tablespoons oil	60 ml oil
	1¼ teaspoons salt	6 ml salt
	1 egg	1 egg
	1½ teaspoons rum flavoring	8 ml flavoring
	2 cups flour	500 ml flour

Cover and let rise in warm place until double in bulk, about 2 hours.

Spread on	2 cups flour	500 ml flour
kneading flat		

Pour dough onto the floured surface and knead, adding more flour if required. When smooth and light, divide dough into two parts and roll into strips each 12 × 6 × ¼ inches (30 × 15 × 1 cm). Brush with butter.

Sprinkle on	4 tablespoons sugar	60 ml sugar
each strip	4 tablespoons raisins	60 ml raisins

Roll as for a jelly roll from the long side, keep pulling dough out at edges to keep it uniform and seal by pressing edge with water. Roll should be 15 inches long (36 cm). Cut each roll crosswise into slices ¾ inch (2 cm) thick. Place rolled biscuits on a greased tin and let rise until double, about 1 hour. Bake at 400°F (200°C) for 15 minutes and as soon as the biscuits are removed from the oven brush tops with icing:

Mix	1 cup powdered sugar	250 ml pow. sugar
	1 tablespoon hot water	15 ml water
	1 tablespoon butter	15 ml butter
	1 tablespoon rum flavoring	15 ml flavoring

Cool briefly and eat. Rum rolls are nice to serve when company arrives at 11:00 A.M. to spend the day; fragrant, fresh from the oven, they start things right.

BASIC DINNER ROLLS

These sweetish mellow rolls may be baked the same day or the dough refrigerated and used within 2 weeks.

Preparation time: 20 minutes to mix and store in the icebox, plus a 2 hour warming period and a 1½ hour rise in the pan and bake time if you serve at a later date. Preparation time: 2 hours to make, bake and serve the same day. *Makes:* about 30 rolls.

	U.S. CUSTOMARY	METRIC
In bowl	1 package dry yeast	1 pkg. yeast
dissolve	4 tablespoons warm water	60 ml water

Add and mix	1 cup warm milk	250 ml milk
well	1 teaspoon salt	5 ml salt
	6 tablespoons oil	90 ml oil
	4 tablespoons sugar	60 ml sugar
	1 egg	1 egg
	5 cups flour	1.25 liters flour

Pour dough onto a well floured board and knead until the surface feels smooth and elastic. Return dough to bowl, grease top and cover. If you plan to use the same day, allow dough to rise in a warm place until double, about 1 hour, knead down, form into rolls, rise about 45 minutes and bake at 450°F (230°C) for 15 minutes. To store dough, grease top, cover well and place immediately in the refrigerator after the initial kneading. Remove from icebox approximately 2 hours before kneading, forming into rolls, allowing dough to rise on cookie sheets or in pans and baking.

Basic Dinner Rolls dough can be shaped into Parkerhouse, Cloverleaf, Pretzel and Crescent Rolls. There is no end of fun shapes to be created with dough: dinner rolls, egg shaped with egg white gloss; Vienna rolls, turkey egg shaped, baked crisp with corn starch and water topping; twists, a circle of pencil thin dough flipped into a figure 8; and donut buns. Snails, Butter Horns, Hot Cross Buns, Kolace and Butterfly Buns may be shaped from Basic Dinner Roll dough and iced while hot with confectioner's sugar and butter that has been moistened with vanilla.

With the exception of sugar frostings, toppings for dinner rolls should be glued to almost-baked buns with a fingertip application of raw egg white, then the rolls immediately popped back into the oven for a 3 or 4 minute toast. Topping ideas: garlic, onion or celery salt, grated cheese, paprika, curry, white pepper, or any of the zesty herbs. Cumin and chili powder, sage and black pepper, or parsley make interesting roll toppings. All kinds of chopped nuts or seeds, pumpkin and sunflower seed kernels, sesame, poppy and caraway are good and don't forget the wild ideas: seeds of lambs' quarters, amaranth as well as smartweed all create interesting toppings. Seeds burn readily so if you don't want your rolls to smell like incense or pot, toast them briefly on the bun at the last moment.

Early Virginia Federal Loaf

On a journey southward from Philadelphia the great orator, Daniel Webster, was reported to have requested Federal Loaf at every wayside inn. After numerous regrets a dusky maid in south Virginia was said to have produced a buttery pull-apart loaf and Mr. Webster thanked the shy lass with a glowing tribute.

A modern version of the early Virginia bread may be made by using the Basic Dinner Roll Dough recipe. Use refrigerated dough. Take from the icebox and immediately shape into two loaves. Working fast, immerse a sharp knife into 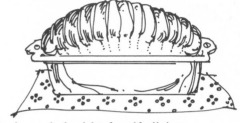 cold water and slice all the way through the unbaked loaf as if slicing bread. Butter the slice generously and lay aside on a floured surface. Dip knife in water and cut a second slice, butter it and lay aside. Dip knife blade between each slicing, butter each piece and lay on flour until the loaf is sliced. Finally, replace the slices until the loaf resumes its original shape, place in a greased bread pan that fits the loaf snugly. Repeat process with the second loaf. Butter tops and allow to rise for 2 hours before baking at 400°F (200°C) for 30 minutes. Served warm, the bread pulls apart and its buttery goodness complements any meal. Federal Loaf is excellent as a tea snack served with delicate violet jelly or with bits of smoked spiced beef.

PECAN ROLLS

Use Basic Dinner Roll dough plus 1 cup (250 ml) nuts.

	U.S. CUSTOMARY	METRIC
Boil for 5 minutes	¾ cup water	175 ml water
	1 cup plus 2 tablespoons brown sugar	280 ml brown sugar

Place 1 teaspoon (5 ml) of syrup in the bottom of each of 20 sections of well buttered deep muffin tins and arrange 4 pecan halves or a pinch of nuts in each. Turn dough onto a lightly floured board and roll to ½ inch (1 cm) thickness; cut into 2 inch (5 cm) rounds. Form into balls by folding under edges. Place one ball in each section, cover, let rise in a warm place until double and bake at 425°F (220°C) for 12-15 minutes. Remove rolls from pans immediately so that the sugar will not cool and harden in the pan and turn upside down on a buttered plate so that the pecan side will be up.

FLANNEL CAKES

To my taste these pancakes have a cleaner flavor than those made with sourdough.

	U.S. CUSTOMARY	METRIC
In a bowl dissolve	1 package dry yeast	1 pkg. yeast
	4 tablespoons warm water	60 ml water
Add and mix well	2 cups warm milk	500 ml milk
	½ teaspoon salt	2 ml salt
	2½ cups flour (scant)	600 ml flour
	1 cup corn meal	250 ml meal

Cover and set in a warm place overnight. In the morning:

	U.S. CUSTOMARY	METRIC
Stir in to make batter	1 egg	1 egg
	2 tablespoons oil	30 ml oil

If the batter is too thick add a second egg. Fry by spoonfuls on a hot, lightly greased griddle and serve. Like stillroom cooks, I enjoy honey, sorghum or maple syrup, but sometimes I boil brown sugar and water, 2 parts sugar to 1 of water for Flannel Cake syrup.

GRAHAM GRIDDLE CAKES

Graham flour griddle cakes are made similarly except that 3 cups (750 ml) of graham or whole wheat flour is substituted for the white flour and corn meal in the above recipe.

LIGHT BREAD

This has been the work horse, the everyday bread of many American homes.

Preparation time: 5 hours 30 minutes. *Makes:* 5 loaves.

	U.S. CUSTOMARY	METRIC
In large bowl dissolve	1 package dry yeast	1 pkg. yeast
	1 cup warm water	250 ml water
	1 teaspoon sugar	5 ml sugar
Add and mix	3 cups liquid	750 ml liquid
	½ cup dry milk	125 ml dry milk
	4 teaspoons salt	20 ml salt
	4 tablespoons sugar	60 ml sugar
	4 tablespoons oil	60 ml oil
Stir in	10 cups flour	2.5 liters flour

Pour dough onto a well floured surface:

	U.S. CUSTOMARY	METRIC
Knead in	2 cups flour (Approx.)	500 ml flour

Knead until dough is smooth, satiny and elastic. Grease top, return dough to the bowl, cover and place in a cozy spot and let rise until 'light,' that is, the pressure of a finger leaves a dent and the dough does not spring back, about 2 hours. Knead briefly, grease top, cover and let rise a second time for 1½ hours to about three-fourths the size of the first rising. Turn dough onto a lightly floured board, knead briefly and divide into five parts. I save one loaf-size piece of dough for storage in the icebox (grease top and cover) to be used for pizza, filled squares or sweet buns. Shape four parts into loaves, put them into greased pans, insert them upside down then turn loaves of dough over in order to grease bread tops evenly. Cover with a tea towel and let the dough rise in the pans until doubled in size. Bake at 450°F (230°C) for 20 to 30 minutes.

Roll-Up Buns

Light Bread dough is superb for making jelly rolls, cinnamon or fruit rolls, minced meat rolls, anchovies, slivered pepperoni, stuffed olive-cheese spread rolls, or sticky buns. Simply roll out the rectangle of dough to about ¼ inch (0.5 cm) thick, spread with butter and filling, and roll up from the long side, pulling the dough toward you as you roll away from yourself. Seal outer lip of the roll by pinching it with water and slice into ½ inch (1 cm) biscuits. Top with butter after placing them rather closely together in a well greased pan. Let your rolled buns rise in the pan as you would bread and bake at 400°F (230°C) for 12 to 15 minutes.

For Sticky Buns I swizzle a bit of honey over the cinnamon or fruit-filled (diced apples are good) buns about 5 minutes before they are completely baked and put them back into the oven to stew in their own juice for 5 more minutes. Remove all rolls from the pan immediately because sugar sticks when it gets cold. Flip the Sticky Buns over onto a buttered plate so that the gooey side is up.

Interesting buns may be made by filling rolled out Light Bread dough with sauted onions, 2 cups (500 ml) finely chopped onions fried until transparent; or nuts sprinked on the dough with brown sugar; or chopped ripe olives as filling for rolled buns are delicious with Italian food. I lubricate my rolls with olive oil when filling with olives and sometimes sliver a nibble of cheese on them, too.

Filled squares made from Light Bread dough that has been saved, unbaked, in the icebox are good filler-uppers, inexpensive and easily prepared dishes that may be served solo or embraced by sauce.

SAUSAGE SQUARES

Preparation time: 30 to 40 minutes. *Makes:* 10 squares.

	U.S. CUSTOMARY	METRIC
In skillet	½ pound hot sausage, bulk	250 g sausage
brown for	1 onion, chopped	1 onion
7 minutes	1 teaspoon salt	5 ml salt
Stir in	2 cups turnips and	500 ml turnips,
to heat	potatoes mashed together	potatoes

Mix ingredients well. While the filling is cooking roll out Light Bread dough on a lightly floured board and make ten 6 inch (15 cm) squares about ¼ inch (1 cm) thick. Place approximately 3 tablespoons (45 ml) of filling on each square. Moisten edges of the dough and fold the square across to make a triangle. Pinch the moistened edges together to seal, place on a cookie tin, slash tops for steam and bake at 400°F (200°C) for 20 minutes. I have found that the thinner you can roll out the dough, the better these are.

MEATLESS SQUARES

A meatless meal-in-itself from Light Bread dough.

Preparation time: 30 to 40 minutes. *Makes:* 8 squares.

	U.S. CUSTOMARY	METRIC
In skillet	2 tablespoons oil	30 ml oil
cook for 5	1 cup chopped onions	250 ml onions
minutes	½ cup sliced mushrooms	125 ml mushrooms
	1 teaspoon salt	5 ml salt
	¼ teaspoon pepper, basil	1 ml pepper, basil
Stir lightly	1 cup cooked rice	250 ml rice
and add,	½ cup cottage cheese	125 ml cheese
cover and cook	1 cup shredded cabbage	250 ml cabbage
5 minutes	1 tablespoon soy sauce	15 ml soy

Roll out Light Bread dough about ¼ inch thick (1 cm), cut into five 6 inch (15 cm) squares. Place about 3 tablespoons (45 ml) of filling on each square. Moisten edges of dough and fold across to make a triangle. Pinch moistened edges to seal, place on a greased cookie tin, slash tops for steam, and bake at 400°F (230°C) for 20 minutes.

My neighbor adds tiny shrimp to the Meatless Squares and they are delicious. I have tried leftover meatloaf lubricated with a bit of barbecue sauce as a filling for Light Bread squares and also cubed chicken precooked in a white sauce with peas and celery. If you have any gravy lurking in the icebox, puddle it over the filled squares about 10 minutes before taking them from the oven. And sometimes a daub of sour cream popped on top just before serving brightens this all-in-one meal. Served with salad and peach cobbler, you will be favored by all who dine with you.

PIZZA

Light Bread dough that has been refrigerated for one day to two weeks makes an excellent pizza base. In fact I have found that older dough rolls out more easily than freshly made dough. It does not spring back as if frightened, nor does a wad pout in the corner of a tray. As a tipsy cook once told me, "Good pizza dough's like them women that got a little age on them, they stays put."

Take Light Bread dough from the icebox and let rise about 2 hours before using. Roll very thin, place on a center-greased cookie tin, pull carefully to each side and pinch edges to form a standing rim of dough. Cover the surface with Marie's Pizza Sauce or an 8 oz. can (225 g) tomato sauce sprinkled with garlic salt, chopped onions and green peppers, chili powder, a touch of cumin and a dash of oregano. The real creativity of pizza-making lies in the topping. Anything goes, anything but turnips; somehow turnip pizza did not say anything to Lewis. Top your pizza with any kind of cheese, anchovy or fish, clams, baby smoked oysters, or any meat that you have. Great pizzas can be made with poultry, of course mushroom or onion, ripe or green olives, bean or leftover chili con carne, cubes of yesterday's tamale pie, slivered almonds or chopped nuts, crunchy bean sprouts, blue cheese with bacon, or corned beef bits. I have put corn flakes under Mozzarella for texture, crab meat pizza is superb, black-eye peas, lamb patty. . . . I almost wrote, peanut. I'll have to try peanut pizza some day. The list is endless, as my tippling friend said, "Anything but a black cigar." Bake pizza at 450°F (230°C) for 15 minutes.

'Making Pizzas' is a grand way for a gang of young people to spend an evening. Music turned up, three or four doughs rolled out, what fun our trio have had with their friends in the kitchen! The only drawback is that you have to take a putty knife to the floor the next day.

CALZONE

A creative answer to the ham and cheese sandwich doldrums.

Preparation time: 30 minutes.

Roll Light Bread dough very thin, cut into rounds with a tea cup and fill the round on one side with a slice of ham and cheese, a bit of oil, salt and pepper. Fold over into a half circle, press with water to seal, poke a hole for steam and bake at 400°F (200°C) for 20 minutes or fry slowly in a tiny bit of olive oil.

CRISPELLO

Roll Light Bread dough thinly, sprinkle with garlic salt, cut into rounds with a cup, prick with a fork all over and fry in hot oil, 375°F (190°C) until crisp. Serve with chili con carne or sauerkraut soup.

Away-From-Home-Homemaker Light Bread

A good way to serve Light Bread for supper even though you work.

Preparation time: All day. 10 minutes in the morning, a daylong stay in the icebox, 2 hours at room temperature and rise in the pan, plus 30 minutes baking.

Get up about 10 minutes earlier than usual and make Light Bread dough. Knead, replace in bowl, grease top of dough, cover and set bowl over a pan of hot water, about 140°F (60°C). Just before you leave for work punch down dough, grease top, cover and set bowl in the refrigerator. Ever since the day that I went to town for 8 hours and left dough rising over a pan of hot water and spent another 8 hours picking the gas burners clean, I hang a note to myself on the front door knob: PUT BREAD IN ICEBOX. A note also helps the first child home to remember to remove the dough from the refrigerator and punch it down. Kids love to fool with dough. After an hour at room temperature, form into loaves, and for an hour or so, let rise in the pans, then bake at 450°F (230°C) for 20 minutes. I have read that some professional bakers prefer cool rising for 8 to 12 hours rather than allowing dough to rise in a warm place; they say a cool rise gives bread more body and better texture and I have found that it works.

To cut hot bread, do not press down with the knife. Lift up the sides of the loaf as you gently score the crust and slice. A sharp serrated bread knife seems to work best.

Store or freeze bread after it is thoroughly cooled. Wrap in an airtight bag, seal tightly and store in a cool, dry bread box or freeze immediately. To thaw frozen bread takes about 2 hours, do not unwrap until just before serving and if you wish to crisp a loaf, warm in an oven at 375°F (190°C) for 20 minutes.

Polish Pizza

A variation of Italian Pizza for sit-down suppers with knife and fork.

Preparation time: 30 minutes.

Roll Light Bread dough as for regular pizza, spread with sauce and topping, then roll into a long jelly roll loaf sealing edges with water.

Transfer the filled loaf to a greased, square 'corn bread' pan and curve the loaf slightly to form a crescent. Bake at 400°F (200°C) for 15 minutes, remove from oven, pour additional sauce over the filled loaf, top with your favorite cheese and return to oven for 5 minutes or until the cheese drizzles. Serve immediately, cut slices and spoon over with sauce. As a main dish served with avocado-lettuce salad, succotash, fried milkweed pods and vanilla ice cream topped with crushed peanut brittle as dessert, your Polish Pizza supper will be long remembered.

I knew a lady who cut her unbaked Polish Pizza loaf into gooey biscuits, 1 inch (2 cm) slices, baked them in a well greased cake pan and a few minutes before taking them from the oven, poured over extra sauce and slivered cheese on top. She said that it was easier to eat than the Polish Pizza in a loaf. Any way you serve it, Polish is perfect.

Leftover Bread

Light breadmaking used to be a daily stillroom chore but I bake twice weekly and if any 'old bread' is left in the box, I cube it and toast the cubes on a cookie tin in the oven, about 20 minutes at 350°F (175°C) or until golden brown. These toasted bread cubes keep almost indefinitely in a tightly-lidded canning jar; they can be crushed for crumbs and they are great for instant topping, croutons, stuffing or warmed with nuts for a jiffy party snack.

BREAD ROAST

A totally different flavored casserole from toasted cubes.
Preparation time: 45 minutes. *Serves:* 5.

	U.S. CUSTOMARY	METRIC
Soak for 5 minutes	2 cups toasted bread cubes	500 ml cubes
	2 cups milk, part cream	500 ml milk
Beat and mix in	2 eggs	2 eggs
	1 teaspoon salt	5 ml salt
	2 teaspoons grated onions	10 ml onions
	1 cup chopped nuts	250 ml nuts

Pour into a buttered baking dish, cover and bake at 350°F (175°C). Delicious for non-meat eaters.

DEVILED OYSTERS IN THE SHELL

When you go to the waterfront or fish stand beg or liberate 18 oyster shells, scrub them well and douse with boiling water. This dish may be served in a casserole but it's more fun in the shell.

Preparation time: 45 minutes. *Makes:* 18 deviled oysters.

	U.S. CUSTOMARY	METRIC
Drain and save juice	18 select oysters about a pint	18 oysters about 500 ml
Soak in juice until moist	1 cup bread cubes 1 teaspoon salt 2 raw eggs	250 ml cubes 5 ml salt 2 raw eggs
Mix well	2 chopped hard eggs 1 teaspoon chop. parsley ¼ teaspoon thyme the oysters	2 eggs, hard boiled 5 ml parsley 1 ml thyme oysters
In small skillet melt	3 tablespoons butter	45 ml butter

Pour the moistened bread and oyster mixtures into the skillet, stir once or twice, cover and cook slowly for 15 minutes. Do not brown. When heated through spoon into the washed and buttered oyster shells, making sure to get one oyster in each shell, sprinkle over with bread crumbs and a lump of butter. Set shells on a cookie tin and bake at 350°F (175°C) for 15 to 20 minutes. Some people top each serving with cayenne pepper, but our family prefers the delicate flavor of oysters.

BLACK BREAD

Preparation time: 6 hours. *Makes:* 2 large loaves.

	U.S. CUSTOMARY	METRIC
In large bowl dissolve	2 packages dry yeast 1 cup warm water	2 pkgs. yeast 250 ml water
Warm over low heat and pour into yeast bowl	1½ cups strong coffee 1 tablespoon onion juice 4 tablespoons molasses 4 tablespoons vinegar ½ cup oil	375 ml coffee 15 ml onion juice 60 ml molasses 60 ml vinegar 125 ml oil
Mix separately and gradually add to the yeast and liquid in	4 cups rye flour 4 cups flour 3 tablespoons cocoa or one square chocolate, melt 1 tablespoon sugar 2 teaspoons salt	1 liter rye 1 liter flour 45 ml cocoa or chocolate 15 ml sugar 10 ml salt

bowl. Stir	2 cups bran or cereal	500 ml bran
well	2 tablespoons caraway seed	30 ml caraway
	½ teaspoon fennel or anise	2 ml fennel

Stir with a spoon until ingredients are well mixed and soft dough forms.

| Spread on | 1 cup flour | 250 ml flour |
| kneading flat | | |

Turn out the dough, knead in flour adding more if too soft and knead until dough is manageable. Dough will be sticky but when light, cover and allow to stand for about 30 minutes. Return to knead a few minutes, place dough in bowl, grease top, cover and let rise for 2 hours in a warm place. Punch down, knead briefly, let rise again in a bowl for about 1½ hours. Turn out onto a floured surface, divide into two rounds about 6 inches (15 cm) and place each ball of dough in a greased, round cake tin. Cover and let rise a third time in the pan. When doubled, about 1 hour, bake at 400°F (200°C) for about 45 minutes. When done to a rich brown remove from oven and brush with cornstarch glaze, return bread to the oven and bake 5 more minutes.

CORNSTARCH GLAZE

To give your bread a bright, professional look, combine 1 tablespoon (15 ml) cornstarch with ½ cup (125 ml) cold water. Stirring constantly, cook over a low heat until it boils and boil for 1 minute. Brush on hot bread, or refrigerate and use when needed.

CORN MEAL BREAD

This supergood old-fashioned, corn-molasses yeast bread is especially fragrant and nutritious.

Preparation time: 4 hours, 30 minutes. *Makes*: 3 loaves.

	U.S. CUSTOMARY	METRIC
In large bowl	1 package dry yeast	1 pkg. yeast
dissolve	½ cup warm water	125 ml water
In a pan mix	2 cups cold water	500 ml water
cold, boil	½ cup corn meal	125 ml meal
for 1 minute	2 tablespoons butter	30 ml butter
and cool	½ cup molasses	125 ml molasses
	1½ teaspoons salt	7 ml salt

When lukewarm combine corn meal with yeast mixture in a bowl.

| Stir in | 5 cups flour | 1.25 liters flour |

Pour the soft dough onto a floured surface and knead in enough flour to make a firm dough. Place in bowl, grease top and let rise in warm place until doubled, about 1½ hours. Turn out onto a lightly floured surface, knead briefly, return to bowl and allow dough to rise a second time for about 1 hour. When not quite doubled in bulk, punch down and form into loaves. Place into 3 greased 1 pound (500 g) loaf tins and let rise in pans until doubled. Bake at 400°F (200°C) for about 45 minutes.

We enjoy warm Meal Bread drenched in butter and eaten with an everyday meal of fried fish, hot slaw, butter beans and pears in a light syrup with a touch of anise. If there is a cubbyhole of room left, another piece of Meal Bread with a bite of damson preserves does the trick.

I baked this bread on the Yukon and received two separate proposals for marriage in one evening. Very embarrassing!

FRENCH BREAD

An unconventional but delightful bread.

Preparation time: 3 hours. *Makes:* 2 loaves.

	U.S. CUSTOMARY	METRIC
In large	1 package dry yeast	1 pkg. yeast
bowl	1½ cups warm water	375 ml water
dissolve	1 tablespoon sugar	15 ml sugar
Add, mix well	1½ teaspoons salt	7 ml salt
with spoon	1 tablespoon oil	15 ml oil
	4 cups flour	1 liter flour

Work the dough with a spoon by scraping down the side of the bowl, up again, across the top and cutting through the center. The dough should always be worked with a large spoon, not kneaded. (I use a wooden spoon because the Frenchman who taught me used wood. He was a Liberator, he liberated 40 gallons of my best wine, but looking back it was a good exchange.) Work the dough for about 1 minute at 10 minute intervals. Do this 5 consecutive times. Cover dough between workings to keep it warm. Turn the dough onto a lightly floured surface, divide into two balls, roll them back and forth in the flour, cover, let them 'heal' on the board for 10 minutes, then roll out into a 9 × 12 inch (22 × 30 cm) rectangle. With your hands roll the dough tightly the long way to form an elongated jelly roll-type loaf. Place on a greased baking sheet, score the top diagonally 6 times with a sharp knife, cover with a towel and let rise 1½ hours. Bake at 400°F (200°C) for 30 minutes. For a glossy pate, dip your fingers into egg white and brush tops as soon as the loaves come from the oven, or rub with butter. Cool slightly and pull apart to eat.

DIET BREAD

A salt-free bread for persons on special diets.

Preparation time: 3 hours, 30 minutes. *Makes:* 3 small loaves.

	U.S. CUSTOMARY	METRIC
In large bowl	1 package dry yeast	1 pkg. yeast
dissolve	2 cups warm water	500 ml water
	2 tablespoons sugar	30 ml sugar
Mix in	1 cup powdered dry milk	250 ml milk
	4 tablespoons oil	60 ml oil
	7 cups flour	1.75 liters flour

The last of the flour may be spread on a kneading surface, the dough poured onto it and kneaded. Knead for about 5 minutes or until the dough is smooth and elastic. Place in bowl, grease top, cover and let rise in a warm place until double, about 1½ hours. Punch down and turn onto a lightly floured surface, knead briefly, return to bowl, cover and let rise until about three-fourths the size of the first rising, about 45 minutes. Punch down, shape into loaves and place in greased tins. Cover, let rise until doubled in bulk, about 45 minutes and bake at 400°F (200°C) for 30 minutes.

SALT RISING BREAD

Contains no sugar or fat except what is naturally in the milk, and contrary to its name, Salt Rising Bread calls for only a small amount of salt.

Preparation time: A few minutes plus the overnight stay and about 4 hours of mixing and rising the following day. *Makes:* 3 loaves.

	U.S. CUSTOMARY	METRIC
To be started the evening before:		
In large bowl mix	½ teaspoon salt ½ cup flour	2 ml salt 125 ml flour
Pour on while mixing to make a stiff paste	4 tablespoons boiling water	60 ml water

Cover and set in a warm place overnight. I wrap it in a blanket.
The following morning:

Mix in to make a batter (use fingers or fork to mash lumps)	2 cups warm milk ½ teaspoon salt 4 cups flour	500 ml milk 3 ml salt 1 liter flour
Dissolve and add to bowl	1 package dry yeast ½ cup warm water	1 pkg. yeast 125 ml water

Mix well. Dough will be soupy. Set the bowl over a pan of hot water, 140°F (60°C) and let stand covered for about 1½ hours or until the batter bubbles and rises.

Add, stir and knead in	2½ cups flour	625 ml flour

Pour dough onto floured surface and knead well. This dough will not have the sheen of regular bread dough but it will become pliable. Return dough to bowl, cover and set to rise in a warm place for 1 hour. Punch down when double in bulk and form into loaves. Put into greased tins, cover with a towel and allow to rise 1 hour. Bake at 450°F (230°C) for 20 minutes.

WHOLE WHEAT HONEY BREAD

Preparation time: 3 hours. *Makes:* 4 loaves.

	U.S. CUSTOMARY	METRIC
In a bowl dissolve	2 packages dry yeast 2 cups warm water	2 pkgs. yeast 500 ml water
Add and stir well	4 teapoons salt ½ cup honey 6 tablespoons oil	20 ml salt 125 ml honey 90 ml oil
Mix in	4 cups whole wheat flour 4 cups white flour	1 liter w. w. flour 1 liter flour

Pour dough onto a heavily floured board and knead, adding more flour if necessary to make an elastic dough. Place in bowl, grease top, cover and let rise 1 hour. Knead down, replace in bowl, cover and let rise a second time for 45 minutes. Shape into loaves, put into greased pans, cover, let rise in pans until double, about 45 minutes, and bake at 450°F (230°C) for 20 minutes.

BRIOCHES

Whimsical breakfast muffins to be started the evening before. The word brioches is said to mean "to make a blooper." When a musician in an early day band hit a sour note he was obliged to pay a fine. In time, the sum of fines went for a brioches blast, a party where the whole orchestra got their fill of these light buns.

Preparation time: 30 minutes to mix, the overnight stay, plus 40 minutes to rise and bake the following morning. *Makes:* 16 buns.

	U.S. CUSTOMARY	METRIC
In a bowl dissolve	1 package dry yeast 1 tablespoon warm water	1 pkg. yeast 15 ml water
Add and beat vigorously	3 eggs 2 tablespoons sugar	3 eggs 30 ml sugar
Mix in	1¾ cups flour	425 ml flour

Beat dough until smooth and satiny.

Add	¾ cup creamed butter	175 ml butter

Beat vigorously a few more minutes, let dough rest, cover for 20 minutes, stir down, sprinkle with a little flour and refrigerate overnight. The following morning punch down dough and spoon into greased muffin tins or small molds until half filled. Cover and let rise about 30 minutes. Bake at 450°F (230°C) for 8 to 10 minutes.

Brioches are a bright treat for Sunday breakfast. Serve with poached salt herring, eggs scrambled with cooked carrots and a dish of home canned peaches.

DANISH COFFEE TWIST

A large coffee cake that goes well at a holiday brunch.
Preparation time: 3 hours, 30 minutes. *Makes:* 2 twists.

	U.S. CUSTOMARY	METRIC
In a bowl	2 packages dry yeast	2 pkgs. yeast
dissolve	1½ cups warm water	375 ml water
	1 teaspoon sugar	5 ml sugar
Add and	2 eggs	2 eggs
mix in	½ cup honey	125 ml honey
	1 teaspoon salt	5 ml salt
	½ cup oil	125 ml oil
	1 tablespoon slivered lemon or orange peel	15 ml peel
Gradually add	7 cups flour	1.75 liters flour

When dough is formed turn onto a floured board and knead, adding more flour if required to make a firm, glossy dough. Return dough to bowl, grease top, cover and let rise until double, about 1 hour. Punch down, knead briefly, divide into two parts and on a lightly floured surface roll out into long, narrow sheets, 18 × 6 × ½ inches (45 × 15 × 1 cm).

Spread over	4 tablespoons soft butter	60 ml butter
dough sheet	½ cup brown sugar	125 ml sugar
	2 teaspoons cinnamon	10 ml cinnamon

Roll up dough the long way to make an elongated roll, seal by pinching edges together with a little water and twist the whole roll slightly by rotating each end of the roll in the opposite direction. Carefully lift the roll onto a buttered cookie sheet and knot into a large pretzel shape. Wet each end of the dough with a bit of water and tuck under the edge of the knot so that the ends will not untwist. Cover and let rise for 1 hour and bake at 400°F (200°C) for 20 minutes. Remove from oven, drizzle a bit of honey over the loaf and sprinkle with chopped nuts or slivered almonds. Return to the oven for 5 minutes. Cool briefly and eat. The clear-blue-eyed lady who gave me this recipe sported four diamond rings each of which would choke a goose. Asked how she had caught so many husbands, she replied without blinking, "Danish — the next morning."

RAISED DOUGHNUTS

My grandmother used to make yeast doughnuts before Lent and called them Fastnachtskuchen.

Preparation time: 3 hours. *Makes:* 24 doughnuts plus 36 holes and squiggles.

	U.S. CUSTOMARY	METRIC
In a bowl	2 packages dry yeast	2 pkgs. yeast
dissolve and	1½ cups warm water	375 ml water
let stand	2 teaspoons sugar	10 ml sugar

Stir in	½ cup sugar	125 ml sugar
	4 tablespoons oil	60 ml oil
	1 teaspoon salt	5 ml salt
	⅓ cup dry milk, powdered	80 ml dry milk
Alternately	4 cups flour	1 liter flour
mix in and	3 eggs	3 eggs
beat well	1 teaspoon nutmeg	5 ml nutmeg

Cover and let stand for 10 minutes before turning onto a well floured surface and kneading until smooth; dough will be soft. Replace in bowl, cover and let rise until double in bulk, about 1 hour. Divide dough into two sections, roll out each section to ½ inch (1 cm) thick and cut with a floured cookie cutter. Arrange doughnuts well apart on a floured cookie tin, cover and let rise until almost double in size, about 30 minutes. Heat oil in deep fryer to 375°F (190°C) — a cube of bread should brown in 45 seconds — and fry doughnuts a few at a time turning them once but being careful not to prick them with a fork. Drain on paper and coat with sugar.

CRISPIES

A cross between breakfast rolls and a dessert, a super treat and a real favorite with my family.

Preparation time: 3 hours. *Makes:* 24 Crispies.

	U.S. CUSTOMARY	METRIC
In bowl dissolve	1 package dry yeast	1 pkg. yeast
	4 tablespoons warm water	60 ml water
Heat to lukewarm and add	4 tablespoons milk	60 ml milk
	4 tablespoons butter	60 ml butter
Mix in	¾ cups flour	175 ml flour
	4 tablespoons sugar	60 ml sugar
	½ teaspoon salt	2 ml salt
Beat into the batter	1 egg	1 egg
	4 tablespoons flour	60 ml flour
Stir in to make a soft dough	1½ cups flour	375 ml flour

Turn out onto floured surface and knead until smooth. Return dough to bowl, grease top, cover and let rise until double, about 1 hour. Punch down and let rise a second time for 45 minutes.

| Chop and mix | ½ cup nuts chopped fine | 125 ml nuts |
| | ½ cup sugar | 125 ml sugar |

Punch down dough, turn onto a lightly floured surface, roll dough into 9 x 18 x ½ inch rectangle (23 x 45 x 1 cm). Brush with butter, sprinkle the dough sheet with half of the sugar-nut mixture, roll up from the long side as for a jelly roll and seal edges by pressing together with a bit of water. Cut the roll into 1 inch (2 cm) slices, sprinkle the remaining half of the sugar-nut mixture on kneading surface, place each slice of dough on the sugared surface and roll with a rolling pin so that the bun makes a flat 3 inch (5 cm) round. Turn the flattened Crispie and press into the sugar so that both top and bottom are coated with sugar and nuts. Place carefully on a greased cookie tin, cover, let rise in a warm place about 30 minutes and bake at 375°F (190°C) for about 10 minutes. Cool, and if you can keep the young people away from these crisp, nutty beauties, serve with a nip of wine when your man comes in from work.

SUPER STICKS

I made Super Stick dough one day and when my Cub Scouts romped into our celler meeting den I marched them up to the kitchen where one boy cut sticks, one buttered, one sugared, another put them on a cookie sheet and there was one baker. One tyke, all fizz and sparkle, elected himself taster. We baked Super Sticks and retreated to the den to eat them while exploring the wonders of yeast. The name of these simple, sweet bread treats was made-up by my indomitable Cubs — they ate the whole batch!

Preparation time: 2 hours. *Makes:* 75 Super Sticks.

	U.S. CUSTOMARY	METRIC
In large bowl dissolve	2 packages dry yeast	2 pkgs. yeast
	3 tablespoons warm water	45 ml water
	1 teaspoon sugar	5 ml sugar
Heat to lukewarm and add	2½ cups milk	625 ml milk
	1 cup sugar	250 ml sugar
	½ teaspoon salt	3 ml salt
Stir in	8 cups flour	2 liters flour

When dough becomes too stiff to use a spoon, turn out onto floured surface and use hands. Knead in flour to form a firm dough and work for 5 minutes. Replace dough in bowl, grease top, cover and let rise until double in volume, about 1 hour. Punch down, replace dough in bowl, grease top, cover and allow to rise again for about 45 minutes. Punch down, roll out into a sheet about ½ inch (1 cm) thick and about 12 x 18 inches (30 x 45 cm) to form a rectangle. Cut rectangle in half lengthwise and then into strips about 6 inches long (15 cm) by ½ inch wide (1 cm).

For dipping	½ cup melted butter	125 ml butter
	1 cup sugar (scant)	240 ml sugar

Dip the strips of dough in the melted butter and then into sugar. I put part of the sugar on wax paper and cradle the dough strips in it after dipping them in butter. Place sticks on a greased cookie tin and bake at 400°F (200°C) for about 10 minutes.

Hors d'Oeuvres

Light Bread, prepared ahead, but baked in tiny pans after the guests have gathered, fills the house with delicious yeasty good feeling. Cooled briefly, sliced and served with spreadables or a bite of pepper jam; there's just no better way to say, "I'm glad you came." Men actually melt at the odor of fresh baked bread. It must somehow conjure up thoughts of boyhood, Grandmother and good times past. I serve Powhatan fingers with a skillet of meatball nibbles and toothpicks; the name Po' wa-ta in an Alaskan Indian language means, "Men from over the horizon," or Russians, which is a conversation starter. Rusks, served with spiced smoked beef is a popular sweet-tart treat and both the dough and the baked rolls can be refrigerated ahead of time. As my grandmother said, "Dough in the icebox is like money in the bank." Ingenuity: cheese, herb and spice happiness, can be baked right into Basic Dinner Rolls. Specially shaped and flavored diminutive motif rolls are a delightful way to carry out a party theme. I have found that large or small gatherings seem to flow more pleasantly if there is a single purpose for getting together, and there is nothing like eating the theme to set the mood and internalize the thought. Simple finger food is a clue to relaxed guests. Canapes of devilish eggs with crab meat stuffing, laid on rectangles of toasted Bachelor's Loaf; caviar on Black Bread wedges; pigeon-egg-sized Baby Jeans heaped with a dip mixture of sour cream and Gruyere. . . . Yeasty breads used to be the bulwark of stillroom cookery; today homemade bread can still uplift the heart and uphold many, many happy times.

IV

Beverages: Soft, Spurious and Strong

F or generations my family has brewed all sorts of will-o'-the-wisp and spiritous drinks as well as some mighty heady wines and other mischief.

Although the name, stillroom, carries the stigma of illicit hootch and muffled signals in the night, stillrooms distilled homemade wines into brandy and grains into spirited liquor as a matter of course. Many American homes possessed a still just as they owned a hand pump or sported slop jars. The naughty-naughty cloud that enveloped the concept of home distillation blew across our land, not because distilling spirits was offensive to our mores, but because avoiding tax on distilled liquor was, and still is, illegal.

It is true that many beverages produced in the stillroom were of a fermented nature: low-alcohol beers, stronger brews and highly alcoholic drinks, but cider also has played a significant part in our culinary culture.

Cider

Cidermaking, the pressing of juice from apples, constituted a near-religious fall ritual in rural homes across America. Cider time was a family affair: boys and uncles picked the fruit; grandmothers selected varieties to be included; girls washed apples and jars and watched the boys; mothers toted apples to the press and cleaned out pulp; the mule turned the wheel to grind and press fruit; grandfather fed the pulp to the hogs and fathers 'tended' the cider.

Blending different varieties of apples is said to make the best cider. Baldwin, Rome Beauty, Delicious and Grimes lend a sweet, acidy flavor; Stayman, Winesap, Johnathan, Spy and Pippin give a slightly tart touch; for fragrance Golden Delicious and McIntosh are added; and for astringency a few crab apples or Red Siberian are thrown into the grinder. The juice is squeezed out of the apple pulp by means of a screw press and the juice runs into a wooden trough and sometimes through cloths which remove escaped apple bits. Most cider is then settled for a day at a temperature of about 40°F (5°C). Although we used to drink cider at the time it ran from the press and anytime thereafter, cider to be preserved had to be refrigerated at temperatures between 32° and 36°F (0 and 2°C); or frozen in containers that allowed for expansion; or pasteurized by heating the cider to 170°F (76°C) and holding it at that temperature for 10 minutes, or treated with chemicals such as potassium sorbate. All cider must be held in sterilized, lidded containers.

Hard Cider

'Tending' cider included the making of the hard stuff. Plain cider, if not preserved, will go hard naturally and many a cidermaker has been snockered by his own accidentally hard cider. I have never made hard cider but people who know about such things add a cup (250 ml) sugar that has been dissolved in a little warm water to each gallon (4 liters) liquid, plus a package of dry yeast to every 10 gallons (40 liters) of juice. They cover the crock and allow the cider to ferment at room temperature for 10 days before jugging. In the old days jugged cider was corked lightly until fermentation stopped, then the corks were bunged home, that is hammered into place, and sealed in wax. Today, cider tenders siphon the fermented drink from the crock into gallon jugs being careful to leave the sediment in the bottom of the crock. The jugs are fitted with fermentation locks that allow gasses to escape but do not permit vinegar-producing bacteria into the liquid. Hard cider should be kept for 3 months in sealed containers and 6 months is said to be optimum. This mildly alcoholic cider, about 9% alcohol by volume, makes a pleasantly dry drink.

Fermented Drinks

The basics of making soft drinks, homebrew, whiskey and wine are the same. Ingredients are: liquid, sugar, yeast, nutrients and flavoring. Liquids may be water, fruit juices, grain infusions, vegetable or sap decoctions. Sugars may be household sugar, invert sugars, demerara or brown sugars, syrups such as corn syrup, treacle, heavy molasses, plain molasses or honey. Sugars are sometimes manufactured from fruits or from vegetables such as potatoes or stock beets. Sugars may come from grains and sprouted legumes.

Brewers' or wine yeasts are best; however, dry or bakers' yeasts are often used to ferment beverages. Nutrients such as raisins, the skins of fruit, grains, vegetables or tea supply tannin and citrus fruit supply acid necessary to keep yeasts healthy. The yeasts of soft beers do not enjoy a long fermentation so they do not require additional nutrients. Flavoring may be artificial extracts, fruits, grains, vegetables, herbs or spices.

Process: yeast plants feed on sugar and excrete alcohol and carbon dioxide, CO_2. Roughly half the weight of sugar is given off as fizz or CO_2 and half as alcohol. From the moment that fruit ripen and manufacture sugar, airborne yeasts start their fermenting chores and the same thing happens with man-made mixtures of liquid, sugar and yeast. Near freezing temperatures, lack of air, lack of food, lack of moisture, plus modern day chemicals or excessive alcohol will all retard yeast growth.

Soft beers made from liquid, sugar, yeast and flavoring must be sealed promptly to cut off the yeasts' air supply and thus stop the fermenting action. The yeast eats a bit of sugar and gives off a bit of CO_2 to sparkle soft drinks, but little alcohol is produced and the flavor does not change in the bottle after sealing.

Hard beers are made of liquid, sugar, yeast, flavoring plus nutrient, and they are allowed to ferment until nearly all of the sugar has been eaten by the yeast. When only a little yeast activity is evident, hard beers are bottled and fermentation is stopped because the yeasts' air supply is cut off. Thus both hard beers and soft drinks appear to be the same when opening a bottle, but each is at the opposite end of the fizz spectrum. Hard beers contain 6 to 10% alcohol and a flavoring change takes place during fermentation.

Sweet beer, as whiskey mash is called, is made from liquid, sugar, yeast, flavoring and nutrients that have been allowed to ferment until enough sugar has been eaten by the yeasts to elevate the alcohol content sufficiently to begin killing the yeasts. The liquid is then distilled, or heated and the alcohol, which boils at a lower temperature than water, is condensed, collected and called hard liquor.

Wine runs out the whole string. Liquid, in this case fruit juice, sugar, yeast, flavoring and nutrients are mixed and allowed to ferment until the alcohol inhibits further yeast action; the wine is usually about 14% alcohol by volume when this happens. Wine is bottled and allowed to mature or undergo a second fermentation, before consumption.

There are other considerations such as aging, blending, cutting and coloring, but basically fermenting soft drinks or hard booze and wine is like climbing a mountain, one step follows the other.

Proper equipment makes the job a joy. One needs a 10 gallon (40 liter) crock or plastic trash container, a hydrometer, siphon hose, bottles, caps, capper, corks and a calendar for keeping track of what gets done to what, when.

A crock is traditional but if you go the trash can route it is advisable to buy a smooth-sided one with a cover and to use it only for brew. A hydrometer for brewing is required unless you possess an educated eyeball. Readily available in many hardware stores, hydrometers tell when to bottle as well as indicate the percentage of sugar present in the liquid. When first inserted into the mixture to be brewed, the hydrometer rides high because of the weight of sugar, and it indicates the amount of alcohol you can probably expect in the end product. Sugar content determines potential alcohol content, but don't fall into the "if a little is good, more is better" trap. Yeasts are ambitious but they are also sterilized at about 14% alcohol, so if you add too much sugar your brew will suffer and so will the drinker's head.

Other needs are a funnel, cloth bags, plastic water buckets, a bottle brush, plus a large stainless steel or enamel pan. A low chair or bench is handy for the crock to stand on as an assist in siphoning into bottles, which should be lined up on a lower level than the crock. And of course a still is needed to distill spirits — which you should not do.

The federal government allows the head of a household to produce up to 200 gallons of wine per year tax free. The only requirement is that you register by filling out Form No. 1541 and sending it to your local Bureau of Alcohol, Tobacco and Firearms, Treasury Department.

LEMON FIZZ

This soft drink is popular with young and old alike and in stillroom days it was said to quiet uneasy stomachs.

Preparation time: about a week. *Makes:* about 20 quarts.

	U.S. CUSTOMARY	METRIC
Sterilize 20 quart (liter) bottles and caps by rinsing with boiling water.		
In pan, boil for	1 quart water	1 liter water
10 minutes to	8 cups sugar	2 liters sugar
make syrup, cool	2 tablespoons lemon peel	30 ml grated peeling
In cup, activate,	½ teaspoon dry yeast, SCANT	2 ml dry yeast
set aside	1 cup warm water, 110°F	250 ml water, 45°C
	1 teaspoon sugar	5 ml sugar

Place large	4 gallons warm water	16 liters water
container on	1 quart lemon juice	1 liter lemon juice
chair and stir	the sugar syrup	syrup
into it	the yeast mixture	yeast
	1 teaspoon salt	5 ml salt

Mix thoroughly. Taste liquid, add more sugar or lemon if needed. Let stand at room temperature for 15 minutes while arranging the sterilized bottles on the floor around the container. Siphon the liquid into bottles leaving ½ inch (1 cm) headspace. Do not siphon the dregs of grated lemon peeling, rather, drop a few pieces of slivered lemon peeling into each bottle. Cap immediately, using cork-lined caps and capper or screw-on caps, and tighten securely. Lay bottles on their sides in a protected place at room temperature for 4 days. I put 8 bottles of 'working' soft drinks into a cardboard box, close the top and set them on the floor in a closet. At the end of 4 days I stand each bottle upright in a cool dark place such as in the basement so that the sediment goes to the bottom. One always handles beers and homemade drinks with gentleness. Refrigerate each bottle for a day before opening. Pour carefully into a pitcher leaving the sediment in the bottom of the bottle.

Other fresh fruit fizz drinks may be made using Lemon Fizz directions but the amount of fruit juice varies.

Strawberry and Raspberry Fizz: Use 2 quarts (2 liters) strained fruit juice to 4 gallons (16 liters) warm water, plus the syrup, including the grated lemon peeling and the juice of one lemon. Add the yeast mixture and process as for Lemon Fizz.

Grape, Cherry and Orange Fizz: Use 1½ quarts (1.5 liters) of strained juice mixed with 4 gallons (16 liters) warm water, plus the sugar syrup and the yeast mixture. The juice of one lemon helps to bring out the flavor of all juices; taste fruit fizz drinks before bottling and add juice or sugar if needed and stir well. Process as for Lemon Fizz.

Ginger Fizz: Use 1 pint (500 ml) of strained lemon juice, plus 1 quart (1 liter) water that has been boiled for 30 minutes with 3 tablespoons (45 ml) cracked ginger and 3 tablespoons (45 ml) cream of tartar. Add to 4 gallons (16 liters) warm water with the sugar syrup and the yeast mixture. Drop a few pieces of the cracked ginger from the bottom of the crock into each bottle and process as for Lemon Fizz.

It is important to remember that yeasts are tricky. They enjoy no greater ecstasy than to ride high on exploding beer and this is particularly true with soft beers. Use SCANT yeast measurements, ferment in a protected place and always chill thoroughly before opening.

Root Beer and Cola

When using commercial extracts, pour the extract over the sugar and rub the sugar between your palms until it looks like brown sugar. Add the lukewarm water, the activated yeast, using a few grains less than directed, stir well and bottle in sterilized bottles immediately. Remember to allow ½ inch (1 cm) headspace so that yeasts will have a bit of air in which to work and create fizz before they expire. Cap tightly. Place bottles on their sides in a protected area at room temperature for the period specified, then set upright, chill and open.

BASIC HOMEBREW

In spite of purists' assertions to the contrary, good homebrew can be made simply and inexpensively. In some areas the ingredients may be purchased at grocery stores; if not available inquire, most grocers will order. Bakers' yeast will work in beer; however, if brewers' yeast is available, by all means use it.

Preparation time: 20 minutes to mix, 5 to 7 days to ferment and optimally 6 weeks in the bottle. Although not recommended, the homebrewers on Bootleg Alley in Seward, Alaska, used to "drink quite a hole in the batch" while bottling. 3 to 6 weeks cure in the bottle is suggested. *Makes:* 40 quarts (40 liters).

	U.S. CUSTOMARY	METRIC
In cup activate, set aside	1 package dry yeast 1 cup warm water, 110°F 1 teaspoon sugar	1 pkg. yeast 250 ml water, 45°C 5 ml sugar
Place a large container on a chair, pour in, mix until dissolved	1 three-pound can LIGHT malt syrup extract 2 gallons warm water, 120°F	1 can malt LIGHT (1.5 kg) 8 liters warm water, (50°C)
Add, stir to dissolve, mix in	5 pounds sugar the yeast solution	2.5 kg sugar yeast solution

Fill container to make 10 gallons (40 liters) lukewarm water. Stir well, cover and allow homebrew to ferment for 5 to 7 days in a cozy, draft-free place. Ecru foam will rise and the brewing mixture will smell like your Grand-father's breath. After the 4th day start testing by inserting a hydrometer into the brew and test each day until the hydrometer reads 1.005. At that point there is only a little sugar left in the brew and the beer is ready to bottle. If you bottle beer too soon it will be volatile. You will have to go outdoors to open a bottle and have a comrade ready with a bucket to catch the brew as it comes down to earth. If time slips by and the hydrometer reads under 1.005, the beer will lack fizz, and you should add ¼ teaspoon (1 ml) sugar to each quart bottle to recharge the brew. Cap and store recharged beer as you would regular homebrew.

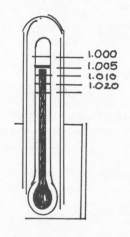

To bottle homebrew, stand the clean bottles on the floor near the beer container, which should be on a bench. Siphon by inserting a ¼ inch (0.5 cm)

hose into the brew until the immersed end is within a few inches of the bottom of the crock. A siphon hose, fitted with a non-metallic weight that hangs 2 inches (5 cm) below the end of the hose is best because the weight can lie on the bottom and sediment will not be drawn into the bottles. With head lowered below the bottom of the crock suck on the siphon hose and as soon as the liquid starts to run transfer the end of the hose from mouth to a bottle. Fill each bottle to about ½ inch (1 cm) from the top, cap securely and allow homebrew to mature, standing upright, in a cool, dark place for 6 weeks. Chill and taste a bottle after 2 weeks, if you must set your mind at rest, remembering that green beer is not the greatest, then forget the batch and start a second brew a-brewing. Soon you'll be hatching homebrew and clucking like a hen over her biddies. Each batch will be the best.

Start simply even if purists and salespeople scorn. Use commercial supermarket extract and plain sugar, and if no brewers' yeast is available use plain yeast. As your eyeball and taste buds become more aware, branch out. There are grand yeasts and multitudes of malt flavors with which you may wish to experiment, or you may wish to sprout, roast and malt your own barley. Finings, acids, hops, corn sugars, brewing Bock beer, Ales and Stouts — there is no end of the mischief a true-blue brewer can brew; the key is to start simple; Basic Homebrew can be made in a few weeks, Purists' Brews sometimes require 6 months before drinking.

I have included only one beer-making recipe, Basic Homebrew, but you can make any of the following variations on this basic recipe:

Light Beer, Ale Flavored

Use Basic Homebrew directions with malt extract that is marked LIGHT. Add 1 cup (250 ml) lemon juice and a pinch of salt. Light Ale is tawny colored, mildly flavored and an all 'round lighthearted drink.

Bitter Beer

A facsimile of the svelte Slavic brew; use LIGHT malt and add a handful of hops (tied in cheesecloth) and a quart of strong, freshly made black tea to the brew when you mix in the activated yeast. Proceed with Basic Homebrew directions.

Mild Stout

Use LIGHT malt but substitute 2 pounds (1 kg) dark brown sugar and 3 pounds (1.5 kg) white for the white sugar in Basic Homebrew directions.

Dark Stout

Use DARK malt extract plus 4 tablespoons (60 ml) black strap molasses and a teaspoon (5 ml) of salt in the Basic Homebrew recipe.

Lager

Lager beer should be made with its very own lager yeast. If you don't have lager yeast you can use the Basic Homebrew recipe and add a small handful of hops, tied in a cheesecloth, plus ½ cup (125 ml) lemon juice and ½ teaspoon (2 ml) salt. This will give you a full-bodied, yet not strongly flavored brew.

Continental Beer

Use DARK malt, a licorice stick or about 2 ounces (60 g) licorice flavored candy and half and half brown and white sugar and proceed with the Basic Homebrew directions.

Pale Beer

This hopped brew is light colored but, contrary to its name, it is strong of character. Use LIGHT malt but add a large handful of hops (tied in a cheesecloth) plus 7½ pounds (3.7 kg) instead of 5 pounds (2.5 kg) sugar and proceed with the Basic Homebrew recipe.

Bock Beer

A springtime brew made to "clean out the tubes" and as a remedy against the "poisons of winter." Basic Homebrew directions are followed and DARK malt extract is used instead of LIGHT, plus ½ cup (125 ml) of black or green treacle, a very strong flavored molasses.

Brown Beer

Use malt extract that is marked DARK and proceed with the Basic Homebrew directions.

Barley Beer

Guaranteed to level even the most loquacious relative. Crack, cook for 2 hours, 8 cups (2 liters) of regular barley in 2 gallons (8 liters) water, cool and add to the Basic Homebrew recipe. This beer will take longer to ferment but it is worth it if you want to put someone to sleep gently.

If some homebrew does not come up to the pleasant, clean-flavored drink that you desire, whether from improper brewing, temperature, bad yeasts or other reasons, do not give it the heave-ho (even though beer is good for cesspools.) Use it in cooking. Stillrooms maids were not backward about dipping into beer as a flavoring for food; in fact, during the years before condiments were commonplace, many dishes were seasoned or cooked with beer. I have found that cooking with beer is great fun, beer lends its very own mystique and adds an ever-changing flavor. Homemade beers and commercial beers may be used interchangeably.

GERMAN BEER SOUP
This is a very old recipe.
Preparation time: 20 minutes. *Makes:* 5 bowls.

	U.S. CUSTOMARY	METRIC
In large pan heat and simmer for 10 minutes	3 cups beer	750 ml beer
	½ teaspoon salt	3 ml salt
	¼ teaspoon black pepper	1 ml black pepper
	¼ teaspoon cinnamon	1 ml cinnamon
	1 tablespoon sugar (optional)	15 ml sugar (I do not use)
In skillet melt	2 tablespoons butter	30 ml butter
	2 tablespoons flour	30 ml butter

Pour the beer mixture into the skillet, mixing vigorously. Boil for 3 minutes, if too thick add a bit of water.

Stir in	1 cup rich cream or half and half	250 ml cream or half and half

Heat thoroughly but do not boil. Serve at once. Good!

Shrimp 'n Beer

Shrimp are always best when cooked in beer. Place 3 pounds (1.5 kg) raw shrimp on a rack in a large pan and season with 2 bay leaves and 2 red pepper pods, crumbled. Pour over 2 cups (500 ml) of beer and simmer, covered for 5 minutes. Turn off heat and let shrimp cool in liquid. Serve as a "shell yourself" shrimp feast, or shell, devein, chill and serve with sauce on a bed of lettuce.

Beer Chuck Roast

Instead of water add beer to a floured and browned-in-oil chuck that has been seasoned with brown sugar, bay leaf, thyme, pepper and salt. Cover, simmer until almost tender. Add cut up potatoes, onions, carrots, and celery, and when done, remove, thicken juice and serve as a happy-man supper. If you wish to put on the dog, saute a handful of mushrooms in butter using a small skillet, squeeze a drop of lemon over them, and when not quite done, spoon a little beer juice from the roast over them, drop in a dozen oysters, cover and bring to a boil. Spoon the oysters and mushrooms over the chuck on a serving platter, add a little unthickened juice and make up some elegant name for your creation.

BEEF IN BEER GRAVY
A Children's Supper

Preparation time: 25 minutes. *Serves:* 4.

	U.S. CUSTOMARY	METRIC
In large	1 pound ground beef	500 g beef
skillet	1 onion, chopped	1 onion
crumble and	1 teaspoon salt	5 ml salt
brown	¼ teaspoon pepper	1 ml pepper
Add and stir	2 tablespoons flour	30 ml flour
When blended	1 cup potato water or milk	250 ml water or milk
mix in	1 cup beer	250 ml beer
vigorously	1 tablespoon soy sauce	15 ml soy sauce

Cover, simmer for about 3 minutes and serve over boiled potatoes together with buttered corn and applesauce. Then light the candles and get ready to serve Lamb Chops a la Biere to your lovely man and self.

Lamb Chops a la Biere

Saute seasoned lamb chops in oil until nicely done, heap in a second skillet, cover and put into a warm oven. Saute a handful of mushroom buttons and drained Spanish olives in the lamb pan, cover, shake a few times and when limp and drizzly, spoon into a corner of the warm skillet in the oven. Cover. Using either fresh, or drained whole canned to-matoes, heat them through without mashing in the covered lamb-mushroom pan. On a hot metal platter arrange chops, spoon over with mushrooms and olives, garnish with the small stewed tomatoes, basil, cover and put into oven to keep warm while you empty ½ cup (125 ml) beer into the cooking pan. Bring quickly to a boil while you set previously prepared plates of cucumber-on-lettuce-hearts salad, surrounded by quartered hard-boiled eggs and sprinkled with oil, vinegar, paprika and a finely chopped brush of onion. A dome of brown rice and buttered corn will complement this dish. At the last moment, pour the scalded beer over the lamb chop platter, turn out the lights and have yourselves a memorable twosome. P.S. Bribe, cajole, threaten the children but inspire them somehow to play quietly while Mom and Dad enjoy.

Curried Beer Balls

Combine 1 pound (500 g) ground beef, ½ teaspoon (3 ml) curry powder, ⅓ cup (80 ml) minced onion, 1 teaspoon (5 ml) salt, ½ teaspoon (2 ml) Tabasco, 2 eggs, 1½ cups (375 ml) bread crumbs, 2 tablespoons (30 ml) oil, ¼ teaspoon (1 ml) garlic powder, 2 tablespoons (30 ml) flour and 1 cup (250 ml) beer. Form into balls, brown and serve smothered in white sauce or sour cream. Excellent over broad egg noodles or rice.

When cooked in beer most meat dishes: shish kebab, soup meat, chili con carne, ribs, veal chops, wursts, hot dogs, kielbasa, kidney stew. . . . all take on a piquant personality. Simmer a slice of ham in beer; pork chops, browned, then cooked in beer and lastly smothered in sliced apples, steamed and seasoned with a bit of cinnamon; sausages or loin blossom with the beer treatment; and poultry, any style, captures a unique flavor when dressed with beer.

Chicken in the Oven with Beer

Dip cut-up chicken in egg that has been beaten with a little water. Then dip into crumb mixture made of one-half Parmesan cheese and one-half fine cracker crumbs. Sprinkle on a bit of pepper, salt and garlic and lay each piece in a well oiled flat baking pan. Bake chicken for 1 hour at 350°F (175°C) turning once. Turn off oven, remove chicken from pan but keep warm while you scrape the brown chicken leavings, and on top of the stove cook the drippings into a gravy by adding 2 tablespoons (30 ml) flour and stirring in 1 cup (250 ml) beer. Boil for 2 minutes. At the last moment add 1 cup (250 ml) milk. Season with pepper and salt, scald but do not boil the beer gravy with milk. Serve the chicken and gravy separately with mashed potatoes, a heaping bowl of kale, pickled beets, squash cooked with creamed onions and cherry pie.

BEER BATTER

"Bonnie made the batter but she made the batter bitter so she added beer and butter and she made the batter better." While you're saying that old tongue twister you can make a bit of beer batter. Good for when you are out of eggs.

	U.S. CUSTOMARY	METRIC
In a bowl mix	1 cup flour	250 ml flour
	1 cup beer	250 ml beer
	½ teaspoon salt	3 ml salt
	¼ teaspoon pepper	1 ml pepper
	1 tablespoon catsup	15 ml catsup

Dip filleted fish, shellfish, precooked tongue, slices of okra, green tomatoes or squash in Beer Batter, and fry briefly in hot oil.

We recently had a German dinner of smoked pork loin, marinated asparagus, hot potato salad dressed with sour cream, red cabbage seasoned with juniper and Camembert fried in beer dough and the beer dough gave a new dimension to batter.

Cheese Fried in Beer Dough

I tried this recipe using cheddar that had stayed in the icebox too long and though not as elegant as Camembert, the dough gave new life to the old cheese. Combine ½ cup (125 ml) flour with ¼ cup (50 ml) beer, 1 egg yolk, ½ teaspoon (2 ml) salt and a good shake of nutmeg. Coat a cracker-sized slice of cheese with the dough and fry until brown in oil.

EGGS BAKED IN BEER

Preparation time: 20 minutes.

	U.S. CUSTOMARY	METRIC
Butter muffin	1 tablespoon beer	15 ml beer
tins liberally,	1 egg, yolk unbroken	1 egg
place in each	salt and pepper	salt, pepper
	1 tablespoon cream	15 ml cream

Bake in oven 350°F (175°C) for about 10 minutes and serve on buttered toast or over briefly cooked and buttered spinach.

BEER BEEF IN A BLANKET

An elegantly classic dish for a special dinner party.
Preparation time: 2 hours. *Serves:* 8 or 10.

U.S. CUSTOMARY	METRIC

There are four steps in addition to eating this delicious meat.

I. Make a pastry blanket, wrap in waxed paper and refrigerate for 1 hour.

	U.S. CUSTOMARY	METRIC
In a bowl mix	3½ cups flour	875 ml flour
with hands until	¾ teaspoon salt	4 ml salt
texture of peas	1 cup shortening	250 ml shortening
Stir in, shape into ball, refrigerate	¾ cup cold water	175 ml cold water

	U.S. CUSTOMARY	METRIC
II. Trim fat from	6 pounds tenderloin beef	3 kg beef
Marinate for	salt and pepper	salt, pepper
10 minutes in	1½ cups beer (1 can)	375 ml beer
(save marinade)	2 tablespoons vinegar	30 ml vinegar

Remove beef from marinade, tie with string to form a loaf, lay bacon strips across top and place on a rack in a baking pan. Bake at 400°F (200°C) for 45 minutes. Remove from oven and let stand for 30 minutes.

III. While meat is preroasting make a filling paste.

	U.S. CUSTOMARY	METRIC
In a saucepan	¼ cup dry mustard	50 ml dry mustard
combine, cook,	½ teaspoon salt	3 ml salt
stirring	2 tablespoons corn starch	30 ml corn starch
constantly	1 tablespoon sugar	15 ml sugar
until thick	1 teaspoon caraway seeds	5 ml caraway
	the marinade	marinade

Roll out dough into a 18 × 14 inch (45 × 35 cm) rectangle, spread with filling paste to within 1 inch (2.5 cm) from edges.

IV. Remove bacon strips and strings and place meat, best side down, lengthwise, in the middle of the rolled out dough. Brush long edges of dough with 1 egg mixed with a teaspoon water. Fold long sides of dough over the meat to overlap and seal the seam by pinching. Measure short sides of pastry, trim if necessary, brush with egg mixture, fold over as for a package and seal by pinching.

Place the packaged beef, seam side down on a greased cookie sheet, poke in a steam hole or two and slightly score a fern design as decoration. Brush top with the remaining egg and bake at 400°F (200°C) for 30 minutes or until nicely brown. Take from oven 10 minutes before serving and place in a bed of watercress on a platter. Garnish with stuffed olives or radish roses for color. Sliced at the table, this rich main dish is bound to be a triumph, but practice once on the family because timing is the clue to success with this dish.

BEER COFFEE CAKE

This "hair of the dog that bit you" is a fine way to set things straight in the morning.

Preparation time: 1¾ hours. *Makes:* 2 loaves.

	U.S. CUSTOMARY	METRIC
In a cup activate	1¼ cup warm beer, 115°F	300 ml warm beer (47°C)
	1 package dry yeast	1 pkg. yeast
When yeast shows activity add, beat, pound and knead in	¼ cup sugar	50 ml sugar
	3 tablespoons oil	45 ml oil
	1 lemon, juice and slivered peel	1 lemon
	1 egg slightly beaten	1 egg
	½ teaspoon salt	2 ml salt
	½ teaspoon cinnamon	3 ml cinnamon
	4 cups flour	1 liter flour

Work dough on a floured surface until easy to handle, about 10 minutes. Form into 2 loaves, slash diagonally 4 times, oil tops, place on greased cookie tray, cover and let rise over a pan of warm water until double. Bake at 425°F (220°C) for about 20 minutes. Remove from oven when lightly brown and spread with topping.

For topping mix	6 tablespoons melted butter	90 ml butter
	¼ cup beer	50 ml beer
	1 teaspoon vanilla	5 ml vanilla
	½ cup brown sugar	125 ml br. sugar
	1 cup coconut	250 ml coconut
	¼ cup quick oats uncooked	50 ml oats

Crumble over the top of the baked and hot coffee cake, return to oven and broil for about 4 minutes or until drizzly. Serve at once with a lean and lanky tumbler of icy tomato juice and lots of hot coffee.

I substitute dark beer for spirits in holiday fruit cakes and for liquid in applesauce and spice cakes. Beer adds an earthy fragrance to baked goods.

Beer Beverages

A friend mixes beer and ginger ale half and half for a cooling drink, or if you want a speedy wicket, Beer-Scotch Boilermakers are recommended by a man who seems to know the way to go. Dry fizzy insurance that you'll awake with no headache the next morning, he told me.

Spirited Liquor

At the present time the home manufacture of distilled spirits is illegal, therefore I do not recommend making whiskey. However, since early day stillrooms sported corners where copper kettles and coils were kept, a Stillroom Cookery book would be remiss not to tell a little about the ancient art of distilling.

As with other fermented drinks the ingredients of illicit whiskey are: liquid, sugar, yeast, flavoring and nutrients. Sweet beer, the name given to moonshine's mother lode, is allowed to ferment and produce alcohol, the alcohol is separated from the rest of the liquid by heating and vaporizing, and the vapor is condensed back into spirited liquor, as whiskey was called.

Other than a large crock or trash container in which to ferment the sweet beer, bottles, caps and a spot in which to conceal your illicit friend, a still is the only other requirement necessary to make distilled spirits.

The making of practical household stills is nearly a lost art. I have seen a number of pre-prohibition "commodities," as my now deceased kin used to call distilling equipment, and they were of two basic designs. One type was generally made from a converted oil drum; lengths of copper tubing ran to a second drum that usually reclined in a cold spring and which was fitted with condensation coils. This kind of an operation was called a "straight shot." One such straight shot that we accidentally ran across in a wood was fitted with galvanized pipes. This probably produced straight poison because all tubing and containers used in distilling should be made of copper, stainless steel or glass.

The second type of still, though horrendously harder to hide than a couple of oil drums in the woods, no doubt produced a more healthy product. It consisted of copper pots, funny shaped heads, copper tubing and a wash boiler.

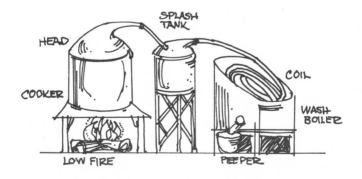

The still that I remember most clearly, God rest its burping little heart, now lies under the mud of the Missouri River. The COOKER was a copper kettle with a top that looked like an inverted funnel that had been mashed to one side. A twist-on connector converted the funnel nipple opening to the size of the ¼ inch (0.5 cm) copper tubing which carried vapor from the Cooker to the copper SPLASH TANK. Less than genteel people used to call this second apparatus the slobber jar. The Splash Tank, smaller than its look-alike Cooker, wore a petcock on its bottom. Vapors that perked out of the Cooker often contained water that was released in the Splash Tank, but the important elements continued through and re-entered a copper tube exit opposite from where the vapor had entered. To describe more clearly: as I remember, the Splash Tank was a miniature Cooker-type kettle with a miniature, lopsided and upside-down funnel as a cover. It contained 3 openings. The entrance tube brought vapor from the Cooker into the Tank. The exit was a tube opening opposite the inlet and located on the tip end of the squashed funnel top. The Splash Tank also contained a petcock at the bottom to drain off water that had been burped into the Tank when the Cooker cooked.

My relatives used to assert that the most important part of the Commodity was the COIL or condensing worm that wrapped around the inside of the washboiler and exited through the boiler to form an appendage called the PEEPER. A jar was placed under the Peeper to catch the runoff. To condense vapor the washboiler was filled with snow in the winter and watery ice in the summer. The ice wagon used to stop by the chicken yard on days when the still was in operation and I used to get all the ice I could chew.

Uncle Frank, now deceased, was keeper of the Commodity and a purist. He ran everything twice because the first run tasted like 'shine.' Most folks around the chicken yard said his stuff was good. Clear as sparkling spring water, it coated the jar in slick repose. I remember the sight and the feel and the smell although I never tasted his stuff.

Recipes for corn liquor are hard to come by. It is difficult to establish rapport with people who have been up the river or who have a river view. Trust is a two way street but the law recognizes only one way: whiskey making and the possession of a still are illegal.

During stillroom times most households raised a field of corn and quite naturally they used corn in making whiskey, although a variety of grains: barley, wheat, oats, rye can be converted into the MASH, as the ingredients that create sweet beer are called. Old books state that the ratio was 1 to 2 to 4:

1 part grain, 2 parts sugar, 4 parts warm water, plus yeast. Some stillroom experts cooked the cracked grains first, then mixed the cooled, cooked cereal with sugar, added warm 110°F (45°C) water together with activated yeast, and let the mixture ferment. Others mixed the cracked grains with warm water, sugar and yeast. I have heard would-be purists declare that they have used no yeast. Of course that is possible, yeasts are in the air, but there is the problem of apprehension. Corralling natural yeasts takes a long, long time. Whichever way, the fermentation process that our forefathers developed was quite simple. One book states that a distiller empties 4 quarts (4 liters) cracked grain, corn, oats or hog feed into a 10 gallon (40 liter) container and scalds with 2 gallons (8 liters) boiling water. I would not take the direction about using hog feed too literally. Today's esoteric livestock feeds containing hormones, dewormers and insect repellants would probably do little for booze. After the grain was scalded and stirred, it was allowed to cool to lukewarm and 8 quarts (8 liters) sugar — which would convert to about 15 pounds (8 kg) sugar — was added together with 4 cups yeast or 4 packages of yeast. The container was filled with warm 110°F (45°C) water. The quantity of water added after the grain and sugar were put into solution was optional so long as it was equal to, or above the 1: 2: 4 ratio. Some distillers wrote that additional water made the grain work better.

	U.S. CUSTOMARY	METRIC
In a 10 gallon (40 liter) crock put	4 quarts cracked grain or meal	4 liters grain
Pour in, stir and let cool to lukewarm	2 gallons boiling water	8 liters boiling water
Mix in and stir until dissolved	8 quarts or 15 pounds sugar	8 kg sugar
	16 quarts or 4 gallons warm water	16 liters warm water
	4 packages dry yeast	4 pkgs. yeast

If desired, fill container with warm water.

The sweet beer was covered, wrapped in a blanket and allowed to ferment in a warm place, 70 to 85°F (20 to 30°C), for a week or two. During the first few days the beer would rant and rave the old books said, and I remember that it smelled like homebrew on the rampage. In about a week however the brewing had settled into baby burps and distillers, not wishing to lose the tiniest mite of alcohol through evaporation, scattered a thin layer of bran or chick feed over the surface of the crock. This cover soon became soggy and not only retarded evaporation but also protected the sweet beer from bad yeasts that live in air.

After about 10 days in the crock, the middlings or layer on top was separated and a glass of sweet beer was dipped for tasting. When Uncle Frank pronounced the brew ready to 'still, the whole neighborhood went into high gear. I was allowed to taste sweet beer and it used to make my nose tingle and tears come to my eyes.

Distilling sweet beer on the washday wood stove located between the chicken coop and the pigpen at the far end of Uncle Frank's garden began when the rooster crowed and lasted long after the cock had tucked his head under his wing. Running the stuff and running it through the distiller a second time was a day-long job, there were no instant reruns in those days. When the fire was steady Uncle Frank brought out the Cooker and put it on the stove. After skimming off the surface paste he dipped enough sweet beer to half fill the Cooker. He covered the copper pot with its funny funnel, ran to the stillroom to get the Splash Tank and Coils, calling as he ran for someone to bring the washboiler and for another to make dough.

Dough was a very important part of early day stills. All joints and lids of homemade distilling equipment leaked under the pressure of steam. Leaks leaked potential alcohol so it behooved a distiller to have a quantity of doughy flour and water on hand, or to distill liquor on his wife's breadbaking day.

A short copper tube was inserted into the nipple end of the big Cooker's funnel head and the joint was plastered with dough, the theory being that dough would heat and bake hard, sealing the connection. Next, the tube was inserted into the back end of the Splash Tank head, its funnel nipple being the front end, and the fitting sealed with dough. The Splash Tank was placed on a high stool next to the stove and a copper tube was screwed into its funnel point and run to the Coil that circled the inside of the washboiler which sat on a table nearby. All connections as well as the two funnel-shaped lids were sealed with dough.

Tending the fire was the most technical part of distilling. "Slow and low" was the password. If the Cooker boiled too rapidly steam slushed out with vaporized alcohol. The idea was, I have heard Uncle Frank explain, "to boil the alcohol but not the water." Those words always puzzled me, in fact I thought that he was teasing because he always had a twinkle in his eye when his batch was ready to run. I have since found out (H. S. Chemistry, where I suspected the teacher of running a few batches himself) that alcohol boils at 173°F (78°C) while water boils at 212°F (100°C). Thus it was indeed possible to boil alcohol and not boil the water. Grandma had a metal and asbestos circle called a Flame Guard that she loaned Uncle Frank to insert between the stove and the Cooker once the batch started to sing. It sang quietly like a teakettle as it heated. Contrary to legends about teakettle songs, it was believed that if the Cooker sang shrilly the run would be thin; and a soft, comfortable song meant the batch would be clear and burn blue. Some people used to fill a cake tin with pebbles and put it under the Cooker to insulate the brew against too hot a fire.

As the Cooker heated, excitement around Uncle Frank's chicken yard rose. One person was put in charge of seeing that the condenser or washboiler was kept filled with slushy ice; another, the 'keeper of the dough', was assigned to plop pasties on any spurt of vapor; another periodically checked the petcock at the base of the Splash Tank and released water; another was a tester, who did not drink his test, rather he felt the run between his fingers as it dripped from the Peeper and he watched for signs of water. Uncle Frank kept his eye on the fire and repeatedly checked the heat of the Coils. When the first sputter slobbered into the Splash Tank and a short time later when heat progressed down into the Coils, everyone watched the Peeper. Initially the drops that trickled from the washboiler tubing were slow, gradually they increased to a steady stream and everyone helped the tester 'feel'. A practiced distiller could feel good whiskey; cool and smooth, the distillate had a distinct slickness. I have seen Frank's stuff burn blue, a sign that it was the real thing.

In theory sweet beer would register about 10% alcohol which meant that under perfect conditions distillers could hope to recover about ½ gallon (2 liters) of 100 proof whiskey for a 5 gallon (20 liter) run. This rarely happened.

The tester watched the Peeper carefully as soon as it began to run freely and when he felt that the fluid had lost its slick and saw that it would not burn, he yanked away the jar and gave the signal for the Cooker to be hauled off the fire. Tubes and containers were cleaned and a second run of sweet beer was put on to boil. The residue was given to the pigs and they oinked in delight from beyond the fence.

"Never boil your Cooker dry," Uncle Frank admonished some young men who stopped by to ask advice, "and never run the soup." By soup he meant the dregs of sweet beer from the bottom of the crock. He saved the mushy mother of his operation, added more warm water and sugar and started them on their way to fermentation a second time. This latter day distillation which he ran off in about a week was the "Priest's bite, a bit to pave the way to heaven." It yielded only a pint or so of whiskey.

I have read about manufacturers who closed down operations right then; they distilled their sweet beer once and that was it. That procedure was a sacrilege against good corn according to Frank who was a 'doubler.' He believed that tiny droplets of sweet beer invaded the Coils and when they soured, they tainted the batch. Because of the small total amount of alcohol collected from the first run distillation, the second run, or second distillation went fast. The take was about ⁴/₅ of the first run, or about 1½ quarts (1.5 liters). This was called double run whiskey, and by rule of thumb, the amount that could be distilled from 5 gallons (20 liters) of sweet beer.

The amount seemed to me to be an awfully little bit of bright, clear happiness to be gleaned from so much concern. But those who were involved in the art of distillation probably justified their pastime as a musician justifies time spent capturing a perfect rendition of Bartok, or a poet in searching for a distillate of joy.

For perfection, a double run batch had to be aged for 6 months in charred white oak wood. Aging gave whiskey a mellowness as tannic wept and the subtleness of its tears lent color and glow. Old Frank was a poet and a musician and an artist all rolled into a whiskey barrel, his friends said. My grandfather had been a barrelmaker and the two men got along fine. They took a white oak keg and charred it by putting red hot wood coals into it, turning it onto its side and slowly rolling it along the walk. As the fire burned down they put in more coals until the inside was black as pitch. The head of the barrel was charred separately and put into place before the barrel was filled with clear water. The water was used to make the barrel swell so that it could be entrusted with the precious distilled spirits. I have heard since those days that oak flavoring can be made by charring white oak chips, smothering the blaze, washing the chips and dropping them into gallon jugs of hooch. I have never seen this done nor tasted the mock product. I would warn against the use of commercial charcoal for this purpose if you are tempted, but in a word, don't be tempted to make whiskey. Stillroom days are past and gone; only the magic of their ways lives on and the Treasury Department takes a dim view of such magic.

According to stillroom legend, "Cut with caution." When whiskey was cut from its natural 95% ethyl alcohol content to a more palatable 85%, it was recommended that distilled water be used because "pump water spoilt the product of God and rusted the pipes of man."

Wine

Rats, plants, feathered friends, fishes, yeasts: no biological species can long survive in its own pollution. Modern man is becoming acutely aware of that problem. In the marrying of liquid, sugar, yeast, flavoring and nutrients to make wine, the yeast is allowed to excrete sufficient alcohol to kill itself. Thus the fermentation of wine creates its own preservative except when wild yeasts invade and they succumb to the action of the fungus MYCODERMA ACETI and produce vinegar.

To make wine you will need fermentation containers, siphon hose, bottles, corks, a hydrometer, plus a mechanism to outwit the undesirable yeasts. Because they live in the air, it seems logical that if you exclude air from your winemaking process after the initial brewing, you will be able to exclude the 'bad buds.' To do this a fermentation lock is necessary. Various equipment is available today in winemaking shops, but our stillroom compatriots simply hollowed out a hole of predetermined size in a cork, or in a bung if a barrel was used. They inserted a piece of copper tubing through the hole, sealed it with wax or in some cases, the hot insides of freshly baked bread. They connected a curved tube to the cork insert and placed the opposite end of the tubing into a bottle of water. This allowed fermenting gasses, carbon dioxide, to escape and bubble off through the water without permitting air to enter the wine container.

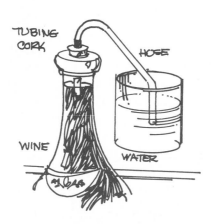

TUBING
CORK
HOSE
WINE
WATER

The process of winemaking begins with the fruit. Grapes contain nearly enough sugar and in many instances their own yeasts clustering in the 'bloom' or the frosty flush on their skins. Do not wash grapes (assuming that they have not been sprayed) nor remove them from their handy tannin-bearing stems. Pick them over and discard green or split grapes. Pour the grapes to half fill a sterilized 5 gallon (20 liter) crock that has been placed on a chair, and with both hands squeeze and press until juice oozes over the fruit. Continue adding fruit and pressing until the container is filled with solids and juice. Cover and allow grapes to ferment at room temperature for 4 days, at which time the grapes should be floating in a cake on the top. Using your fingers as a sieve, remove handfuls of the mass, squeezing as you do, until the wine is mostly free of floating debris. Winemakers call the fermenting juice that is left in the crock MUST. Taste the must, add sugar until it tastes like sweet grape juice but add no more than 2 pounds (1 kg) sugar to a gallon (4 liters) of must. Too much sugar will ruin the wine. Keep the fermenting crock covered in a warm place and let the wine work for 8 or 10 more days. Using a sterilized hose, siphon the must into sterilized gallon (4 liter) jugs that you have previously outfitted with fermentation locks. Do not drain the crock when you siphon because there will be sediment that will cloud the wine and cloudy wine is eyed with suspicion. Fill each jug to within ½ inch (1 cm) of the top. Air will spoil the secondary fermentation of wine so the airspace should be small. Attach a fermentation lock to each jar making sure that the hose end in the bottle is not immersed in the wine, and store the "working wine" in a cool dark place for 4 months.

Do not stir or shake. Using gentleness, siphon only the clearest wine from the jugs into sterilized wine bottles and fill them to within ½ inch (1 cm) of the top. Leave sediment in the bottom of the fermenting jugs. Cork the bottles tightly, label and lay them on their sides on a wine rack to mature for at least 4 months or, if you are bestowed with patience, for a whole year. Remember to set the bottles upright for about two weeks prior to decanting into sterilized bottles for chilling and serving. And don't forget to fill out your U.S. Treasury Form 1541 and send it in.

Some winemakers exhibit their purple hands as a badge of honor and they let the stain wear off; the more discreet purple handed winemaker can rub his hands with lemon juice and work cream of tartar around his fingernails.

Fruits such as berries or cherries are easiest to start with if you want to try something other than grape wine, and they should be handled essentially as grapes; the only exception I make is to cover all other fruits with an equal quantity of boiling water. I allow the squashed or chopped fruit to steep for 4 days, strain through a cloth bag and I add a sprinkle of wine yeast and 4 cups (1 liter) of sugar per gallon (4 liters) of must to help the natural buds and sugars communicate. The idea is to encourage wine yeasts to grow as fast as possible because if they get their bud in the door first they discourage delinquent yeasts. Proceed as with grapes. Wines, like your own children, sometimes mature into fascinating entities, so do not give up if adolescent wines smell terrible and taste worse. After the fermentation in the 'locked' jugs is complete, bottle the wine and seal.

Blossom wines such as rose, honeysuckle, daisy and elderberry blow, generally require a week or two to get them on the vintage path. Cover edible and fragrant flowers containing little or no greenery with an equal quantity of boiling water. Allow the blossoms to steep 4 days, strain through a cloth and add a teaspoon (5 ml) of wine yeast together with 5 cups (1.25 liters) sugar per gallon (4 liters) liquid. Blossoms require tannin and acid for a healthy yeast sex life so drop in a handful of tea leaves or raisins plus a thinly sliced lemon or orange. Proceed as with grape wine, only strain through a cloth and allow the must to settle for 24 hours after the second fermentation but before you put the strained juice under fermentation lock.

Add heat to blossom and fruit wines by dropping a dozen peppercorns or a small handful of cracked ginger into the bottom of the jars before you attach the fermentation lock, or a pinch into the bottles before you seal them. Watch the peppercorns, however, when decanting into the final bottles, they'll blow your head off if any get crosswise in your throat. Cassia buds impart a cinnamon flavor to wine, star anise gives a licorice taste and a few drops of juniper essence in a bottle of white wine makes a glamorous mock gin. Dried orange peeling is nice for that mystique in sweet wine and peppermint contributes a carnival air to pallid fruit wines.

If your wine has the foggies, a crushed eggshell might line up the particles and march them to the bottom. And if you desire that "full bodied feeling" add an ounce (30 g) of glycerine per gallon (4 liters) of wine just before the final bottling.

Wine Recipes

To red meat soup, tomato, minestrone or sour red cabbage soup, add 1 cup (250 ml) dry red wine just before serving. Simmer for 1 minute, ladle into individual bowls and daub each bowlful with sour cream.

Onion soup, fish, cream of mushroom and chicken soups are enhanced by 1 cup (250 ml) of white wine added a minute before removing from the fire. Do not boil cream soup.

CELERY SOUP

Preparation time: 20 minutes. *Makes:* 3 servings.

	U.S. CUSTOMARY	METRIC
In pan boil, covered until soft	4 stalks celery chopped fine	4 stalks celery
	1 cup dry white wine	250 ml wine
In skillet melt and add	2 tablespoons butter	30 ml butter
	2 tablespoons flour	30 ml flour
	salt and pepper	salt-pepper
Mix in, stirring over low heat	2 cups milk	500 ml milk
	the celery mixture	celery mix

When scalded turn off fire and add a little cream, a bit of white wine for fragrance and a sprinkle of fresh chopped parsley.

ELDERBERRY SOUP

Preparation time: 30 minutes, plus 30 minutes if dumplings are added. *Makes:* 4 servings.

	U.S. CUSTOMARY	METRIC
Wash, stem and cook	1 cup elderberries	250 ml elderberries
	1 cup water	250 ml water

When soft the berries may be rubbed through a sieve to remove seeds if desired.

Thin puree with	1½ cups water	375 ml water
Add and cook until soft	2 apples finely chopped	2 apples
	½ teaspoon salt	3 ml salt
	1 orange, grated peel and juice	1 orange
	1 tablespoon sugar	15 ml sugar
Add, heat but do not boil	1 cup wine such as apple or grape	250 ml wine

Serve with a dollop of sour cream or with German dumplings.

SEMOLINA GERMAN DUMPLINGS

	U.S. CUSTOMARY	METRIC
In bowl mix	1 cup semolina, flour of coarsely milled wheat	250 ml semolina
	1 teaspoon sugar	5 ml sugar
	pinch of salt	salt
	2 tablespoons oil	30 ml oil
	2 eggs	2 eggs
	milk to make a light dough	milk

Mix well and drop hazel nut-sized dumplings into the elderberry soup before the last cup of wine has been added; more hot water may have to be added depending upon the thickness of the soup. Cover and steam dumplings gently for about 20 minutes. Remove dumplings, add the wine to the soup, heat to scald and serve.

RUMP IN WINE

Cooking meats in wine retards shrinking and tenderizes as it flavors.

Preparation time: 2½ hours. *Serves:* 6.

	U.S. CUSTOMARY	METRIC
Bake in an oven dish with cover	2 cups red wine	500 ml red wine
	3 pound rump roast laced with bacon, salt, a crumpled red pepper and bay leaf	1.5 kg meat, bacon salt, red pepper, bay leaf

Before adding the smoked bacon turn the roast over and over in the spiced wine for 2 minutes, poking the meat with fork tines as you do so. Place upright, top with lubricating pork and cover tightly. Bake at 400°F (200°C) for about 2½ hours. Turn once. Thicken gravy by mixing 2 tablespoons (30 ml) flour in a little cold water, then adding cold water to fill cup and stirring the mixture into the wine-beef juices. Blend in 1 tablespoon (15 ml) crab apple jelly or other tart sweet and boil gravy until thickened.

Serve with Yorkshire pudding, baked butternut type squash, avocado, shredded cabbage, celery cube salad and a big chocolate cake.

Ham Slice in Wine

Using a covered skillet, simmer a slice of ham in red wine, turn it when the liquid is almost cooked down, turn again and sprinkle over with a bit of ginger and brown sugar. Fire out, keep lid on and let the ham gather all the goodness until ready to serve.

PORK AND PRUNES

My grandmother bought prunes in bulk and we ate prunes in everything. I have used mixed dried fruit in this recipe; they are great.

Preparation time: 1½ hours. *Serves:* 4.

	U.S. CUSTOMARY	METRIC
Boil for about 10 minutes and let stand	1 cup red wine 1 box dried prunes, about 15 ounces	250 ml wine 450 g box prunes
In lightly oiled skillet, brown	4 pork chops, floured, salt and pepper	4 pork chops salt, pepper
Add, cover and simmer for ½ hour. Turn once	½ cup red wine	125 ml wine

Pour prunes and juice over chops, boil 10 minutes, with a slotted spoon remove pork and prunes and keep them warm.

	U.S. CUSTOMARY	METRIC
In a cup mix and stir into pork juices, boil briefly	1 tablespoon corn starch ½ cup water ¼ teaspoon mace ¼ teaspoon cinnamon	15 ml corn starch 125 ml water 1 ml mace 1 ml cinnamon
Add	1 cup cream	250 ml cream

Stirring all the while, scald the cream-wine gravy and pour over the chops that have been arranged on a platter with some prunes. Scatter a few shiny plump prunes over the top and garnish with parsley.

Spaghetti

Spaghetti is enchanting with a small tumbler of plum wine in its sauce and use some of the same tart amber with olive oil to dress a crisp Neapolitan salad.

Mock Veal

Soak thinly sliced cutlets of beef in potato wine for 45 minutes, beat with the base of a cup to complete the tenderizing and create a Veal Parmesan that even a chef would swear was milk fed calf.

FRYER FRICASSEE

Preparation time: 1 hour. *Serves:* 5.

	U.S. CUSTOMARY	METRIC
Split, bone, cut into large cubes and dip in	2 chicken breasts 1 egg slightly beaten	2 breasts 1 egg
Dress cubes with mixture	¼ cup of grated cheese ¼ cup fine bread crumbs 1 teaspoon salt sprinkling garlic ¼ teaspoon pepper ½ teaspoon oregano	50 ml cheese 50 ml crumbs 5 ml salt garlic 1 ml pepper 2 ml oregano
Fry brown in	2 tablespoons oil	30 ml oil

Remove chicken cubes from skillet and keep warm.

	U.S. CUSTOMARY	METRIC
In skillet saute and add	1 onion chopped 2 cups stewed tomatoes ½ cup white wine, sweet ½ teaspoon oregano	1 onion 500 ml tomatoes 125 ml wine 2 ml oregano

Arrange chicken in a greased casserole, pour sauce over, top with slices of sharp cheese, cover and bake in oven at 350°F (175°C) for 40 minutes. Serve with rice, fresh buttered peas, a salad of endive and celery bits with a strip of anchovy and wine vinegar and oil dressing seasoned with a breath of garlic. A blackberry turnover may be cooked in the oven at the same time as the casserole and served hot with ice cream for dessert.

DATE NUT QUICK COOKIES
Preparation time: 30 minutes. *Makes:* 1½ dozen cookies.

	U.S. CUSTOMARY	METRIC
In saucepan melt,	2 tablespoons butter	30 ml butter
remove from fire	½ cup sugar	125 ml sugar
and mix in	1 egg slightly beaten	1 egg
	2 tablespoons sweet wine	30 ml wine
Add and stir	¾ cup flour	175 ml flour
to make a	¼ teaspoon salt	1 ml salt
soft dough	¼ teaspoon baking powder	1 ml baking pow.
	¼ teaspoon baking soda	1 ml baking soda
	1 cup chopped dates	250 ml dates
	½ cup chopped nuts	125 ml nuts

With a rolling pin roll out on a greased cookie tin to ¼ inch (0.5 cm) thick. Bake at 350°F (175°C) for about 10 minutes. Remove from oven, cut into finger shapes with a pizza cutter.

Fresh Peaches in Port Wine

Blanch, peel, pit and slice ripe peaches. Cover with 1 tablespoon (15 ml) sugar per peach and 2 tablespoons (30 ml) elderberry or port wine per peach. Set in a cool place for 3 hours. Taste. Add sugar if needed and lemon juice if too sweet. To serve, place a spoonful of peaches in individual bowls, cover with vanilla ice cream, a second layer of peaches with juice and crown with whipped cream. You may wish to serve the juice in tiny brandy glasses and the liquid is super over crushed ice, too.

Mock Peach, Plum, Cherry or Berry Brandy

In sterilized ½ gallon (2 liter) canning jars layer sugar and raw fruit to fill, making sure that a layer of sugar is on the top. Fill each jar to within ½ inch (1 cm) of the top with inexpensive wine. Rub the canning jar lids heavily with paraffin to prevent rust. Screw down the jar lids tightly and store jars in a cool, dark place until the sugar is dissolved. I used to store my brandy down in the spring run-off until some thirsty SOB found my cache and drank the juice. One consolation: blackberry anything acts as a purgative and the thirsty thief drank a gallon of the stuff.

Wines, beers and natural soft drinks were all conceived, as it were, by nature. Stillrooms were the birthing places, man, a concerned midwife. Comprehending this, it is easy to understand the poet's toast, "All nature is sinless and smiles."

V

Vinaigres Bons and Saucy Secrets

G ood sauces enliven meals with that bracing tonic quality that gives meaning and enjoyment to otherwise ordinary fare, and I have found that with faith, a heavy skillet, a low fire and a pinch of seasoning, successful sauces can be created with certainty. One problem: today we are deluged with flavorings. When a person has too many choices, positive and negative ideas cluster and lead to uncertainty. Like a kitten in a huge sand pile, multitudes of choices make us dig holes, change our minds, dig again,....Abundance confounds our tastebuds.

Flavoring in stillroom days did not crowd the senses because, dependent upon garden, woodlot and fermentation, cooks had fewer choices. Savory stillroom sauces relied upon homey ingenuity and herbs such as lemon verbena for fresh lemon flavor and fragrance, basil for flavor reminiscent of mint and cloves, borage for a refreshing cucumber-like flavor, lovage for flavor similar to celery, fennel for licorice flavor, garlic, chives, parsley and horseradish roots. Whole cloves, cinnamon bark, ginger root and bay leaves were store-bought treats. Celery leaves, turnip, carrot, pepper and onion slices were dried and used as welcome aids with which to flavor stock. Dried herring contributed provocative seasoning to sauces as did cured meats. Whole nutmegs were basic to spice cupboards and, as with peppercorns, were purchased by the tin. Dried native mushrooms, wild marjoram, mustard seed and mints together with the cress cousins were foraged to be used in sauces; black birch was a substitute for wintergreen, jellies gave sweet tartness, orange and lemon peelings were dried for a citrus bite, and red hot peppers sparked meals. Of course there were also dried cheeses, butter, eggs, cream, salt and sugar. But paramount to field flavorings or spices was the queen of the stillroom: Mere Vinaigre.

Vinegar

The matronly condiment, vinegar, is the product of fermentation by the fungus MYCODERMA ACETI in wine, cider or beer. The ACETI work best at temperatures between 60 and 85°F (15 and 30°C) to form their veil and to penetrate the liquid. A good vinegar is clear and may be colorless, pink, tawny or dark. Wine vinegar holds the aroma of wine, cider vinegar is less acid and beer vinegar is more bitter.

"Vinaigres bons" are not only beautiful in sauces, marinades and pickles, but they are excellent for table use, especially when flavored with tarragon, garlic, dill, shallot, mustard or basil. A cruet of vinegar, its crabby sour self sitting beside a spoon holder on dining tables, used to be ready to add gusto to any dish: greens, beans, eggs, salad, meat, a dip for bread or a dunking for doughnuts.

To make vinegar deliberately in stillroom days was like deliberately breeding the cat: kittens and vinegar came naturally. True, if wine was not sealed at the proper time, ACETI invaded the liquid and the wine was on the vinegar trail; but no winemaker started out with visions of vinegar dancing in his head.

For wine vinegar, mash 3 pounds (1.5 kg) fruit in a crock, cover with a gallon of warm water, 115°F (47°C), mix in 2 cups (500 ml) sugar and a starter of 1 cup (250 ml) good vinegar. If mother has formed on the starter transfer part of the thick, slick mother skin to the new batch, cover lightly and let her inoculate and incubate the brew in a warm place, 60 to 85°F (15 to 30°C) for about 2 months. Stir from time to time, taste and when a full vinegar flavor permeates the juice, strain, pour into bottles and seal tightly. Use the mother to start another batch of solids that has been squeezed from wine or jelly makings. She will rise to the occasion and ferment the pulpy leftovers into vinegar. If you are 'vinegar rich' flush mother down the toilet, she does wonderful things for septic systems and you don't need competition from excessive ACETI floating around your house. Vinegar should be settled and cleared before being decanted into cruets or shaken with herbs for flavoring.

Cider vinegar may be made by allowing unpasteurized apple juice to stand open at room temperature for about a week and when it has finished active fermentation, it may be decanted into a second bottle, leaving the sediment in the jug. Cork lightly and cure for about 6 months.

Beer or malt vinegar is created by adding a starter, 1 part good vinegar to 5 parts of homebrew that has been mixed but to which no brewer's yeast has been added. To state another way: make Basic Homebrew but before adding the yeast, dip out as much potential vinegar as you want and inoculate the liquid removed with 1 part vinegar, mother included, to 5 parts Homebrew. Proceed making beer and proceed as for making wine vinegar with your borrowed brew. Keep your "Winegar Works" separated from your beer brewing operation otherwise you will end up with Winegar Brew. The fungus fun boys from the ACETI gang like nothing better than to invade a brewmeister's turf, rumble and corrupt innocent beer yeasts.

The specific gravity reading on the hydrometer should be about 1.050 when you steal from the homebrew and that will give about a 6% acetic acid content in finished vinegar. If vinegar is too strong, cut with distilled water. To clear vinegar drop a crumbled egg shell into the jug and let the shell settle out the fog.

Herb Vinegar

Florence Williamson, a prominent Virginia herb grower who has bounced through her gardens with the vitality of a healthy puppy for half a century, lives in a fragrant house and creates zesty herb vinegars. For herb vinegar she fills a container about ⅔ full of herbs and covers the lightly packed greenery with hot to the touch vinegar. Stronger plants such as tarragon or garlic require fewer herbs to flavor vinegar. Florence uses no metal, stirs her infusions with a wooden spoon and caps jars with plastic. Laughing merrily when I inquired about recipes, she said that old-timers used ingenuity and rule of thumb, which I have discovered is prerequisite to most stillroom cookery. After the herbs have completed a 3 week or longer vinegar incarceration, during which time Florence regularly stirs or shakes them, the herb vinegars are strained through a heavy cloth sack, allowed to settle and carefully decanted leaving the sediment on the bottom of the jar. Blended or straight herb vinegar captures the pleasures

of a green garden and beginning where nature leaves off, it brings harmony to any meal.

Sauces, liquid flavoring for food, may be tart, sweet, thick, thin; they may bite back, doze around your tonsils, vibrate giddily, slither about with arrogant defiance or wander indolently to your stomach. Here are the best of a bevy of favorites.

Vinaigrette

The simplest sauce to be served with everything from salads to fish is made by whisking 1 part vinegar to 3 parts oil and a dash of salt and pepper. Vinaigrette is especially tempting when made with odd colored wine vinegars; elderberry vinegar is superb. Variations on vinegar and oil dressing include the addition of a bit of sugar, chopped parsley, onion, dill, sage, borage, watercress, garlic, curry powder, mashed anchovies, cubed ham or fresh cream.

Horseradish

Using a gas mask and the fine grate, grind a fresh horseradish root. Cover this pulp with vinegar, add a little sugar, put on a lid and let stand in a cool, dark place for 3 weeks. This sauce may be used with its pulp as a dressing or the liquid may be strained and sprinkled over cold pork, head cheese, salads, fish or corned beef. Horseradish vinegar is tasty but brutal on the sinuses.

Mustard Sauce

Pound ½ cup (125 ml) mustard seed, cover with vinegar, about 1 cup (250 ml), and let steep overnight. Strain, and to the juice add 4 tablespoons (60 ml) honey, 2 tablespoons (30 ml) cinnamon, ½ teaspoon (2 ml) salt. Stir until dissolved and handle with care because this stillroom sauce will mar your table top. Mixed 1 part with 2 parts cream, it is akin to a keen Dijon mustard and sparks salmon or game with an enticing flare. A daub mashed with butter is a nice dressing for steak as it comes off the grill, or on herring or fresh pork.

Mustard Paste

Make a paste of 4 hard-boiled egg yolks, 2 tablespoons (30 ml) prepared mustard, 1 teaspoon (5 ml) sugar, salt and pepper. Beat in ½ cup (125 ml) oil, a trickle at a time, and whip until smooth. Sprinkle with a bit of lemon juice and serve with shellfish, venison, duck or cold cuts. Mustard loses its nippy personality when heated, so add to hot dishes at the very last moment.

PLAIN SALAD DRESSING

A delicate dressing for lighthearted salads.

Preparation time: 5 minutes. *Makes:* ½ cup (125 ml).

	U.S. CUSTOMARY	METRIC
In a pint jar	2 tablespoons vinegar	30 ml vinegar
with a top,	5 tablespoons oil	75 ml oil
mix and shake	¼ teaspoon sugar	1 ml sugar
	⅛ teaspoon pepper	0.5 ml pepper
	¼ teaspoon salt	1 ml salt
	dash of Tabasco, mustard,	Tabasco,
	curry powder and garlic	mustard, curry,
		garlic

Cover, shake for a minute to get the ingredients into solution and pour over crisp, dry salad makings. My friend adds ½ cup (125 ml) sour cream to this plain dressing and it is delicious on cabbage or sliced cucumbers.

Mayonnaise

"Good mayonnaise hides a multitude of sins," my grandmother used to say and she had sins to hide. Although she was one of this planet's better housewife cooks, the art of saladmaking escaped her. Bless her heart, she tried, and like hers, my salads often lie limp and shamed on the plate. With this forewarning, I offer Mayonnaise that is good, but you will have to build your own salad.

Olive oil is the clue. *Makes:* 3 cups (750 ml).

	U.S. CUSTOMARY	METRIC
In a bowl beat	3 egg yolks, room temp.	3 egg yolks
together	1 teaspoon salt	5 ml salt
	⅛ teaspoon cayenne	0.5 ml cayenne
	¼ teaspoon vinegar	1 ml vinegar
Gradually,	2½ cups olive oil	625 ml olive oil
very slowly add	3 tablespoons vinegar	45 ml vinegar

Have the olive oil at room temperature. Whisk or beat with an electric blender as drop by drop the oil is mixed in. Increase the addition of oil to a tiny stream as soon as the color lightens, continue to beat as hard as you can. If the mayonnaise seems too thick add a few drops of vinegar, then a drop or two of oil, and, little by little add all of the required oil and vinegar, beating all the while. Finally, beating continuously, slowly add 3 teaspoons (15 ml) boiling water. Whisk or beat the water in while the water is still hot. When smooth, light colored and mellow, cover and refrigerate. Cover mayonnaise with a circle of wax paper to keep a skim crust from forming.

Sauce Tartare

Sauce Tartare is mayonnaise mixed with minced gherkins, mashed anchovies, chopped chives, hard-boiled egg yolks, and seasoned with tarragon and a touch of prepared mustard. A squeeze of lemon over the sauce keeps Tartare bright-flavored and fresh. A natural accompaniment to any french-fried seafood.

Green Mayonnaise

This dressing is created by mashing watercress or spinach in a blender or mortar and straining the juice into mayonnaise. Served with lemon gelatin dishes or citrus salads, the green touch reaches out to grab the eye of the diner and makes him smile.

Remoulade

Mayonnaise, a bit of mustard sauce and horseradish, mashed kippers mixed with minced celery and onion. Piled high on shrimp, tomato and lettuce, it creates a fine lunch.

Russian Supreme

Mayonnaise with the 'butter' or creamy parts of crab or lobster and a whisper of lemon. Absolutely super on crackers when enjoying a shell-fish feast, or with thin strips of celeriac and curly endive.

Salads may consist of a single kind of vegetable or they may embrace a variety of vegetables plus mushrooms, hard-boiled eggs, diced fish, poultry, tongue, etc. Colors should contrast with little heaps and bunches arranged decoratively, and whether for family fare or for an elegant dinner, salads should be served with simplicity. The role of the dressing is to satisfy the mood created by the salad.

ITALIAN DRESSING

In bowl blend	U.S. CUSTOMARY	METRIC
	¾ cup olive oil	175 ml olive oil
	¼ cup red wine vinegar	50 ml wine vinegar
	1½ teaspoons onion, chopped	8 ml onion
	1 teaspoon oregano	5 ml oregano
	½ teaspoon basil, fresh chopped	2 ml basil
	¼ teaspoon garlic powder	1 ml garlic
	¼ teaspoon salt	1 ml salt
	⅛ teaspoon pepper	0.5 ml pepper

FRENCH DRESSING

In bowl blend	U.S. CUSTOMARY	METRIC
	¾ cup oil	175 ml oil
	½ cup vinegar (scant)	115 ml vinegar
	3 hard-boiled eggs, chopped fine	3 eggs
	3 tablespoons gr. olives, ch.	45 ml chopped olives
	3 tablespoons shallots, ch.	45 ml shallots
	1 tablespoon catsup	15 ml catsup
	¼ teaspoon salt	1 ml salt
	⅛ teaspoon pepper	0.5 ml pepper

HEALTH DRESSING

In bowl blend	U.S. CUSTOMARY	METRIC
	¾ cup oil	175 ml oil
	¼ cup vinegar	50 ml vinegar
	½ cup yogurt	125 ml yogurt
	1 teaspoon wheat germ	5 ml wheat germ
	2 teaspoons honey	10 ml honey
	¼ cup nuts, chopped	50 ml nuts

Few kitchen gardeners cultivated tomatoes in the late 1800s, thus tomato sauces and catsups as we know them today were not widespread. The following sauces are of recent vintage.

TOMATO SAUCE

Heat until mushy, unpeeled and chunked, washed ripe tomatoes. Press through a sieve and reheat pulp to boiling.

	U.S. CUSTOMARY	METRIC
To each quart (liter) of juicy	1 teaspoon salt	5 ml salt
	1 teaspoon sugar	5 ml sugar

pulp, add   ¼ teaspoon ginger   1 ml ginger
                      ¼ teaspoon cinnamon   1 ml cinnamon
                         dash of garlic, cayenne   garlic, cayenne
                         and basil   and basil
                      2 tablespoons vinegar   30 ml vinegar

Boil briefly so as not to destroy the bright tomato flavor. Use at once as a base for soup or pizza sauce, or pour boiling hot into hot, sterilized pint canning jars and seal at once.

TOMATO CATSUP

Preparation time: 2½ hours. *Makes:* 10 to 12 pints (5 to 6 liters).

	U.S. CUSTOMARY	METRIC
Boil until soft, strain through a sieve	8 pounds tomatoes, washed, chunked but unpeeled	4 kg tomatoes
	5 onions, roughly chopped	5 onions
	2 cloves garlic, crushed	2 garlic
	2 sweet peppers, seeded, ch.	2 peppers, seeded
	2 bay leaves	2 bay leaves
	1 teaspoon salt	5 ml salt
	½ cup sugar	125 ml sugar
Return pulp to fire, add spices tied in a bag	1 teaspoon celery seeds	5 ml celery seeds
	1 teaspoon allspice	5 ml allspice
	¼ teaspoon red pepper	1 ml red pepper
	2 inch stick cinnamon	5 cm stick cinnamon

Boil slowly stirring from time to time, until the liquid is reduced by half. Remove spice bag.

Stir in and boil   2 cups vinegar   500 ml vinegar
for 10 minutes

Pour the boiling catsup into hot, sterilized pint jars, seal immediately. My neighbor reduces this catsup by putting it in a very low oven overnight. She brings it to a boil on the top of the stove the next morning, adds vinegar, brings it back to a boil for 10 minutes and seals it into jars.

MARIE'S PIZZA SAUCE

Preparation time: 15 minutes. *Makes:* 2 cups (500 ml).

	U.S. CUSTOMARY	METRIC
In pan boil	2 cups tomatoes	500 ml tomatoes
	1 onion, chopped	30 ml onion
	2 tablespoons green pepper, ch.	30 ml gr. pepper

4 teaspoons chili powder	20 ml chili powder
¼ teaspoon garlic powder	1 ml garlic powder
¼ teaspoon oregano	1 ml oregano
1 teaspoon sugar	5 ml sugar
½ teaspoon vinegar	2 ml vinegar
3 tablespoons catsup	45 ml catsup

Boil until a little thickened, spread on rolled out pizza dough, dot with pepperoni, cheese, a sprinkle of oregano, salt and pepper and bake pizza for 15 minutes in a 450°F (230°C) oven.

Tabasco

Grind 2 ounces (60 g) or a large handful of dried red hot peppers, seeds included, mix with 1 tablespoon (15 ml) salt and 2 cups (500 ml) vinegar. Bring to a boil, pour into a jar, cool and cover. Let stand for a week, strain and use sparingly. Though this is brown, it is as hot as its commercial cousin, and covered, it keeps indefinitely in a cool place.

Walnut Sauce

Pound ½ cup (125 ml) of walnuts, black, white or English, with 2 cloves of garlic, season with a little salt. Beat in a little at a time, drop by drop at first, ½ cup plus 2 tablespoons (155 ml) olive oil. Whip continually as you gradually increase the olive oil to a trickle. A drop at a time while you beat, add ½ teaspoon (3 ml) vinegar. Continue to beat the mixture until a thick sauce is formed. Serve as a spread on fresh bread, as a dip for celery sticks or with cold cuts.

Sweet and Sour Sauce

In a pan mix ¾ cup (175 ml) sugar, ¼ cup (50 ml) vinegar and ¼ cup (50 ml) oil. Heat, stirring constantly until dissolved. Add 1 chopped green pepper, 1 chopped pimento, 2 slices of cooked pineapple. Thicken by mixing 1 tablespoon (15 ml) cornstarch in a little water, add, bring to boil, cook slowly for 5 to 7 minutes and serve over ham, rice or, for a change of pace, pour over heated, drained sauerkraut. If this sauce is to be used over plain boiled rice, add ¼ teaspoon (1 ml) salt and 1 teaspoon (5 ml) soy sauce.

WORCESTERSHIRE SAUCE

The list of ingredients seems endless, but this sauce keeps well and tastes better than "boughten," expert tasters attest.

Preparation time: 2 hours. *Makes:* about a pint (500 ml).

	U.S. CUSTOMARY	METRIC
Tie loosely in a cloth	1 onion, chopped	1 onion
	3 tablespoons mustard seed	45 ml mustard seed
	½ teaspoon red pepper pod	2 ml red pepper
	2 garlic cloves, crushed	2 garlic
	1 teaspoon peppercorns	5 ml black pepper
	½ teaspoon cracked ginger	2 ml cr. ginger
	1 inch cinnamon bark	3 cm cinnamon
	1 teaspoon whole cloves	5 ml cloves
	½ teaspoon cardamon seeds	2 ml cardamon
Simmer spices in a large, heavy pan with	2 cups vinegar	500 ml vinegar
	½ cup molasses	125 ml molasses
	½ cup soy sauce	125 ml soy sauce
	¼ cup tamarind pulp and juice or	50 ml tamarind or
	6 tablespoons lemon juice	90 ml lemon juice
Mix in a cup and add	3 tablespoons salt	45 ml salt
	½ teaspoon curry powder	3 ml curry
	1 anchovy, mashed	1 anchovy, mashed
	½ cup water	125 ml water

While spices are boiling, carmelize ½ cup (125 ml) sugar by putting the sugar into a heavy skillet and stirring vigorously over a lively fire. Move the sugar back and forth as it starts to melt and brown. Lower fire. Move sugar continuously, keep chopping at it, breaking the lumps until it becomes almost black and soupy, but not burned. Remove from the fire.

Take the spice bag from the sauce, squeeze, and carefully pour a little of the boiling spiced liquid into the sugar skillet stirring briskly until dissolved. Return the liquid sugar to the large pan. Boil briefly. Pour into a bowl, replace the spice bag in the sauce, cool and let stand in the refrigerator, covered tightly for about 2 weeks. Stir from time to time and squeeze the bag. Bottle, keep refrigerated and shake well before using.

For Worcesterburgers, paint hamburger patties with sauce, sprinkle with Parmesan cheese and fry until brown. Serve on bun.

HERB BOUQUET

A nice gravy, soup and stew additive to have on hand.
Preparation time: 2 hours. *Makes:* about 1 pint (500 ml).

	U. S. CUSTOMARY	METRIC
Chop fine, put into a pan, cover with water and boil until vegetables are mushy	1 bunch celery with leaves	1 celery bunch
	1 bunch parsley	1 parsley bunch
	2 onions	2 onions
	4 carrots	4 carrots
	½ teaspoon basil	2 ml basil
	2 bay leaves	2 bay leaves
	3 cardamon seeds, cracked	3 cardamon seeds
	1 teaspoon coriander seeds	5 ml coriander
	½ teaspoon grated nutmeg	3 ml nutmeg
	6 peppercorns, cracked	6 peppercorns
	½ teaspoon cracked ginger	2 ml ginger
	1 tablespoon salt	15 ml salt
	1 cup vinegar	250 ml vinegar

Strain through a cloth, squeeze well. Return juice to fire, simmer and reduce to about a pint (500 ml) in volume. While liquid is boiling down, put ½ cup (125 ml) sugar in a heavy skillet over a fire and keep stirring sugar until it gets lumpy and finally melts into a brown-black syrup; you may wish to lower heat as the sugar melts. When melted, immediately pour the boiling liquid into the skillet, stir vigorously, be watchful that the hot sugar does not pop out and burn you, and cook mixture until well blended and a rich brown. Pour into hot, sterilized catsup bottles, cap, cool and refrigerate. Use about a spoonful to color and season sauces.

CHILI SAUCE

Preparation time: about 2 hours. *Makes:* about 6 pints (3 liters).

	U. S. CUSTOMARY	METRIC
Peel, chop	5 quarts (about 30) tomatoes	5 liters tomatoes
Combine with chopped	2 cups onions	500 ml onions
	4 cups sweet peppers, cleaned	1 liter peppers
Mix in	1 red pepper, hot variety	1 red pepper, hot
	2 tablespoons salt	30 ml salt
	1 cup sugar	250 ml sugar
	3 tablespoons pickling spices tied in bag	45 ml pickling spices
	1 tablespoon mustard seed	15 ml mustard seed
	1 tablespoon celery seed	15 ml celery seed
	1 teaspoon cloves	5 ml cloves

1 teaspoon allspice   5 ml allspice
1 teaspoon cinnamon   5 ml cinnamon
3 cups vinegar   750 ml vinegar

Mix until all is in solution and simmer until the chili sauce begins to thicken. Stir frequently to prevent sticking and when the sauce is as thick as desired pour boiling hot into hot, sterilized pint (500 ml) canning jars leaving ½ inch (1 cm) head space and seal at once. If jars do not seal within 3 hours, process for 15 minutes in a Boiling Water Bath.

PICCALILLI

Preparation time: Overnight plus 3 hours. *Makes:* 8 pints (4 liters).

	U. S. CUSTOMARY	METRIC
Chop vegetables very fine, mix in salt and let stand overnight	30 (medium) green tomatoes 2 cups cucumbers 2 sweet peppers, cleaned 2 onions ¼ cup salt	30 green tomatoes 500 ml cucumbers 2 sweet peppers 2 onions 50 ml salt
Mix thoroughly, bring to a boil, fire off and let stand overnight	1 quart vinegar 1 cup sugar 2 tablespoons celery seed 4 tablespoons mustard seed ½ teaspoon ground cloves ½ teaspoon red pepper	1 liter vinegar 250 ml sugar 30 ml celery seed 60 ml mustard seed 3 ml cloves 3 ml red pepper

The following morning drain vegetables and rinse briefly in cold water to remove salt. Press slightly, mix with pickle solution, bring to a boil, cook for 3 minutes, pack hot into hot, sterilized pint (500 ml) jars, seal at once and store.

CORN RELISH

Preparation time: 3 hours. *Makes:* 6 pints (3 liters).

	U. S. CUSTOMARY	METRIC
Cook, cool and cut from cob	12 ears corn	12 ears corn
Clean and chop	6 sweet peppers (red and green)	6 peppers
Chop finely	1 cabbage (small)	1 cabbage
Add to vegetables, cook all ingredients until tender, about 20 minutes	1 quart vinegar 1 cup sugar 2 tablespoons dry mustard 1 tablespoon celery seed 1 tablespoon salt	1 liter vinegar 250 ml sugar 30 ml dry mustard 15 ml celery seed 15 ml salt

Pour hot into hot, sterilized pint jars and seal at once. Process pints for 15 minutes in a Boiling Water Bath.

BEET RELISH

Preparation time: 2 hours. *Makes:* 3 pints (1.5 liters).

	U. S. CUSTOMARY	METRIC
Chop finely	1 quart cooked beets	1 liter beets
	1 quart cabbage	1 liter cabbage
Grate	1 cup horseradish	250 ml horseradish
Mix in, heat	2 cups sugar	500 ml sugar
to boiling	1 tablespoon black pepper	15 ml pepper
	1¼ teaspoons salt	8 ml salt
	1½ cups vinegar	375 ml vinegar

Mix well, press into hot, sterilized jars, seal at once and store in a dark place.

GREEN PEPPER SAUCE

A facelift for meatloaf.

Preparation time: 20 minutes.

	U. S. CUSTOMARY	METRIC

Wash, remove seeds from 2 peppers and cut into 6 or 8 circle slices.

	U. S. CUSTOMARY	METRIC
In skillet,	¼ cup oil	50 ml oil
slightly cook	1 garlic clove, chopped	1 garlic
Add, saute 4	the pepper rings	pepper rings
minutes until	salt and pepper	salt, pepper
warm but crisp		
Pour over and	2 cups tomato sauce	500 ml tomato sauce
cook 4 minutes	¼ cup sweet red wine	125 ml sweet wine

Do not overcook peppers because the crunchiness adds allure. Pour sauce with its large floppy pepper rings over a precooked meatloaf. Sprinkle with a flurry of grated cheese and serve with a pretty smile.

BARBECUE SAUCE

For an outside grill skillet supper or oven barbecue.

Preparation time: 30 minutes plus meat time. *Makes:* 2 cups (500 ml).

	U. S. CUSTOMARY	METRIC
In heavy pot	1 cup water	250 ml water
combine	1 cup catsup	250 ml catsup
	2 tablespoons vinegar	30 ml vinegar
	1 tablespoon brown sugar	15 ml br. sugar
	1 tablespoon Worcestershire	15 ml Wor. sauce
	1 onion, chopped	1 onion
	1 garlic clove, minced	1 garlic
	2 teaspoons dry mustard	10 ml mustard

1 teaspoon paprika	5 ml paprika
1 teaspoon chili powder	5 ml chili powder
½ teaspoon salt	3 ml salt

Cover, simmer over a low fire for 30 minutes. Use sauce to flavor meat in one or a combination of three ways:

1. Dip meat into barbecue sauce before grilling.
2. Baste meat with barbecue sauce while cooking.
3. Marinate meat in barbecue sauce overnight.

If meat is lean, brush with oil; if you like a hotter sauce add ⅛ teaspoon (0.5 ml) cayenne.

Roux Based Sauces

Someone once wrote that the best sauce is a gracious disposition; be that as it may, it has been my experience that a hungry man wants good gravy even if the cook has had an attack of dyspepsia. There's no substitute for high stepping sauce. Drawing upon all of your ESS, "Extrasensory Senses," be aware of flavor, fragrance, texture, sounds from the stove and color. There is nothing worse than leaden gravy unless it's the morning after and the cook has mashed plump oysters in the cream sauce.

Basic needs for roux based sauces are: oil, which may drippings, butter or other shortening; thickening, which may be flour, cornstarch, rice or potato flour, eggs or bread; and liquid, which may be stock, part beer, wine or vinegar, milk, vegetable waters, juices or a combination. Salt and seasonings are the cook's contribution. Sauces may be ravishing, light-headed blondes, sultry auburns, rich and jolly golden blondes, svelte platinum broths or juicy brunettes.

Pour sauce or gravy usually calls for:
2 tablespoons (30 ml) oil
2 tablespoons (30 ml) flour
2 cups (500 ml) liquid.

Coating sauce or puddings call for:
3 tablespoons (45 ml) oil
3 tablespoons (45 ml) flour
2 cups (500 ml) liquid.

To make a roux: melt the butter or oil in a heavy pan over a low heat, add the flour, stir well until smooth. Cook the flour and oil for 2 or 3 minutes, slowly add hot or cold liquid while stirring constantly. Bring the sauce to a boil and stir vigorously until smooth and thick. If it is too thin, an egg, beaten with a little cold liquid, then poured into the sauce will thicken it nicely. Milk sauces are scalded but usually not boiled.

There are all sorts of fancy ways and names for making gravy but I am a skillet and fork person. I melt the oil, mix in the flour, browning it, if required, then I stir in the liquid. I mix with great vigor until the gravy is lump free and slightly thick; lowering the flame to simmer, I add seasoning. This last step is done in great secrecy, like a witch over a steaming cauldron I create the gravy that haunts my taste buds. In thickening meat juices I use the same technique: using a separate pan I melt the oil, stir in the flour and add the juices, stirring all the while. Although it means dirtying another skillet, bumpies are avoided.

Causes for lumpy gravy range from the cook's ill temper to mixing the thickening ingredient with hot liquid. Both will cause miniature dumplings to form and your family will ask you why you put tapioca in the gravy.

Never mix flour into hot liquid. If you object to the skillet and fork route and have stock such as juices of roasted meat or chicken to be thickened, mix the flour or other thickening agent in a cup with a little cold water. You can bind with yolks of eggs or blood but always mix the thickening with cold water added a little at a time. When well blended pour some of the seasoned hot stock into the cup, stirring as you pour, then empty the cup of liquid back into the boiling stock. Mix vigorously with a wooden spoon as you blend, later whisk to make the sauce as smooth as possible. Boil as directed and butter the surface to keep a skim from forming.

Pot Roast Gravy

For taste twists with pot roast, the moment before serving add to the thickened pan juices the juice of one orange and a wee bit of the peeling, or a small glass of port; or a dash of nutmeg and a squeeze of lemon.

PORK CHOP SAUCE

Preparation time: cook the meat plus 10 minutes.

	U. S. CUSTOMARY	METRIC
Drain the grease from fried pork chops, remove chops and keep warm.		
In pan, saute until clear	2 tablespoons oil	30 ml oil
	2 tablespoons onion, chopped	30 ml onions
Mix in with fork	2 tablespoons flour	30 ml flour

| Gradually add, stir, boil | 1½ cups vegetable water salt, pepper, parsley, pinch of ginger | 375 ml water salt, pepper, parsley, ginger |
| When smooth blend in | 1 tablespoon tart jelly ½ cup red wine | 15 ml jelly 125 ml red wine |

Serve separately or smother pork chops in the pink sauce. A side dish of sweet potatoes, spinach cooked briefly then turned in browned butter, fresh fruit salad dressed with oil, lemon juice and basil, hot dinner rolls and brownies complete this hearty meal.

HAM LYONNAISE

Preparation time: cook the meat plus 15 minutes.

	U. S. CUSTOMARY	METRIC
Bake, simmer or grill ham as you will.		
In skillet saute until clear	2 tablespoons ham fat 1 onion, chopped	30 ml ham fat onion
Mix in	2 tablespoons cornstarch	30 ml cornstarch
Stir in	¼ cup vinegar ½ cup white wine 2 tablespoons honey	50 ml vinegar 125 ml white wine 30 ml honey
Boil and add	1 cup ham liquid or water	250 ml ham juice

Simmer until well blended, drain a can of Queen Anne Cherries.

| Stir in | ½ cup Queen Anne Cherries | 125 ml cherries |

Heat through and serve sauce over a ham slice that oozes its own juice or over sliced ham. The salty, smoked, sweet-tart sauce with its shiny cherry lumps creates a pretty dish.

MUSHROOM SAUCE

This sauce makes hamburger patties think that they are steaks that were mistakenly caught in the meat chopper. You'll need 2 skillets.

Preparation time: 20 minutes. *Makes:* 4 servings.

	U. S. CUSTOMARY	METRIC
In skillet #1, saute until limp	¼ cup butter ¼ pound mushrooms, washed and sliced salt and pepper	50 ml butter 125 g mushrooms salt, pepper
Stir in, add liquid, mix, bring to boil, set aside, fire off	1 tablespoon flour ¾ cup white wine 1 tablespoon catsup 1 teaspoon soy sauce ½ cup water	15 ml flour 175 ml wine 15 ml catsup 5 ml soy sauce 125 ml water

| Heat skillet #2, | 4 beef patties, ground | 4 beef patties |
| salt, fry | round or hamburger | |

Sprinkle brown sugar on top side of meat and when seared turn. Lower fire, cover, cook until done and remove from pan onto platter. Sprinkle with crumbled blue cheese. Drain grease from the meat skillet and pour the wine-mushroom sauce into it, bring to boil and serve over the sweet dark meat.

White Sauce

"White sauce should be like a woman's lips," a French chef purred to a class of would-be cooks, "luxuriant, savory, mellow, piquant, spicy and provocative." To this day I do not think "white sauce" without seeing DuBois' quivering mustache.

Basic needs for white sauces are: oil, which may be drippings, butter or vegetable oils; thickening which is usually plain flour; liquid which may be stock, milk, cream, vegetable waters or a combination of these liquids plus 2 to 4 tablespoons (30 to 60 ml) white wine. Wine may be any lighthearted, dry commercial product, or it may be potato, parsnip, honeysuckle or elder blow. White grape is good, too.

Basic White Sauce

Method: for a moderately thick basic white sauce melt 2 tablespoons (30 ml) butter in a skillet over a low fire, stir in 2 tablespoons (30 ml) flour, cook slowly until well integrated and add 1½ to 2 cups (375 to 500 ml) milk. Stirring hard, mix in the liquid, bring just to a boil, or scald, remove from the fire, add salt and pepper. Freshly ground black pepper is recommended to spike most white sauces. Flavor with wine as desired but decrease the amount of other liquid by the amount of wine added. Cover and allow white sauce to steep without added heat but in a warm place for about 4 minutes. Wine is usually added with a brisk blending motion at the very last moment before serving.

White Sauce Variations

Name	Directions	Serve with
ANCHOVY	To Basic White Sauce add 1 tablespoon (15 ml) mashed anchovy or anchovy paste plus ¼ cup (50 ml) white wine.	Fish dishes and tomato base casseroles.

ANISE	To Basic White Sauce add 2 teaspoons (10 ml) sugar, 1 tablespoon (15 ml) vinegar, ½ teaspoon (2 ml) anise seed plus ¼ cup (50 ml) white wine.	Wild meats such as venison or moose.
BECHAMEL	To Basic White Sauce add 1 cup (250 ml) sieved vegetable pulp made by chopping, boiling and mashing an onion, carrot, celery stalk, garlic clove, half small red pepper pod in a little cooking water.	Dry fish such as marlin, halibut or swordfish steaks; chicken and farinaceous vegetables.
CHIPPED BEEF	To Basic White Sauce add 1 cup (250 ml) precooked or fully cured chips of bacon, ham or beef.	Thinly sliced white meat of chicken over toast.
EGG	To Basic White Sauce add 2 finely chopped hard-boiled eggs, plus a pinch of parsley.	Green vegetables, tuna, noodles.
FENNEL	To Basic White Sauce add 1 tablespoon (15 ml) chopped and blanched fennel, a breath of nutmeg and juice of a lemon.	Strong-flavored fish such as mackerel.
ONION	To Basic White Sauce add 1 cup (250 ml) sauteed chopped onion, 1 tablespoon (15 ml) vinegar and a grate of nutmeg.	Lamb, squash dishes or croquettes.
OYSTER	To Basic White Sauce add 12 poached oysters plus their juice, a pinch of cayenne and the juice of ½ lemon.	Steak, bread dressing, roast slices or spinach.
PINE NUTS	To Basic White Sauce add 1 teaspoon (5 ml) sugar, 1 teaspoon (5 ml) vinegar, grated nutmeg plus ½ cup (125 ml) pine nuts. I have substituted hickories.	Hamburgers, fried eggplant, fried okra or squash.
SHRIMP	To Basic White Sauce add ¼ cup (50 ml) chopped shrimp, a pinch of cayenne and 1 teaspoon (5 ml) lemon juice.	Spread on buttered toast and top with poached egg.

Mint Sauce

In a saucepan boil until dissolved ¼ cup (50 ml) water and 3 tablespoons (45 ml) sugar. Pour over 1 cup (250 ml) chopped fresh mint leaves, add ⅓ cup (80 ml) vinegar, cover and let stand for 2 hours. I use cultivated mints or wild mints such as Pennyroyal, *Hedeoma pulegioides,*

Spearmint *Mentha viridis* or Peppermint *Mentha piperita*. Strain and use in basting roasted lamb or serve separately.

Roast Lamb

Remove excess fat from a 6 pound (3 kg) leg of lamb and rub all over with crushed mint leaves. Sprinkle with a teaspoon (5 ml) rosemary, slit meat 2 or 3 places around the bone and push into the openings 2 teaspoons (10 ml) minced garlic. Place roast in a small roaster, lubricate with ¼ cup (50 ml) olive or corn oil, cover and let stand at room temperature for 3 hours. Bake at 450°F (230°C) for 20 minutes, remove from oven, baste with the drippings, salt and pepper to taste. Lower heat to 350°F (175°C) and return lamb to roast for 2 hours for medium done meat. During cooking baste alternately with the pan drippings and mint sauce. When done remove lamb to a platter, skim fat from the pan juices and reduce liquid over a high heat for 5 minutes. Pour over meat and garnish with fresh mint leaves.

BUTTER SAUCE

A rich, thick sauce.

	U. S. CUSTOMARY	METRIC
In a skillet	½ cup butter	125 ml butter
melt, stir in	2 tablespoons flour	30 ml flour
	½ teaspoon salt	3 ml salt
Add, heat, but	1½-2 cups milk	375-500 ml milk
do not boil	2 tablespoons white wine	30 ml wine

If boiled, the butter will turn to oil and the milk will curdle, so if you wish to avoid oily curd, heat butter sauce slowly, bring to the boiling point, cover and remove from the heat. Lastly fold in wine, if desired.

Butter Sauce Variations

Name	Directions	Serve with
CAPER	To Butter Sauce add ⅓ cup (80 ml) drained capers or minced sour pickle.	Baked fish or mutton.
CUCUMBER	To Butter Sauce add briefly sauteed, chopped cucumbers and shallots.	Pork cutlets, beef grill or sweetbreads.
GARLIC	To Butter Sauce add 2 tablespoons (30 ml) garlic liquid made by boiling 4 cloves of garlic in a little water. Brighten with the juice of ½ lemon.	Vegetable casseroles that contain tomatoes or cheese.

HARD-BOILED EGG AND BACON	To Butter Sauce add 2 hard-boiled eggs chopped fine, 2 tablespoons crisp fried bacon and a liberal shake of pepper.	Briefly cooked cabbage wedges or buttered toast.
HERB	To Butter Sauce add a finely chopped shallot, a minced fresh tarragon leaf, a sprig of chopped chervil and a touch of thyme and basil.	Grilled steaks and plain boiled potatoes.
MINCED CLAM	To Butter Sauce add ½ cup (125 ml) minced clams, juice included and a whisper of lemon.	Croutons as a side dish to minute steaks.
SAGE AND ONION	To Butter Sauce add ½ teaspoon (2 ml) powdered sage plus chopped and sauteed onion and a vigorous shake of coarsely ground black pepper.	Pork chops and grits.
SPINSTER'S	To Butter Sauce add ½ cup (125 ml) sauteed mushrooms, ½ cup (125 ml) sliced ripe olives, 1 tablespoon (15 ml) chopped parsley, at the last moment fold in ½ cup (125 ml) whipped cream.	Veal cutlets or large cuts of beef.
WINE AND CARAWAY	Bow to the islands of Madeira by tossing ½ cup (125 ml) Madeira wine and 1 teaspoon (5 ml) caraway seeds into Butter Sauce.	Fried chicken, cheese dishes, braised beef or roast pork.

Sour Cream Sauce

Make a White or Butter Sauce. Reduce the milk to 1 cup (250 ml), add ½ cup (125 ml) white wine and ½ teaspoon (2 ml) paprika. Scald, remove from the heat and fold in ½ cup (125 ml) of sour cream. Serve at once over grilled ground meat, lamb patties are nice, or with steak that has been garnished with a few sauteed onions and mushrooms.

Sour Cream Sauce is good when flavored with dill or with nutmeg and onion juice.

A slice of broiled ham served snuggling in noodles, garnished with baby smoked clams and covered over with Sour Cream Sauce is elegant fare.

Sweet Sauces

Favorite sauces that lighten rich desserts and moisten dry ones.

ORANGE MARMALADE SAUCE

Excellent over sponge cake or mincemeat pie.
Preparation time: 7 minutes. *Makes:* ¾ cup (175 ml) sauce.

	U. S. CUSTOMARY	METRIC
In a cup mix	1 tablespoon cornstarch	15 ml cornstarch
	¼ teaspoon salt	1 ml salt
	2 tablespoons sugar	30 ml sugar
	½ cup cold water	125 ml cold water
In pan, heat	½ cup Tokay (scant)	110 ml wine
and stir until	2 tablespoons marmalade	30 ml marmalade
dissolved	orange or other	

When wine and marmalade are almost boiling pour in cornstarch mixture, heat slowly, stirring constantly and when the sauce clears add 1 tablespoon (15 ml) butter and 1 teaspoon (5 ml) lemon juice. Boil for 1 minute and serve hot or cold.

Strawberry Sauce

Substitute strawberry jam for the marmalade in the above recipe, and serve this luscious sauce over crepes.

Nutmeg or Lemon Sauce

In a cup mix 3 tablespoons (45 ml) sugar with 1 tablespoon (15 ml) cornstarch and ¼ teaspoon (1 ml) salt. Add ½ cup (125 ml) cold water and stir into solution. In pan heat ½ cup (125 ml) water to boiling, stir in the cornstarch mixture, heat slowly, stir constantly and when sauce clears add ¼ teaspoon (1 ml) grated nutmeg, bring to boil and serve over apple or peach turnovers. For lemon sauce, omit nutmeg and at the last moment add 2 teaspoons (10 ml) lemon juice, scald and serve with puddings or turnovers.

RASPBERRY CREAM

Though technically not a pudding, old-fashioned fruit creams were called summer puddings.

Preparation time: 20 minutes. *Serves:* 5.

	U.S. CUSTOMARY	METRIC
If you wash berries, drain thoroughly.		
Chill in icebox or freezer	1 cup raspberries	250 ml raspberries
Whip and set on ice or in freezer	2 cups heavy cream	500 ml cream
In second bowl whip until stiff	4 egg whites	4 egg whites
Slowly add	½ cup powdered sugar	125 ml powdered sugar
When glossy slowly fold in	1 tablespoon cream sherry the raspberries the whipped cream	15 ml sherry raspberries whipped cream

Pour into custard cups and chill or serve immediately. A sprinkle of chopped nuts or slivered almonds on top delights most raspberry cream fiends.

PUMPKIN PUDDING

Preparation time: 50 minutes. *Makes:* 8 servings.

	U. S. CUSTOMARY	METRIC
In large bowl	1 cup sugar	250 ml sugar
mix until well	2 tablespoons cornstarch	30 ml cornstarch
blended	¼ teaspoon nutmeg	1 ml nutmeg
	½ teaspoon cloves	2 ml cloves
	1 teaspoon cinnamon	5 ml cinnamon
	½ teaspoon salt	3 ml salt
Stir in	3 eggs, well beaten	3 eggs
	2 cups pumpkin, cooked or canned	500 ml pumpkin
	2 tablespoons oil	30 ml oil
	2 cups cream	500 ml cream

Pour into a greased baking dish and bake at 450°F (230°C) for 15 minutes, lower heat to 350°F (175°C) and bake about 30 minutes or until a knife inserted into the pudding comes out clean. Cool to firm and serve. Or if you feel like a fling, pour brandy over it, light, and when the blue flame dies down serve while its bubbly top is still smoldering. I have never flamed pumpkin pudding but a hostess did and it was spectacular, especially when the dish broke and tongues of fire licked the table. Make sure that your dish is flameproof. I use this recipe with winter squash too; I quarter and seed the squash, boil it until tender, then scoop out the pulp. It's much easier than peeling the hard rinds and one can save the juice for soup.

Blackberry Pudding

Preparation time: 1 hour to pick a quart of berries, 15 minutes to make.

Put briefly cooked berries through a sieve and sweeten them to taste with brown sugar. Add a sprinkle of salt and thicken with a ratio of 2 tablespoons (30 ml) cornstarch to 2 cups (500 ml) pulp. Boil the pudding for 2 minutes. Pour the cooked pudding into a serving bowl, pour a glass of blackberry brandy over it to keep it from crusting and serve into individual bowls with a daub of whipped cream. The drop or two of brandy in each spoonful seems to explode in your mouth and the cool cream melds it all together in a most delicious manner.

Honey

As a sauce honey may be used plain, drizzled over fruit or ice cream. Whipped cream sweetened with honey gives a homey flavor to fruit cup, applesauce cake or hot gingerbread. Honey creamed with butter and flavored with a jigger of rum provides a provocative hard sauce to be served on mincemeat pie or with fruit cake.

Honey contains the same qualities today that it had in stillroom times. Though flavor, aroma and color vary with the kind of flowers from which bees gather nectar, as a rule the lightest is the mildest; that may be clover, alfalfa or thistle honey. The darkest honey is probably buckwheat. Simple sugars which are easy to digest make up about four-fifths of honey's weight. Honey keeps best in covered containers in a dry place at room temperature; exposed to air it loses flavor and absorbs moisture. If honey seems to turn sugary, place the container in a pan of warm water until the crystals disappear. Honey may be used, measure for measure, in place of sugar in moist foods, but in cakes honey can replace one-half of the sugar and in cookies, about one-third. In both cakes and cookies the honey should be thoroughly mixed with either the shortening or the liquid to prevent a soggy layer on the top.

HONEY BREAD PUDDING

Preparation time: 1 hour. *Makes:* 4 servings.

	U. S. CUSTOMARY	METRIC
In a buttered baking dish crumble	2 cups day-old bread A combination of plain and raisin bread is nice.	500 ml bread
In pan over low heat combine	2 tablespoons butter	30 ml butter
	¼ cup honey	50 ml honey
	⅛ teaspoon salt	0.5 ml salt
	2 eggs, beaten	2 eggs
	1 teaspoon vanilla	5 ml vanilla
	1¾ cups milk	425 ml milk

Stir, and when everything is in solution pour the mixture over the bread in the baking dish. Shake the dish and set it in a pan of hot water in the oven and bake at 350°F (175°C) for 45 minutes. Serve hot and with plain honey as a sauce.

Honey Apple Crisp

Wash, core and chop 2 cups (500 ml) apples and put into a greased baking dish. Spread with 2 tablespoons (30 ml) sugar, 2 teaspoons (10 ml) lemon juice and ¼ cup (50 ml) honey. In a bowl mix ¼ cup (50 ml) flour, 2 tablespoons (30 ml) brown sugar, 2 tablespoons (30 ml) butter and a dash of salt. Crumble over the top of the apples, sprinkle with cinnamon and bake at 375°F (190°C) for about 45 minutes or until the apples are tender and the crust is brown. Serve smothered in cream whipped with honey and watch your young people drool as the frothy sauce oozes into the crumbly crusty top.

Flower Cookery

Stillrooms of the last century were treasure troves of edible flowers. Tossed fresh into salads and fritters, flowers pleased the eye, nose and palate; preserved in vinegars, dried, candied or jellied, they captured floral essences that flavored food.

Spinach and Violet Salad

Tear spinach leaves with violet leaves and mix in a handful of violet flowers, chunked avocado, sectioned orange and at the moment before serving dash over oil and vinegar seasoned with salt, pepper, a bit of garlic, curry powder and a splash of Tabasco. This luscious spring time supper salad complements grilled fish, steamed yellow squash dressed with cream, nutmeg and butter, fresh garden peas and hunks of hot French bread.

Dandelion Potato Salad

Briefly mix 4 cups (1 liter) of cubed, cooked potatoes with 4 minced hard-boiled eggs, ¼ cup (50 ml) chopped spring onions, tops included, and 1 cup (250 ml) dandelion petals. When picking dandelions, hold the heel of the flower and pull out the petals, do not allow any stem or milk into your salad or you will pucker for a week. Dress with salt, pepper, celery seed, and mayonnaise mixed half and half with Italian dressing.

Rose Salad

Make a lemon gelatin. After it has been chilled to the consistency of egg whites, stir in shredded carrots, celery and cabbage bits, bright multicolored rose petals and chopped olives. Refrigerate until set, about 2 hours. Serve on lettuce with sour cream mixed with mayonnaise.

Flower Fritters

Fresh elder flowers, rose and carnation petals, squash and day lily blooms were commonly dipped into a beer batter made by blending ¾ cup (175 ml) beer with ½ cup (125 ml) flour and a sprinkle of salt. Fry in hot oil and serve drenched in powdered sugar to be eaten as finger food.

Flower Vinegar

Place washed and towel-dried edible and fragrant flower petals, no greenery, into a jar and cover with boiling, clear vinegar. Hide the lidded jar away for 10 days, strain and use it to tease salads, roasts and mild-flavored sauces.

Dried Flowers

To dry flowers, spread full-blown flowers on paper in a shady spot, fluff from time to time, and when dry as hay, store in paper bags in a moisture free area. Dried day lily flowers, marigold and nasturtium petals, and elder blooms add an exotic touch to soups, souffles and chowders. Rose petals, lemon flowers and lavender dry into unusual teas. Put dried petals into a plastic bag and freeze for a day to prevent mildew.

Candied Flowers

Candied flowers were decorative treats created by dipping washed and towel-dried rose petals, violets or lilac clusters into slightly beaten egg whites and then into granulated sugar. The flowers were allowed to crystallize overnight on paper and decoratively arranged on cake icing. I do not wash flowers but we do not have poisonous sprays or dust in the woods, "just a little clean dirt," as my husband says.

Poison

Flowers are like women; some are spritely and captivatingly pretty, some innocent and shy, some flamboyant, brassy and some are pure poison. The word is IDENTIFY. Do not experiment. An Indian I knew described his blue flag poisoning as "Awfully hard on the guts," and I believed him. His skin had turned green and his eyeballs, yellow—and that was 2 weeks after he was hospitalized and had his stomach pumped.

Among suspect poisonous pretties are listed: azalea, laurel, daffodil, buttercup, bloodroot, jimson and iris. . . . Serve only known edible flowers and do so with a spirit of joy and a light heart.

COMMON FLOWERS USED IN STILLROOM COOKING

Wash young flowers, old-fashioned varieties, all green parts removed.	Vinegar	Sauce	Fritter	Dried for tea	Candied	Salad	Omelet	Jelly	Tastes similar to:
Carnation	●	●			●	●	●	●	Cloves
Chrysanthemum						●	●		Bitter, pungent
Clover	●			●			●		Sweet hay
Dandelion				●		●	●		Lemon peeling
Day lily			●			●	●		Okra
Elder	●		●	●			●		Old cheese
Lavender	●	●		●				●	Sweet chestnuts
Lemon flower	●				●	●			Citrus
Marigold							●		Oregano
Nasturtium	●		●			●	●		Cress
Rose	●	●	●	●	●	●	●	●	Fragrant tea
Squash			●			●	●		Sweet squash
Violet	●	●			●	●	●	●	Sweet peas
Yucca			●			●	●		Fresh spinach

Whether queens of impudence such as mustard or gentle friends of beef, tart or sweet, sauces give liquid seasoning to foods and may well qualify to be a cook's finest kitchen companion.

CHAPTER **VI**

Cured Meats

"Sing a song of sausage
Bacon, hams and wurste, . . ."

Unlike a homemaker in today's world of refrigerated meat, a stillroom cook had to think about the rapidity with which bacteria changed fresh products. She understood that even after slaughter an animal carcass underwent constant change; that untended, meat became inedible in five days. After briefly feasting on fresh meat our forefathers ate homecured pork products because pigs were generally raised for table meat. As the salt barrel or smokehouse took on "that leane, lanke looke" they ate less meat and more flavor. Throughout the summer, vegetable and grain foods were seasoned with meat remnants and when the butchering moon and pork chop fever rode high, the ritual of putting down pork began.

During the late 1700s and most of the 1800s beef as food was practically unknown. Cattle were regarded as brush eating, field working tools, valued primarily for their leather, secondly for tallow and lastly as meat; on small farms milk was their main product. It was not until after the Civil War that the rangy Long Horns were seen as a money crop of the south and were herded northward to be slaughtered and corned for city food. Tough and unattractive compared to pork, most range cattle were over 4 years old and weighed less than 400 pounds when mature. Today's steer weighs 1000 pounds at 2 years, an accomplishment stimulated by railroads, grain feed, breed improvement, refrigeration and Americans' beefy appetites.

Authorities tell us, however, that a change is at hand. The cost of energy may preclude meat from many tables in the near future. The enormous amount of energy consumed in producing grains and converting it into beef points to the future use of grass fed beef, but pastureland is limited. Commercial pigs too are fed primarily on grain. The high costs of transportation and refrigeration may well lead to more preservation of meat without refrigeration. Agricultural predictions indicate that vege-

131

table and grain protein may be substituted for meat protein in diets, with meat used as flavoring and as holiday fare. America's profligate days of meat consumption are numbered. Our menus with regard to meat consumption will be similar to those of stillroom times.

To preserve meat and inhibit decay, bacterial action must be stopped. As they do in useful fermentation processes such as winemaking, meat-spoiling bacteria require warmth, moisture, air, plus food to thrive; therefore, reason dictates that freezing, drying or vacuum packaging will retard spoilage. If you have ever looked at 700 pounds of freshly butchered meat, the importance of preserving it would come into focus in a hurry. Ham, bacon, corned beef and sausages not only save meat from spoiling, but add variety to mealtimes and once put down they become carefree, and in many cases, instant food.

Drying meat by the addition of salt is the simplest preserving method but unfortunately salt hardens meat and causes it to turn gray. I ran across some gray meat in Alaska once; the owner, a hoary prospector, gummed the moose with gusto and being hungry I joined him. Surprisingly, the old gray moose was flavorful. In ordinary homes, however, sodium nitrate or saltpeter and sugar are added to salt in curing meat; the nitrates stabilize cured meat pigment and sugars soften the product.

People who put down their own hams or beef state that only fresh, non-frozen meat should be cured and that the best temperature for butchering is between 38 and 48°F (3 and 9°C). After the meat has been initially cured in salt, the best drying temperature for large cuts is about 50 to 60°F (10 to 15°C). Men who produce really excellent hams have told me that first the salt draws out moisture, then a fermentation takes place in hams that pickles and flavors the meat.

Equipment for homecuring includes knives, scales and large containers such as plastic trash cans with lids. Storage requires heavy string, paper and a dark, dry, varmint-free area with a current of air where the meat is to be hung. Most cellars are too damp for meat curing but Virginia connoisseurs vow that a little mold improves the flavor.

As in stillroom days, common salt is the main meat curing ingredient. Many people also add a very small amount of saltpeter even though nutritionists regard nitrates as a weak poison. In fact, the U.S. Department of Agriculture stipulates that the addition of nitrates should be no more than 200 ppm in commercial products; as a comparison, seawater is 30,000 ppm salt. Sugar is added to most salt cures at the ratio of 2.5% salt to 1.1% sugar, in order to flavor the meat and to counteract the hardening effects of salt. Sugar also improves the frying characteristics and color of meat. Other curing ingredients include pepper, honey, spices, liquids such as beer and brandy, and smoke.

Meat is generally cured in three ways: by pickling or the immersion of meat in salt water; by rubbing dry salt into the meat, which is called dry cure; or by rubbing on a combination of salt, spices, sugar and nitrates, called sugar cured.

Different sizes and kinds of meat require different amounts of cure and different times in cure. Most cured meat, except that in brine, should be washed, hung to dry, smoked or aged if desired, and wrapped in cloth or paper after the initial salting process is completed.

Sausage may be ground and seasoned from any good quality meat and the principles of curing sausages are the same as those in curing meat. Salt dehydrates the product thus inhibiting the wanton growth of bacteria that causes spoilage. Sausages must be sealed after time in cure is complete, otherwise you'll end up with an overly salty product that even the dog won't eat. Equipment for home sausage making includes knives, a meat grinder or a friendly butcher, a stuffer and casings, plus a varmint-free holding area.

Sausage ingredients are: meat, salt, spices, cereals, sugar, spirits, and in some cases, saltpeter. There are hundreds of kinds of sausage because hundreds of people make them; just as with bread, cheese and fermented drinks, sausage making is an individual art. Most recipes call for pork fat in sausage because it is more mellow and tasty than lamb, beef or game fat, but usually no more than ⅓ fat is recommended.

Sausage making consists of grinding the meat, mixing in salt and spices, rigging the stuffer, boiling the casings and utensils, stuffing, tying, curing or smoking the sausages and sealing them after time in cure is up.

Because of the danger of humans contracting trichinosis, all pork must be thoroughly cooked before eating, or if pork is to be eaten uncooked as some kinds of sausages are, pork should be frozen at minus 10°F (-23°C) for 21 days before processing.

To add flavor, color and cure, both meat and sausages may be smoked after they have been cured in salt. There are two main smoking techniques: hot smoke, temperatures 120 to 160°F (50 to 70°C) for a partially cooked product that requires refrigeration; and cold smoke 90 to 100°F (32 to 40°C) for a longer period of time. Cold smoke dries the meat and seals the outside of it as it is being smoked. Don't do as my daughter and I did. We hung the bacon down the cabin chimney and went for a walk. When we returned, the bacon had charred into an elongated curlicue worm.

Corned Beef

Although most corned beef is made from tough cuts, Lewis and I corn round and rump roasts and find them to be inspired eating. We trim all fat before processing and substitute a sprinkling of oil during cooking. We have discovered that freezing our corned beef after it has been cured, smoked and wrapped, keeps it moist and retards surface molds. People ask why cure if you are going to freeze the beef anyway? Curing beef takes several weeks, by that time our groaning freezer has been relieved of part of its booty and our saturated tastebuds are ready for a flavor change. Additionally we have found that because of its density and pungent flavor, corned beef goes further than plain roast beef. It is instant food, we often slice it very thin and eat it raw on sandwiches or as party snacks. A very little bit stretches greatly when creamed or used in casseroles, and as a bacon substitute, smoked beef can't be beat.

Brine Corned Beef

To corn beef, select thick, well-muscled, boneless pieces, trim fat, cut into uniform sizes and weigh. For a 50 pound (25 kg) batch of meat, rub 4 pounds (2 kg) dry, noniodized salt into the meat and pack it into a sterilized plastic trash container. Allow the salt-rubbed meat to stand for 24 hours, then make a brine by dissolving 1 pound (500 g) salt, 2 pounds (1 kg) sugar, 2 tablespoons (30 g) saltpeter in 2 gallons (8 liters) of water and cover the salted meat. Cover with a plate and weight with a rock to keep meat under the brine, lid the container and hold the beef submerged in cure for 30 days at temperatures between 38 to 48°F (3 to 9°C). After removing a piece of corned beef from its curing brine, wash it thoroughly then soak it in fresh water for 2 hours. Taste the meat for saltiness; it should be acid, somewhat salty, but the beef flavor should come through. Kept submerged in a cool, dark place, corned beef will remain sweet indefinitely. If any off-flavor develops, drain and wash each piece well and cover with a brine made of 1 pound (500 g) salt dissolved in 2 gallons (8 liters) water. Cook the smaller pieces first because salt penetrates them faster. You can sneak a piece of corned beef at any time during the curing process but taste for saltiness and soak or cook accordingly.

Paprika Corned Beef and Cabbage

Soak corned beef for 2 hours. Simmer in fresh water until tender, (about 40 minutes to the pound), add a head of cabbage that has been cut into wedges, 2 teaspoons (10 ml) caraway seeds, ¼ teaspoon (1 ml) pepper and 1 tablespoon (15 ml) paprika. Stew for 15 minutes while you saute 1 chopped onion and a thinly sliced green pepper in a little butter. Drain cabbage and meat, briefly mix cabbage in the onion-pepper skillet and arrange the drained greenery around the corned beef on a large platter. Garnish with a shower of paprika. Served with potted potatoes, buttered corn, pickled beets and prune tarts spiced with ginger.

Corned Beef Sandwiches

Cold, cooked corned beef is royal fare for sandwiches when thinly sliced across the grain; try it with lettuce and a slice of Swiss cheese on buttered rye. Or try some of these ideas:

On homemade bread heap paper-thin corned beef with thick slices of tomatoes;

Grilled corned beef sandwich with Gruyere cheese and slivered black olives;

Corned beef layered with creamed cheese on buttered wheat toast, warmed on a cookie sheet, and served with eggs;

Thin slices of corned beef wrapped around chicken livers and pinned with a toothpick for hors d'oeuvres.

Lewis likes corned beef with a stack of sauerkraut, a slice or two of brick cheese and slivered pepperoni on a big bun. It sounds and looks good, but to me, corned beef and horseradish is just about the greatest.

Sugar Cured Corned Beef

Although we have tried a variety of cures our favored fall back corning process is sugar cure. We cut fresh, unfrozen heavy cuts of beef such as rump, round and brisket into fairly uniform 4 to 6 pound (2 to 3 kg) squares and rub sugar cure right into the meat. Sometimes we use the commercial sugar cure product that can be purchased at rural grocery stores. It contains salt, sugar, nitrates plus seasoning. Some years we make our own sugar cure. For 60 pounds (30 kg) of trimmed meat, we mix by hand 4 pounds (2 kg) salt, 2 pounds (1 kg) sugar, 2 tablespoons (30 g or 30 ml) saltpeter, 8 tablespoons (60 g or 120 ml) garlic powder and 16 tablespoons (120 g or 240 ml) chili powder, which is a scant cup. We divide the dry cure mixture into three portions after it has been blended and rub all sides of every piece of our 60 pounds (30 kg) of meat with one part of the mix and let the meat stand on an enamel topped table at a temperature of about 40°F (5°C) for 4 hours. We then rub the second portion of our sugar cure mix on each piece, put the meat into a plastic trash container, cover it and let it stand overnight in a cool place 38 to 48°F (3 to 9°C). The next day, 24 hours after the meat was first rubbed with cure mix, we remove the beef from the container and apply the last part of our dry cure. Finally we pack the meat in the plastic container, putting the larger pieces as flat as possible on the bottom, cover the container and put it to corn in a cool area, 38 to 48°F (3 to 9°C). The meat must be repositioned or repacked so that each piece is turned upside down after the curing time is about half up. Marking the calendar so that we will not forget, we leave our beef in cure for about 1½ days per pound. We take the average; if we have 10 pieces of beef and the total weight is 60 pounds (30 kg), the average weight per piece is 6 pounds (3 kg). At 1½ days per pound, our beef is ready to be removed from the dry cure in about 9 days. The timing in meat curing, as in other fermentation processes, is flexible. If we're going to the theater on the 9th day and do not wish to smell like garlic, we wait until the 10th day to remove our meat. For a milder cure, some people leave meat in cure one day per pound; others like a stronger product and leave it for 2 days per pound before removing the meat.

When the time in cure is up, wash each piece of meat in tepid water, soak in cold water for ½ hour and hang the beef to dry for about 4 days in an airy place, about 50°F (10°C). For hanging the meat we hammer a hole into each piece with a sterilized spike and poke a clean cord through the hole. A strong wire is needed to hang 60 pounds of meat on a line. This reddish brown beef is corned and may be eaten or wrapped and stored after it is thoroughly dried.

Smoked Beef

Some years we smoke part of our corned beef in the fireplace. First we wash and oil the racks from the gas oven, lay them on building blocks in the fireplace and arrange the cured and dried beef on them so that smoke can circulate around each piece. We make a fire and keep it barely smoldering with green hickory or apple logs, black birch chips and damp sawdust. It takes about a day to smoke a double rack of meat at 90°F

(32°C), and we have to watch it fairly constantly so that no fire gets to the meat, only cool smoke. We reposition and turn each piece several times until the beef takes on a beautiful auburn glow.

When time in smoke is up the smoked corned beef is hung to cool a day or two at room temperature, then wrapped in brown paper and tied tightly. A second wrapping is required to exclude as much air as possible; if you can smell smoked meat through the second wrapping, wrap it again. Lastly we put each piece of beef into a brown paper sack and store it in the freezer. This beef does not have to be thawed to cut it; merely cut that which you need, rewrap and return it to the freezer. Our smoked corned beef is not the dried jerky that back packers carry, so it will not keep indefinitely without refrigeration. Before we had a freezer, however, we hung the thrice wrapped meat in the basement and it kept well for 8 months or until we ate it.

Both smoked and dry sugar cured beef may be eaten as is, thinly sliced, or they may be prepared in any manner that regular brine cured corned beef, bacon or ham is cooked.

BOILED CORNED BEEF WITH HORSERADISH

Soak 3 pounds (1.5 kg) of plain or smoked corned beef for 2 hours.
Preparation time after soaking: 2½ hours. *Serves:* 6.

	U. S. CUSTOMARY	METRIC
Boil for 1½ hours in water to cover	3 pounds corned beef, save the liquid	1.5 kg beef
An hour before serving add and cook until tender	7 whole potatoes	7 potatoes
	6 carrots, halved	6 carrots
	1 peppercorn	1 peppercorn
	3 allspice	3 allspice
In a skillet blend	2 tablespoons oil	30 ml oil
	2 tablespoons flour	30 ml flour
Stir in	2 cups meat liquid	500 ml liquid
When boiling, fold in, remove from fire	2 tablespoons grated horseradish	30 ml horseradish
	½ cup cream	125 ml cream

Do not boil after the horseradish and cream have been added. At the table ladle the gravy over the thinly sliced beef as it is placed on individual plates.

Saltpeterless Corned Beef

Make a brine of 2 quarts (2 liters) water, a can of beer, 1 cup (250 ml) salt, ¼ cup (50 ml) sugar and 2 tablespoons (30 ml) pickling spice. Immerse a 6 to 8 pound (3 or 4 kg) rump roast in the brine, weight the meat with a plate and rock, cover and set in a cool place, 38 to 48°F (3 to 9°C), for 4 days. To cook this corn-flavored but not fully cured beef, remove from brine, wash, soak for about 30 minutes in cold water, rub the meat with ½ teaspoon (2 ml) garlic powder and 1 tablespoon (15 ml) chili powder. Let the spices permeate for about 30 minutes. Cover with cold water and simmer for about 4 hours. This beef may be served warm with cabbage and potatoes, refrigerated and sliced cold, or prepared as you wish.

CORNED BEEF SPOON BREAD

An economical and savory all-in-one supper dish.

Preparation time: 45 minutes. *Serves:* 5.

	U. S. CUSTOMARY	METRIC
In a pan mix	½ cup corn meal	125 ml corn meal
	1 tablespoon parsley, chop.	15 ml parsley
	1 stalk celery, chopped	1 stalk celery
	1 small onion, chopped	1 onion
	2 slices bacon, chopped fine, or 2 tablespoons oil substituted for bacon	2 slices bacon
Blend in	1 cup milk	250 ml milk
	¾ cup water	175 ml water

Heat, boil for 3 minutes or until the mixture has thickened, stir constantly.

Add, stir into mixture	1½ cups cooked, cubed corned beef or ½ can	375 ml corned beef
	1 egg, slightly beaten	1 egg
	¾ teaspoon salt	3 ml salt
	¼ teaspoon pepper	1 ml pepper
	any leftover vegetables	vegetables

Pour into a greased casserole dish, top with 1 piece of bacon cut into small pieces, or cubes of cheese or butter. Bake at 375°F (190°C) for 35 minutes. Serve hot with crisp curls of watercress.

Dried Beef

Dried beef, which may be kept without refrigeration for carrying on ski trips and back packing, can also be used in most corned beef recipes.

You begin by presoaking lean beef rump or round for an hour in a strong brine: 2 pounds (1 kg) salt, 4 teaspoons (20 ml) saltpeter to 1 gallon (4 liters) water. Remove and place the beef to drain for a few minutes but do not allow it to dry. Weigh the meat and figure one-tenth of its weight for salt and one-fortieth of the weight of the salt for saltpeter. A 10 pound (5 kg) piece of beef to be dry cured would require 1 pound (500 g) salt and .4 ounces (12 g) saltpeter. Mix the salt and saltpeter thoroughly before dividing into three parts. Rub one part of the mix into the meat, sprinkle the second part of the mix in the curing container and over the top of the meat after you put it down. Pack the meat tightly into the mix and hold at a cool temperature, between 38 and 48°F (3 to 9°C), for 5 days. Break the pack and reposition the meat, sprinkle it with the third part of the curing mixture and keep the meat in salt 6 days for each inch (2.5 cm) of thickness. A 2 inch (5 cm) piece of beef would be kept in cure for 12 days. Mark the calendar. When time in cure is up, remove the meat from the salt, wash the surface in cold water and hang to dry in a cool place, 38 to 48°F (3 to 9°C), for 2 to 4 weeks, depending upon the humidity of the area. A dry location dries the meat faster. If a white surface layer of salt appears, wash the surface a second time and hang the meat in a warm place, 60°F (15°C), until thoroughly dry. Wrap the meat in several layers of paper or cloth and hang it in a dark, dry place. As an alternative to air drying you may wish to cool smoke your fully cured dried beef. After the meat has been washed in cold water and allowed to dry for 4 days, lay it on a rack or hang in smoke, 90°F (32°C), for 72 to 84 hours. Cool, wrap and store in a dry, dark place. Sliced very thin, or cut into finger-sized strips as jerky, dried beef is excellent as a bacon substitute or as a trail food. In cooking with dried beef, soak in water overnight and use as corned beef.

Quick Sauerbraten

Soak a 3 pound (1.5 kg) corned beef or dried beef overnight. The following morning flour and brown in oil. Taste, salt if necessary. Cover meat with water and cook until tender. Cut the meat into ½ inch (1 cm) diagonal slices, set aside. To 2 cups (500 ml) meat liquid, add ½ cup (125 ml) vinegar, ½ cup (125 ml) catsup, one large onion chopped, 2 tablespoons (30 ml) sugar and a bay leaf. Boil while you make a roux. In a skillet blend 2 tablespoons (30 ml) oil with 3 tablespoons (45 ml) flour, pour the boiling mixture into the skillet, stir, bring to a simmer and add the sliced beef, careful to keep the slices intact. When piping hot, cover and set aside off the fire until dinner time. Reheat and serve. Standing in the gravy, the meat takes on the flavor of catsup and vinegar and is very similar in flavor to the real stillroom sauerbraten.

CORNED BEEF SANDWICH FILLING

A sandwich spread that can be stored in the icebox and used as needed. Use cooked corned beef.

Preparation time: 1 hour. *Makes:* 3 cups (750 ml).

	U. S. CUSTOMARY	METRIC
Finely grind	1 pound corned beef	500 g beef
In a bowl beat together	2 egg yolks	2 egg yolks
	½ teaspoon prepared mustard	3 ml mustard
	½ teaspoon paprika	3 ml paprika
	1 teaspoon sugar	5 ml sugar
	2 tablespoons vinegar	30 ml vinegar
Add at a very slow trickle while beating	1 cup salad oil	250 ml oil

When mixture begins to thicken the oil may be added faster. Beat well.

When thick fold in	2 teaspoons horseradish	10 ml horseradish
	1 teaspoon celery seed	5 ml celery seed
	the ground corned beef	the corned beef

Use at once or store in the refrigerator.

CORNED BEEF AND DRIED BEANS

Preparation time: Overnight, plus 4 hours. *Serves:* 8.

	U. S. CUSTOMARY	METRIC
Soak overnight and drain	1 pound dried pinto beans	500 g dried beans
Cover beans with water, add and simmer 4 hours	½ pound corned beef	225 g beef
	1 onion, chopped	1 onion
	¼ teaspoon pepper	1 ml pepper
Just before serving mix in	3 tablespoons molasses	45 ml molasses
	3 tablespoons catsup	45 ml catsup

If beans are too juicy they may be baked for a little while at 350°F (175°C), or we like them served in a soup bowl with a heap of brown bread and butter.

SPICY BAKED CORNED BEEF

Soak beef in cold water for 2 hours.
Preparation time: 4 hours. *Serves:* 8.

	U. S. CUSTOMARY	METRIC
Cover with	4 pounds corned beef	2 kg corned beef
boiling water	1 stalk celery, chopped	1 celery
	1 tablespoon pickling spice tied in bag	15 ml pickling spice
	1 onion, chopped	1 onion
	1 carrot, chopped	1 carrot

Reduce heat to simmer, cover and cook gently for 3 hours. Remove meat.

	U. S. CUSTOMARY	METRIC
Cover meat with	1 tablespoon prepared mustard	15 ml mustard
	1/3 cup brown sugar	80 ml brown sugar
	1/2 cup sweet pickle juice as from pickled peaches	125 ml pickle juice

Bake meat in a slow oven, 300°F (150°C), for about 45 minutes, baste a time or two. Take from oven and allow to stand for at least 10 minutes before slicing. Serve with sweet potatoes that have a half cup (125 ml) black walnuts mixed in, buttered kale, fried apples, fresh bread and persimmon pudding for a good early winter supper.

CORNED BEEF CHILI

Preparation time: Overnight plus 4 hours. *Serves:* 8.

	U. S. CUSTOMARY	METRIC
Soak overnight and drain	1 pound dried kidney beans	500 g dried beans
Cover with water, add and simmer for 3 hours	the soaked beans 1 pound corned beef, trimmings or one piece	the soaked beans 500 g corned beef
In skillet saute	1 tablespoon oil 2 onions, chopped 2 cloves garlic, minced 1 sweet pepper, cleaned and chopped	15 ml oil 2 onions 2 garlic 1 pepper
Add and simmer until well blended	1 quart tomatoes 1/4 teaspoon Tabasco 2 teaspoons caraway seeds 2 tablespoons chili powder 1/2 teaspoon cumin	1 liter tomatoes 1 ml Tabasco 10 ml caraway 30 ml chili pow. 2 ml cumin

Drain beans and beef when cooked and spoon into the tomato sauce. If the beef does not fall apart, cube into bite-sized pieces, cover the chili and simmer for about an hour. Add salt if necessary. If the mixture boils down add bean juice. A smooth thickening agent may be added by mixing 1 tablespoon (15 ml) flour into 4 tablespoons (60 ml) cream and blending it into the chili moments before serving. The smoked corned beef adds a dash of pioneer savor to this hearty, all-in-one meal, and served with a bowl of freshly chopped onions, hot corn bread and applesauce, it pleases even children.

BEEF CORN SOUP

Preparation time: 20 minutes. *Serves:* 4.

	U. S. CUSTOMARY	METRIC
In skillet saute	2 tablespoons oil	30 ml oil
until slightly	½ cup minced corned beef	125 ml corned beef
brown	1 onion, chopped	1 onion
Add	2 cups cooked corn	500 ml corn
	2 cups milk	500 ml milk
	corn liquid and pepper	corn liquid, pepper

Taste, season with salt if necessary, scald and serve at once.

Beef Stuffed Bakers

Bake and scoop centers from 6 large potatoes. Mash the potatoes with 2 eggs and a cup (250 ml) minced dried beef. Refill potato shells, sprinkle with pepper and bake for 10 minutes, 350°F (175°C), or until peaks brown.

Grinding dried or corned beef is muscle building work. If you are not out to build up your biceps, ask a man with a chopper to mince a piece of beef for you. Cured beef, minced, slivered or coarsely chopped, will keep fresh in a lidded canning jar in the icebox for several weeks and it is handy to add to dishes that need a boost. Some people take their home corned beef to the butcher for slicing or slivering. Smoked or dried corned beef, sliced and wrapped in the icebox is great for instant snacks for unexpected company; most people enjoy tufts of beef tucked with cheese on crackers or on corners of toasted bread.

Cured Pork

Pork may be cured in much the same manner as beef. Hams, bacon, shoulder and clod find new personalities when given a chance in the barrel, or trash can as the case may be. There are as many ways to put down a ham as there are hams, and the philosophy "you can always find something interesting in every person that you would not find in any other," might well apply to hams.

Pork may be brine cured and called pickled; it may be dry salted or sugar cured. The object in each case is the same: to remove moisture quickly and thus inhibit bacterial action. Dry curing meat is faster and in the south, preferred; whichever method you use to cure pork, remember that cleanliness, coolness and speed are paramount.

Dry Sugar Cured Ham

Trim and weigh hams and shoulders. To make a cure for 50 pounds (25 kg) meat, mix in a large dishpan 4 pounds (2 kg) noniodized salt, 2 pounds (1 kg) sugar and 2 tablespoons (30 ml) saltpeter. Rub the ingredients between your palms for about five minutes. Divide the curing mixture into two parts, save one portion for resalting at a later date and rub one part on all surfaces of meat. Poke the salt mix into the shank ends and around the bone, pat and poke until the hams are coated with salt and layer them into a plastic trash container that has been sterilized. Keep cool, 38 to 48°F (3 to 9°C), and covered for a week. On the 7th day rub the remaining half of the salt cure into the hams and reposition the meat so that each piece has been turned over. Put the lid back on the container again. Curing time for hams is usually between 2 to 3 days per pound, minimum 28 days. If your hams average 15 pounds you should keep them in cure for 30 to 45 days. If they average 9 pounds they should stay in cure for the minimum, 28 days. When in doubt leave the heavier cuts of meat in salt an extra day. Give salt lots of time to penetrate.

Dry Sugar Cured Bacon

Trim the meat into manageable squares and weigh the bacon. For each 25 pounds of meat mix 2 pounds (1 kg) salt, 1 pound (500 g) sugar and 1 tablespoon (15 ml) saltpeter. Rub all of the required amount of the cure on the bacons at once. Do not plan to resalt smaller pieces of meat. Place the salted bacon squares on the top of the hams in the curing container, cover and hold in a cool place, 38 to 48°F (3 to 9°C), for 1½ days to the pound, minimum time in cure, 25 days. Most bacons are small enough to come under the minimum time so mark your calendar for 25 days.

We have learned to keep a calendar just for curing, fermenting and gardening chore dates; our problem is remembering to look at it. Lewis suggested that we hang our 'time calendar' in the bathroom. I don't believe that that is such a good idea. I am a bathroom dreamer and he's a reader; we probably would not look at it there either. I suggested hanging it behind the coffee pot but Lewis did not like that idea; he's too sleepy, he says and since we take turns getting up first to put on the coffee, we'd each miss every other day. We are still looking for a happy home for our calendar.

After the time in cure is up, remove the meat, rinse each piece in tepid water, hang the bacon to dry in a cool place and soak the larger pieces of meat for about 20 minutes before hanging them. Meat should dry thoroughly, usually 4 days to a week, and after each piece is fully dry wrap separately in three layers of paper, tie securely and hang in a cool, dark, dry, varmint-proof place.

Smoking Bacon and Hams

Although stillroom rafters were often hung with cured meat, I doubt if many stillroom cooks ever smoked in the fireplace. Most families of the last century had access to a smokehouse. I would not attempt to smoke hams in the fireplace, but bacon can be given the day-long fireplace treatment and it thrives in a cool, medium smudge. The big caution with smoking any pork is heat: 90°F (32°C) is tops. Pork products will drip and catch fire if you do not smoke cool. I have insulted several porkers with heat and they retaliated by shriveling. Dampening the heat with water sends ashes flying up the flue and though charcoal is said to be good for the digestion, it's murder on fillings. To control heat and smoke have a bucket of damp sawdust ready to douse onto any overly ambitious coals. Bacons should be cooled for a day or two after smoking, wrapped in three separate papers, tied securely and hung in a cool, dry place. Eat bacons first because of their higher fat content; fat deteriorates before lean. We freeze our bacon to preserve moistness but freezing is not necessary. Home cured bacon keeps well in a dry cool place and may be used in the same manner as commercial bacon. Some people ask their butcher to slice it for them, a package at a time, others cut it themselves as it is used. Bacon rinds make fine flavoring for beans and good fishing bait.

Early American smokehouses were tightly constructed with varmint-proof ventilators at the top and screened air intakes near the floor. Some were built with a low firebox outside; others had the firepit inside. In the dark they were easy to mistake for outhouses. Contemporary smoke-houses need not be permanent buildings; ventilated boxes, barrels, backyard barbecues will work fine, and the diminutive commercial smokers are uncomplicated to operate, too. An Army sergeant I know smokes meat on his balcony several stories above the trucks and traffic of his street. He rigged a ventilated box with wires and set it over a stove-lid type electric hot plate on which he periodically sprinkled damp sawdust.

Pieces of meat may be crowded but should not touch each other while smoking. Openings at the top of the smoker are essential to circulate smoke, and if you wish to get fancy, a device to raise and lower hams is helpful. Fire is a constant hazard in smoking meat, so whatever your equipment, smokers should be kept far away from combustibles. As a precaution, we have learned to keep the hose or a bucket of water handy.

After hams have completed time in salt cure and have been washed and allowed to dry, they should be hung for from 2 to 4 days in a thin gauze of smoke, 90°F (32°C). Put your hand in the smoke, it should feel cozy warm. When a rich brown glaze covers the meat, hams may be taken from the smoker, hung to cool for several days and wrapped in two layers of paper, a cloth sack, and lastly, secured in brown paper bags. We age our hams for 6 to 9 months before we succumb to need or desire. Other households age their hams for a year or more. A farmer in Missouri once told me, "hams ain't no good until they are old enough to get a little hair on their chest."

Meat storage areas should be scrubbed with soap and water because tiny scraps of meat attract insects and mites that infest meat. Insecticides may be sprayed on the area and will kill insects that crawl over the spray, but the best way is to keep the storage place soap and water clean. If meat becomes infested, cut away the bad parts, cook and eat the rest.

To Cook Ham

To cook a home cured ham one must always soak it in cold water overnight, wash it, scrub off any mold and cut away discolored fat. I tie ham in cheesecloth and simmer it 30 minutes to the pound then let it cool overnight in its own cooking water. The next day I remove the rind and bake the ham with a plain brown sugar coating on top. Sometimes I make gashes across the surface of the rindless ham, stick it with whole cloves, and spread with a mixture of 1 cup (250 ml) brown sugar, ¼ cup (50 ml) flour, 1 teaspoon (5 ml) dry mustard and ½ cup (125 ml) corn syrup. I roast the ham on a rack in a deep pan for 45 minutes at 350°F (175°C) or until blistered and glazed, then cool for 15 minutes before slicing.

Home cured ham, like legendary masterpieces of stillroom meat is sweet, nut-like and salty, winey, yet robust and meaty in flavor, and from the standpoint of economy, it can't be beat. Ham blends with nearly every type of dish and because it is usually stronger than commercial hams and not pumped with water, it lasts and lasts and lasts. If I had a choice of one meat that I could take with me to a desert island I think that it would be a side of country bacon or a slab of ham.

CHICKEN LIVER AND BACON

Nice for weekend guests because it is quick and elegant.
Preparation time: 30 minutes. *Serves:* 6.

	U.S. CUSTOMARY	METRIC
In skillet, fry, remove and drain excess fat	¾ pound bacon, chopped	375 g bacon
Saute and remove from skillet	3 tablespoons drippings	45 ml oil
	1 onion, chopped	1 onion
	1 cup mushrooms, sliced	250 ml mushrooms
Coat with flour, fry for 10 min.	1 pound chicken livers	500 g livers
	½ teaspoon salt	2 ml salt
Mix in	1 cup white wine	250 ml wine
	¼ teaspoon thyme	1 ml thyme
	⅛ teaspoon pepper	0.5 ml pepper
	the onions, mushrooms	onions, mushrooms
Blend, then add and stir	1 tablespoon cornstarch	15 ml cornstarch
	¼ cup cold water	50 ml water
When boiling fold in	¾ cup cream	175 ml cream
	one-half the bacon	half the bacon

Scald, dilute with water if too thick but do not boil after the cream has been added. To serve, spread on toast and garnish each dish with chopped parsley and a sprinkle of chopped bacon.

Note: When cooking with home cured meats do not add much salt until after you taste; saltiness varies in noncommercial products.

POTATO SOUP

Though children are not too fond of potato soup, it is a man's dish.
Preparation time: 20 minutes. *Serves:* 4.

	U.S. CUSTOMARY	METRIC
Peel, dice and boil	5 potatoes	5 potatoes
	½ teaspoon salt	2 ml salt
Chop and fry	¼ pound bacon	125 g bacon
	1 onion	1 onion

Drain excess fat and when the potatoes are tender drain, save the liquid and add potatoes to the bacon and onions.

Blend in   2 cups milk   500 ml milk
                        1 cup potato water   250 ml water

Scald, pour into bowls and season with freshly ground pepper.

STUFFED PORK SHOULDER

An elegant buffet dish when served cold and sliced very thin. Best prepared 2 or 3 days ahead of time and refrigerated.

Preparation time: Overnight soaking plus a day. *Serves:* 12.

U.S. CUSTOMARY	METRIC

Ask your husband (or butcher) to trim and bone a 8 or 10 pound (4 or 5 kg) cured shoulder, soak the meat overnight in cold water, drain and sprinkle the bone cavity with rosemary.

Make a moist   1 pound liver, ground   500 g liver
stuffing by   1 onion, chopped fine   1 onion
mixing to blend   ¼ pound bacon, chopped fine   125 g bacon
well   2 cups bread crumbs, soft   500 ml bread
                    2 eggs   2 eggs
                    ½ cup water   125 ml water
                    2 cloves garlic, crushed   2 garlic
                    1 teaspoon sage   5 ml sage
                    ½ teaspoon oregano   3 ml oregano
                    ¼ teaspoon pepper   1 ml pepper

Fill the cavity with the stuffing, sew or skewer it closed. Put the shoulder, cavity side up, in 1 inch (2.5 cm) water, beer or cider, or for especially festive fare, port wine, in a baking pan with a tight lid. Cover and bake at 325°F (160°C) for about 40 minutes to the pound. Baste from time to time, add more liquid if necessary. This roast should be cooked with moist heat or slowly steamed. When tender, but not falling apart, take from pan, remove any rind and excessive fat, pat on brown sugar that has been mixed with dried bread crumbs and glaze the roast in the oven at 450°F (230°C) for 10 minutes, or until it's bubbly and blistered. Cool in the pan overnight, then refrigerate until needed. To serve, slice paper thin making certain that there is a circle of the savory liver stuffing and nibble of sweet topping with each piece. Combined with dinner rolls such as an enormous basket of rusks, a plate of dill pickles, a golden yam casserole, hot potato salad, peas creamed with mushrooms, a heaping crab meat, lettuce and tomato salad, rice with minced carrots and slivers of almonds and a tray of sweets, Stuffed Shoulder creates a memorable dinner.

Westphalian Ham

A German pig farmer whose neatly fenced farm was located near Merrill Field, Anchorage, Alaska, used to put down Westphalian Hams that he flavored with juniper berries and smoked over alder fires. His

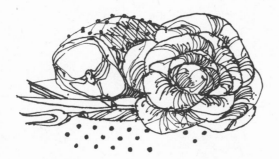

hams were distinctive with overtones of gin and cigars. I liked them.

For every 100 pounds (50 kg) of fresh pork hams and shoulders he mixed 15 pounds (7 kg) plain salt with 2 tablespoons (30 g) saltpeter, and he rubbed the mixture thoroughly into the meat. He placed the hams in a stack on the wooden slatted floor of his curing shed and let them cure there for two weeks. The weather was usually cold but not freezing when he cured. After the two weeks were up he made a brine by dissolving 3 pounds (1.5 kg) of salt in 6 quarts (6 liters) water, a 21 or 22% brine solution reading on a salinometer, and he allowed the meat to cure in brine for 18 more days. The hams were then removed from the brine and stacked in a cool area, about 38°F (3°C), for 4 weeks, during which time they ripened, he said. With a stiff brush he then scrubbed his hams clean of mold and salt using lukewarm water and he allowed them to freshen by soaking them in water for 12 hours. After hanging the hams to dry for about a week he smoked them in a cool, 85°F (30°C) smoke for a week or 10 days. He had juniper twigs and berries shipped into Anchorage from Germany and he threw the green juniper on the alder fire from time to time. Whenever the fire got too hot he loaded on a couple of handfuls of juniper and then covered the whole thing with sawdust. After a few days of cooling in the smoke chamber with the fire out, he hung his hams in a dark area and ate the meat as he needed it. When I used to fly into Merrill Field I'd stop and see him and enjoy his wonderful gin-flavored ham. A piece cooked with sauerkraut is absolutely superb.

No matter which type of ham you create: dry cured, sugar cured, brined, smoked, Westphalian or your very own secret formula, ham may be used interchangeably in most recipes.

When cooking with home cured meats remember not to add salt until after tasting.

Ham and Green Beans

Boil a previously cooked shank with 2 or 3 pounds (1 or 1.5 kg) green beans that have been washed and broken into pieces. About 15 minutes before supper drop in a dozen new potatoes, scrubbed or peeled, and a bit of pepper pod. When the vegetables are tender, drain, save the liquid for soup, pull the meat from the bone and serve as one dish in a big bowl. Salt to taste.

Boiled Dinner

A shank bone is great for boiled dinner. Boil a previously cooked shank together with 3 or 4 onions, a few carrots, small, whole potatoes and pepper. Shortly before supper add a head of cabbage that has been chunked into serving pieces. Cover and boil for 5 more minutes. Remove the meat from the bone and serve boiled dinner in soup bowls with a chewy piece of red meat in each bowl. Horseradish or a daub of sour cream complements this homey dish. Salt if necessary.

French Pea Soup

Boil 1 pound (500 g) split peas and a precooked ham bone in water to cover together with 2 chopped onions and 1 diced carrot. When the peas are soft, press through a sieve and return the pulp to a pan. Add a little water if necessary, heat slowly and just before serving blend in 1 cup (250 ml) cream and a sprinkle of grated cheese. Season with salt and pepper to taste.

HAM STEAK

An instant dinner if you have a precooked ham in the icebox.
Preparation time: 15 minutes.

	U.S. CUSTOMARY	METRIC
Saute a thick ham steak in oil to heat, turn once, remove from skillet.		
To skillet stir in	1 tablespoon flour	15 ml flour
	¼ cup water	50 ml water
	1 tablespoon catsup	15 ml catsup
	½ teaspoon prepared mustard	2 ml mustard
	1 tablespoon brown sugar	15 ml brown sugar
	½ cup wine such as sherry	125 ml wine

When well blended, replace ham and let simmer for 5 minutes before serving.

Cured Lamb or Game Meat

Lamb or game meat such as venison, reindeer, caribou, moose or bear may be dry salt cured, sugar cured, pickled or brined and smoked as you would cure similar-sized pieces of beef or pork. Trim all fat from game and lamb before curing because this fat tends to hold a stronger flavor than other meat, and game fat tends to become rancid in cure. I cured moose in Alaska without trimming fat and I later had to trim away about a third of the meat to avoid the musky off-taste. When cooking cured game or lamb, moisten liberally with oil and use interchangeably with ham or bacon recipes.

Sausage Making

Making sausages in stillroom times was an individual pursuit and just as common a practice as making bread or beer. The main impetus for creating sausage was to use up odd cuts of surplus meat.

Basically sausage is chopped meat. Sausages may be fresh such as Country Sausage; they may be uncooked but smoked, such as Polish Sausage; they may be cooked and smoked, such as hot dogs; they may be fermented to undergo a maturation, such as Lebanon Bologna; or sausages may be dry, such as Salami.

Cleanliness, high quality meat, salt, spices and recipes concerning time in cure and temperatures as well as when and how to stop the action, are the primary requirements of sausage making. Once the procedures are understood sausage making is relatively simple, yet today, with the ever mounting laws, regulations and propagandized reservations, the skill of home sausage making is becoming doomed. As long as guidelines are followed there is small reason why sausage making in a modern home cannot be a family adventure into the wonders of fermentation and good eating. Recipes given on the following pages are for 10 pound (5 kg) batches of sausage.

Steps in sausage making consist of grinding meat, mixing in the spices, preparing and sterilizing equipment, stuffing, hanging the sausages or smoking them, and storage. Except for a stuffer, kitchen utensils can double as sausage making equipment. Muslin sleeves can be sewed together in a jiffy or casings can be purchased if you have a stuffing attachment for your meat grinder.

To get the feel of sausage making, it might be best to start with fresh, uncooked, unsmoked, uncured, unfermented sausage. Because the

high fat content of fresh sausage invites rancidity, it is important to keep sausage making temperatures as close to 38°F (3°C) as possible. There are two rules that apply to all sausage making: sterilize all utensils, and mix spices and salt together before adding them to the meat. Some sausage makers recommend that meats be ground twice, the spices and salt premixed and added before the second grinding. If possible entice your meat man to do your grinding.

FRESH COUNTRY SAUSAGE

	U.S. CUSTOMARY	METRIC
Grind through ⅛ inch (0.3 cm) blade	6 pounds lean pork 4 pounds pork trimmings	3 kg lean pork 2 kg pork trim
In large bowl mix well before stirring into the meat	4 tablespoons salt 3 tablespoons sage 5 teaspoons pepper 1 tablespoon sugar	60 ml salt 45 ml sage 25 ml pepper 15 ml sugar

Thoroughly mix the seasoning into the meat with your hands for 10 minutes or grind the meat a second time with the spices added. Cook a patty to insure that the flavoring is right. Cover and refrigerate until used, or form into patties, separate patties with wax paper and freeze. To cook Country Sausage, poach patties in a tiny bit of water for 10 minutes, let them boil dry and brown in their own moist juice.

SMOKED PORK SAUSAGE

A fresh meat sausage that must be cooked before eating.

	U.S. CUSTOMARY	METRIC
Grind through ¼ inch (0.5 cm) plate	7½ pounds lean pork 2½ pounds pork trimmings	3.5 kg lean pork 1 kg pork trim
In large bowl mix well before stirring into the meat	½ cup salt, scant 1½ teaspoons saltpeter 1 teaspoon sage, heaping 4 teaspoons red pepper 2 teaspoons paprika	112 ml salt 7 ml saltpeter 6 ml sage 20 ml red pepper 10 ml paprika

If the sausage seems too stiff, that is, if it is brittle and not malleable, add ¼ cup (50 ml) wine or brandy and work the liquid in well. For Smoked Pork Sausage grind only once with coarser, ¼ inch (0.5 cm) blade, because too fine grinding increases fat rendering during smoking and the sausage will shrivel; and as a man once told me, "Never trust a shriveled sausage." Mix sausage meat thoroughly with your hands, squeeze it through your fingers, squeeze and mix, mix and squeeze. This is cold, hard work, you may need a nip to lubricate your joints at this time. When well mixed, stuff the meat into commercial casings, medium sheep casings or narrow pork casings. Use the sausage stuffing attachment on your meat grinder or make your own as outlined below. Tie into 4 inch (10 cm) lengths.

To Stuff Sausage

Commercial casings, purchased from independent butcher shops, are delicate and great care must be taken in handling them or they will rupture, and a ruptured sausage is like a ruptured duck; it just won't fly. The casings are usually salted when you buy them and may be cleaned by flushing water through them and soaking them for a few moments before working them onto the stuffing horn of your grinder. Expel all water by stripping the casing between your fingers, as a milkmaid strips a milk cow. Water will cause meat to be discolored, and though the casings should be moist there should be no droplets of water. Place the ground and seasoned meat in the sausage mill and as the casing fills and works off the horn, cradle the new little sausage in your hand to insure that it gets properly started in its new life. At the same time force out any air pockets in the link. To facilitate the tying of sausages, make your twists between the sausages at least 1½ inches (4 cm) long.

When the casing is filled, remove from the grinder and tie twice at each twist with a light string. Tieing two times insures that you can cut between two links and not have one lose its insides. Sausages in commercial casings may be washed with a quick splash of cold water and refrigerated overnight to firm the meat before smoking.

Muslin Casings

I use handmade muslin sleeves for our sausages because they are easier to come by than gut casings, less expensive and I can make the size I want. Authorities say that cloth takes the smoke better but on the negative side, the cloth casing must be peeled from the meat before eating. Buy the cheapest grade unbleached muslin, tear it into strips wide enough so that the casing will easily fit over the end of your sausage stuffer after the cloth has been seamed and also allow about ¼ inch (0.5 cm) for shrinkage of the cloth. I was behind the door when they passed out sewing brains but I make casings by folding the cloth strips lengthwise then sewing across the bottom and up the open side. Turn inside out when sewn. Boil muslin casings and while wet, work onto the stuffing horn.

Handmade Stuffer

For a handy dandy disposable stuffer, we cut the bottom from a gallon plastic milk bottle and tape onto its neck to form a stuffing horn, a 6 fl. oz. (175 ml) frozen orange juice can, top and bottom removed. With two people working together, we can now stuff. First Lewis and I take a good long slurp of beer; you must be relaxed to stuff sausages because everything becomes very slippery and the little fellows try to get away. Next, one person pushes the mixed sausage through the upside down milk bottle into the neck of the plastic bottle, on through the stuffing horn and into the casing. The other person holds the whole contraption while helping to force the sausage firmly into place and evicting air. The sausages are linked by allowing a 1½ inch (4 cm) space and twisting the cloth between the sausages and when the sleeve is filled each twist is tied twice with a string. Refrigerate the sausages overnight to firm the fat before smoking.

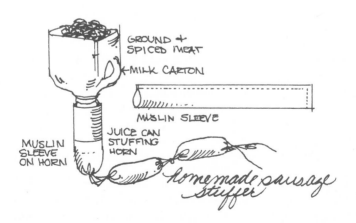

Smoking Sausages

Smoked Pork Sausages are smoked but not cooked, so they must be treated as fresh meat. Smoking destroys surface bacteria as well as flavors and colors meat, but excessive heat will cause pork fat to drip and your sausage will shrivel like a raisin. Always start with a cool light smoke and gradually increase the heat to about 90°F (32°C) with a high concentration of smoke. Raising the temperature too high too fast will cause your sausages to pop. I have scooped up more popped sausages because I tried to speed the process. There is no way to hurry a sausage; low and slow is the rule with smoking. Two hours of 90°F (32°C) dense smoke is usually sufficient. These sausages may be hung to cool overnight before being refrigerated and cooked, but if you can't wait to try your product, cook one and eat immediately. Do not store sausages in plastic bags, they will sweat and spoil.

I have smoked sausage over an oak or hickory smudge in the fireplace on a grate taken from the gas oven. A simple cardboard box, holes poked in the top, may be set on rocks over your barbecue grill; wire lines may be strung in the box or the oven grate may be laid on bricks inside to handle the sausages. Also, numerous small commercial smokers are on the market and they work beautifully for sausage.

To keep Smoked Pork Sausages fresh, wrap them securely in several layers of wax paper and freeze. In the icebox they will keep about 2 weeks. Grilled, poached, fried or sliced into casseroles or boiled with vegetables, this sausage is zesty. And in the morning there is no food like sausage to make you look the world in the eye and say, "You're great, Mr. Earth, I think I'll try to save you today."

POLISH SAUSAGE

	U.S. CUSTOMARY	METRIC
Grind, using ¼ inch (0.5 cm) plate	3 pounds lean beef	1.5 kg beef
	5 pounds pork trimmings	2.5 kg pork trim
	2 pounds lean pork	1 kg lean pork
In large bowl mix well before stirring into meat	½ cup salt, scant	112 ml salt
	1½ teaspoons saltpeter	7 ml saltpeter
	2 tablespoons black pepper	30 ml black pepper
	2 teaspoons coriander	10 ml coriander
	4 teaspoons garlic powder	20 ml garlic

Work the meat thoroughly. If the sausage falls apart add a little brandy or wine. Stuff into 1½ inch (4 cm) commercial pork casings and tie in 7 inch (17.5 cm) lengths, or stuff into muslin sleeves of the same size. Polish sausage is perishable and must be kept as close to 38°F (3°C) as possible. Smoke Polish Sausage in a cool, dense smoke 90°F (32°C) for 2 hours or until the color deepens. Cool overnight and refrigerate or wrap tightly in several thicknesses of wax paper and freeze. Sliced and fried, poached whole, baked with sauerkraut, boiled with black beans or cubed into potato casseroles, this lovely Polish Sausage stretches into meals and meals. I sometimes peel the casing, cube the meat and roll it in bread dough for a baked treat. Any way you cook it, Polish Sausage is a proud food.

Cooked sausages such as Liver Sausage or Frankfurters are possible to make in the home but the internal temperature of cooked sausage must be exact for safekeeping, the stabilization of good color and for flavor. I cannot see the thrift in poking a thermometer into every little hot dog; I'd rather go out and buy cooked sausages than to mess with making them.

Fermented sausages: the creating of both semi-dry and hard sausages are amiable, easy-paced pursuits and in most cases the products are ready to serve without further cooking. There is one major caution however: if the sausage is to be eaten uncooked, pork must be frozen and held at minus 10°F (minus 23°C) for 21 days before it is thawed and processed into sausage. This eliminates the "tricky" as my country friend calls trichinosis. Semi-dry sausages should be held under refrigeration after curing.

The meat used for fermented sausages is usually ground twice, once through a ½ inch (1 cm) plate, after which the spices are mixed in, and the meat is ground through a finer plate.

Some fermented sausages require a preliminary cure before being stuffed. Most fermented sausages take a hotter smoke for a longer period of time than fresh sausages because smoking helps to dry as well as to flavor and preserve them. Always raise the heat slowly.

SUMMER SAUSAGE

	U.S. CUSTOMARY	METRIC
Prefreeze pork at minus 10°F (minus 23°C) for 21 days. Thaw.		
Grind meat using ½ inch (1 cm) plate	4 pounds pork trimmings 6 pounds lean beef	2 kg pork trim 3 kg beef
In large bowl mix well before stirring into the meat	½ cup salt, generous 3 tablespoons sugar 1 teaspoon saltpeter 5 teaspoons black pepper 1 tablespoon mustard seed	135 ml salt 45 ml sugar 5 ml saltpeter 25 ml black pepper 15 ml mustard seed

Grind the spiced meat a second time with a ⅛ inch (0.3 cm) plate. Mix in 3 tablespoons (45 ml) vinegar by hand. Cure meat by piling it on a flat pan, cover and place in the refrigerator, the fresh meat holding area is about the right temperature, 38°F (3°C) and hold for 48 hours. Take from the icebox 2 hours before stuffing. Stuff into sleeves 2 or 3 inches (5 or 7.5 cm) in diameter, tie twice in 8 inch (20 cm) lengths and allow to cure a second time at 55°F (13°C) for 48 hours. Smoke Summer Sausage by raising the smoker heat slowly to about

110°F (45°C) and hold for 6 hours in a medium, hardwood smudge; the temperature is then raised very slowly to 165°F (75°C). The elevation of the heat should take 6 hours. I place a pie tin of water in my smoker to maintain humidity when I hot smoke sausages. Cool the sausages gradually when time in smoke is up by removing the coals or heat from the smoker and letting the sausage hang overnight. The next morning lay Summer Sausages on their sides in a drying area that is about 55°F (13°C) for 24 hours. Laying the sausages flat firms the meat into straight links. Summer Sausage may be eaten immediately or refrigerated and eaten anytime after this point. Some people hang this sausage to cure for a third fermentation period in a varmint-free area; 2 or 3 weeks at 60°F (15°C). Summer Sausage should either be eaten at the end of this last 3 week cure or preserved by coating with paraffin and hung in a cool place, or wrapped in several layers of wax paper and frozen. If the fermenting and drying action is not stopped sausages have the habit of transmigrating to salty shoe leather. Summer Sausage may be eaten raw as a sandwich meat but, as with other home cured meats, it should be sliced paper thin because the flavor is intense. I like to slip nubbins of sausage under an unsuspecting Yorkshire pudding batter and watch the pleased looks on my family's faces; with a cheesy squash or eggplant casserole, a dish of briefly cooked spinach, applesauce and gingerbread, a little sausage stretches into a big meal.

LEBANON BOLOGNA

	U.S. CUSTOMARY	METRIC
Grind, using ½ inch (1 cm) plate	10 pounds lean beef	4.5 kg beef
	3½ tablespoons lard or vegetable shortening	48 ml lard
In large bowl mix well before stirring into meat	5 tablespoons brown sugar	75 ml br. sugar
	7 teaspoons pepper, scant	33 ml pepper
	2 teaspoons nutmeg	10 ml nutmeg
	2 teaspoons mace	10 ml mace
	9 tablespoons salt	135 ml salt
	1 teaspoon saltpeter	5 ml saltpeter
	1 teaspoon ground cloves	5 ml cloves

Regrind the meat and spices through a ⅛ inch (0.3 cm) plate, mix with hands and if the meat falls apart and does not hold together add a jigger or two of brandy. Stuff the meat into 2½ to 4 inch (6 to 10 cm) diameter casings, allow to hang at 55 to 65°F (13 to 18°C) for 4 days and smoke for 7 to 9 days in a slow, cold smoke, 70 to 80°F (20 to 25°C). After smoking, Lebanon Bologna may be eaten at once. Because this is a dry-meated sausage containing no moisturizing pork, it tends to dehydrate readily; if you plan to keep Lebanon Bologna more than 3 or 4 weeks, dip it in paraffin or wrap it in wax paper and freeze. Although I used to paraffin sausages with good results, I freeze them now because I can cut off a piece, re-wrap and return the sausage to the freezer. If mold develops at any time, wipe it off with a wine dampened cloth.

In the 19th century, stillroom cooks made dry sausages during the winter when temperatures and humidity could be controlled because they learned that if sausages dried too fast the surface hardened and its rind did not allow the meat to mature properly. Early books on sausage making state that the drying room, or wintertime stillroom should be maintained between 48 to 60°F (9 to 15°C). Today's packing houses maintain these same temperatures in drying rooms with a relative humidity of 70%. Fully dried sausages are dried between 60 to 90 days after being cured or smoked like other sausages and for best results it is advisable to paraffin or freeze them after that time, although it is not absolutely necessary. Sealing sausages retards shrinkage. During processing fresh meat sausages shrink about 20%, semi-dry sausages shrink about 30% and fully dried sausages shrink 40%.

SALAMI

	U.S. CUSTOMARY	METRIC
	Prefreeze pork at minus 10°F (minus 23°C) for 21 days. Thaw.	
Grind using	2 pounds chuck beef	1 kg beef
½ inch (1 cm)	5 pounds lean pork	2.5 kg lean pork
plate	2 pounds pork trimmings	1 kg pork trim
	1 pound shoulder fat	500 g fat or lard
In large bowl	10 tablespoons salt	150 ml salt
mix well before	½ teaspoon saltpeter	2.5 ml saltpeter
stirring into	2 teaspoons white pepper	10 ml wh. pepper
meat	1 teaspoon whole pepper	5 ml wh. pepper
	1 teaspoon garlic powder	5 ml garlic
Optional spices	1 teaspoon nutmeg	5 ml nutmeg
may be added	1 teaspoon cloves	5 ml cloves
	1 teaspoon paprika	5 ml paprika
	½ teaspoon cinnamon	3 ml cinnamon

Regrind the meat and seasoning through ¼ inch (0.5 cm) plate. Add a jigger or two of red wine if the meat does not hold together. Stuff into 2½ to 4 inch (6 to 10 cm) casings and hang at 55 to 65°F (13 to 18°C) for 3 days. The sausage is wrapped around with twine making a half hitch every half inch (1 cm) for a professional look, and it is hung or laid to dry on the icebox door at about 50°F (10°C) for about 10 weeks. Wipe off mold with a wine soaked cloth and seal in paraffin or wrap in wax paper and freeze after time in cure is complete. . . . Or, better still, eat this grand sausage.

Sometimes a bacterial starter such as yogurt or sour milk culture is added to dried sausages to increase acidity and give a tangy flavor. A starter also speeds the time in which sausages ferment.

THURINGER

Prefreeze pork at minus 10°F (minus 23°C) for 21 days. Thaw.

	U.S. CUSTOMARY	METRIC
Grind, using ½ inch (1 cm) plate	9 pounds beef 1 pound pork trimmings	4 kg beef 500 g pork trim
In large bowl mix well before adding to meat	10 tablespoons salt 1⅓ teaspoons saltpeter 7 teaspoons sugar 9 teaspoons pepper 11 teaspoons anise	150 ml salt 6.5 ml saltpeter 35 ml sugar 45 ml pepper 55 ml anise
When well blended mix in	¼ cup yogurt or sour milk	50 ml yogurt

Grind the spiced meat through the ⅛ inch (0.3 cm) plate and if too stiff add a little more sour milk. Stuff immediately into casing about 2½ inches (6 cm) in diameter. Allow stuffed sausages to cure at about 40°F (5°C) for 3 days; the meat keeper area of the refrigerator is about that temperature. Smoke Thuringer for 12 to 18 hours at 85°F (30°C), gradually raise the heat in the smoking chamber to about 100°F (40°C) and hold that heat for about 24 hours. Slowly raise the smoke density and heat to about 140°F (60°C) and hold for about 4 or 5 hours. Cool the smoker by removing the coals and let the sausages hang in the smoker overnight. Thuringer may be eaten at once, or it may be paraffin sealed and hung in a cool dry place, or it may be wrapped and frozen. We like dried sausages slivered on pizzas and this spirited sausage goes a long, long way.

CERVELAT

Prefreeze pork at minus 10°F (minus 23°C) for 21 days. Thaw.

	U.S. CUSTOMARY	METRIC
Grind, using a ½ inch (1 cm) plate	3 pounds chuck beef 6 pounds pork trimmings 1 pound pork fat	1.5 kg beef 3 kg pork trim 500 g pork fat or lard
In large bowl mix well before adding to meat	10 tablespoons salt 1 teaspoon saltpeter ½ teaspoon whole pepper 8 teaspoons white pepper ¼ cup yogurt or sour milk	150 ml salt 5 ml saltpeter 2 ml whole pepper 40 ml white pepper 50 ml sour milk

Grind the spiced meat a second time through the ⅛ inch (0.3 cm) plate. After mixing thoroughly, pile the meat in a flat pan, cover and place in the meat keeper area of the refrigerator where the temperature should be about 40°F (5°C) and hold for 4 days. Warm at room temperature for 2 hours before stuffing into large casings, 4 inch (10 cm) rounds. Tie 11 inches (27 cm) long. Smoke Cervelat sausages in a hardwood smudge for 12 hours at 85°F (30°C) and gradually raise heat to 100°F (40°C) and hold for 24 hours. Raise heat to 140°F (60°C) and hold for 4 or 5 hours. Cool sausages slowly by removing coals and let the sausage hang in the smoker overnight. Cervelat sausage is a nippy-hot treat that may be thinly sliced and eaten as a luncheon meat or layered with cream cheese on crackers. Although it will hold unsealed for several months I usually paraffin or freeze sausages to insure that their personality does not change.

There is no waste in the sensible and savory world of sausages. Sausage slices cooked in butter, dashed with lemon, arranged with croutons then covered with white sauce make a delightful luncheon dish. Sausage slivers, raw oysters, bread crumbs and beaten eggs baked in a pan like a meat loaf, drained of grease and served as a main course titillates the taste buds. Sausages simmered with sauerkraut, sausages with hard rolls on a pack trip, sausages baked between layers of cornbread; all thrill and tempt hungry people. Sausage nibbles after the theater, served with sipping sherry in a darkened room, call up moments of memory and desire.

Sausages leave no room for staleness or boredom; they are frank and sympathetic to all manner of meals. Though they come from scraps and bits and pieces of meat, homemade sausages leave their second class status behind the moment they hit the grinder; for the rest of their little lives they are first class fare.

CHAPTER VII
Fish and Fowl

E ver since the time while pulling a crab trap in Alaska I was flung end up by the whack of a flying skate tail, I have respected fish. Learned men can write all they want about punishment and alienation, but I believe that a good thump on the rump simply deters self-willed behavior; I am not and never have been alienated from fish.

Whether it's to trap in Alaska's majestic waters or to wade the tranquil Chesapeake with net in hand, the invitation, "Let's go crabbing," conjures memories of good friends, rollicking times and sumptuous feasts.

Crab

Crabs, clams, craw daddies, lobsters and oysters must be alive when they arrive in the kitchen. If there is any doubt, throw them back in their watery homes. Shrimp may be less than alive if well iced.

To steam crabs, bulky Dungeness or dainty Blues, pour 2 inches (5 cm) liquid, vinegar or beer and water, half and half, into a large pot, insert a perforated false bottom to hold the crabs out of the liquid, boil and when steam fills the pan, add live crabs. Sprinkle liberally with salt, red pepper or seafood spices. Put a lid on the pan and steam about 30 minutes. Spread papers on the table, open a box of crackers, pour beer and dig in.

CALVERT COUNTY CRAB CAKES

Preparation time: 1 hour to pick crabs, 20 minutes to mix and cook.

	U.S. CUSTOMARY	METRIC
In a bowl mix	2 cups soft bread crumbs	500 ml crumbs
	2 eggs	2 eggs
	½ cup mayonnaise	125 ml mayonnaise
	½ teaspoon salt	3 ml salt

161

¼ teaspoon dry mustard	1 ml mustard
¼ teaspoon black pepper	1 ml pepper
3 teaspoons soy sauce	15 ml soy sauce
2 cups crab meat	500 ml crab meat

Mix all ingredients well and lastly add the crab. Stir gently so as not to mash the meat. Form into small cakes with your hands and if the cakes do not hold together add a little water and slightly flour each cake. Fry in a lightly greased skillet until brown.

Crab Fritters

In a bowl beat 2 eggs and mix in 1 cup (250 ml) flour, 1 cup (250 ml) cooked rice, 2 tablespoons (30 ml) lemon juice, a dash of garlic salt, ¼ teaspoon (1 ml) each of pepper and salt and 1 cup (250 ml) crab meat. Add milk to make a batter and fry in a lightly oiled skillet until brown.

Crab Snack

Mix crab meat with cream cheese, lubricate with lemon juice and a drop of milk. Flavor this delicate hors d'oeuvre with chopped walnuts that have been briefly sauteed in butter, a touch of Worcestershire sauce and garlic. Serve cold with crackers.

Soft-Shell Calvert Crabs

If you are fortunate enough to inherit a dozen soft-shell crabs, use your large scissors to clip off the head and snip out the spongy tissue located beneath and on each side of the apron. Do this under cold running water. Dry crabs, salt and pepper, coat with flour and fry in a lightly greased skillet for about 5 minutes on each side. Serve hot as a main course with lots of homemade bread, potatoes escalloped with cheese, endive salad flavored with oil and lemon, plain buttered crunchy green beans and a simple yellow cake or vanilla pudding. Or serve with plain bread, butter and catsup for sandwiches.

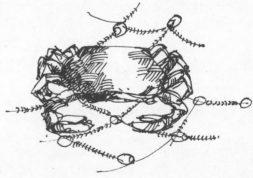

Lobster

To boil lobster, allow 1½ pounds (750 g) lobster in the shell per person. In a large pot boil water and salt, 2 tablespoons (30 ml) per quart (liter). Plunge the lobster, head first, into the boiling water, lower heat and allow about 20 minutes cooking for 1½ pound (750 g) lobsters. When done, remove and wipe dry. Males contain firmer flesh, their shells are brighter red, and their tails are narrower and sport stiff, hard fins. You can tell hen lobsters by their broader tails. Split open the lobster body and tail and crack the claws to extract the meat. The sand pouch found near the throat of the lobster should be removed together with the feathery, tough, gill-like lungs found under the body shell. The head of a lobster is not eaten. Serve lobster hot with melted butter and a bit of lemon.

Oysters

Oysters will keep in the shell for several weeks by covering their basket with wet burlap and storing in a cool, dark place where they will not freeze. Wash well before using. To open oysters hold the shell cupped side down in the palm of your gloved hand. Using an oyster knife insert the point into the finely layered oyster shell on the end opposite the hinge. After you've found the soft, crumbly protruding lip, insert knife, press down on the handle so that the blade will cut the muscle along the top of the oyster. Repeat by raising the handle of the knife and cutting along the inside of the lower shell. Partly withdraw the knife, twist to pry open the two shells. Now with your hands open the oyster all the way. Free the oyster and empty it into a bowl or into your mouth if it's closer. If your biceps won't cooperate or if you can't tell an oyster lip from its hinge, don't despair. Wash your oysters well, line them on a cookie tin, put them in a 400°F (200°C) oven for 10 minutes. When they have opened slightly, it is time to take them out and eat, fritter, fry or stew.

Fricasseed Oysters

Preparation time: 35 minutes. *Serves:* 5.

Cube a slice of ham into ½ inch (1 cm) sized pieces and simmer for 20 minutes in 1⅓ cup (333 ml) chicken broth or bouillon together with 1 small onion, minced fine, a little chopped parsley, marjoram and pepper. Drain 1 quart (1 liter) of oysters and add the liquor to the broth. Mix 1 tablespoon (15 ml) of corn starch into ½ cup (125 ml) milk, stir into the broth. Stir constantly, and when it boils add the oysters and 2 table-spoons (30 ml) butter. Bring the fricassee back to a boil, with a slotted spoon remove the oysters to a deep dish, beat one egg and add to the egg some of the hot broth, stir and empty it back into the pan. Season to taste with salt, bring just to a boil and pour over the oysters. Garnish with a squeeze of lemon juice and a sprinkle of cayenne. I serve Fricasseed Oysters over hot buttered toast or boiled rice and have found it a tasty way in which to stretch oysters to feed a family.

Smoked Oysters

Plump oysters by heating them in their own juice for 4 or 5 minutes. Drain and spoon oysters a few at a time into a small bowl of oil. Lay the oiled oysters on a greased screen and place the screen over the barbecue grill or on bricks in the fireplace. Using a hardwood smudge such as hickory or oak, smoke the oysters at a temperature not hotter than 90°F (32°C). When they start to darken, turn, and when the edges curl over each fat oyster belly, remove from the smoke, cool and serve. Smoking preplumped oysters at an informal cocktail party is fun to do; have lots of paper towels and napkins on hand because these juicy friends like to drip. To store smoked oysters immerse them immediately after smoking in a jar of oil, put on the lid, and place them in the refrigerator. Oysters, like seeds of charity, divert men from inward thinking and solitary pursuits; they are so good that they cry out to be shared. And happiness, the process of discovery and sharing, envelops all who taste these luscious little creatures of the sea.

Clams

Hard-Shell, Cherrystone, Chowder, Little Necks, Soft-Shell or Surf Clams, all are delicious when chowdered, chopped, stuffed, steamed or stripped and fried.

Soft-Shell and smaller clams may be steamed and eaten from the shell. Wash, place the clams in a large pan with a rack, add water below the rack and boil for 15 minutes or until the shells are "grinning big." Serve each person a small cup of the liquid and a bowl of melted butter. Store the rest of the clam broth for chowder. Eat the clams by removing them from the shell, peeling the neck skin, turning the neck partly inside out over your forefinger and dipping the clam in and out of the cup of hot clam liquid. This removes the grit from the neck where it likes to hide. Dip the broth-washed clam into the warmed butter and pop it into your chops. Beautiful!

To remove grit from clams such as Surfers or Razors, put them in a tub of sea water, sprinkle with cornmeal or breadcrumbs and set overnight in a cool place. The meal or crumbs are ingested and flush out grit.

Baked Clams

Wash and steam large clams on a rack over boiling water until they open. While they are boiling make a bread stuffing enriched by double the amount of melted butter and an extra egg. Flavor with a little sage and black pepper. When the clams have opened, scoop them onto a board, chop medium fine and mix into the bread stuffing together with a little clam liquid from the bottom of the steamer. Avoid the grit. Rinse off the biggest shells, butter their insides and fill to heaping with clam stuffing. Squeeze a twist of lemon over each stuffed clam and bake in the oven at 400°F (200°C) for 10 minutes. Serve in the shell. These may be prepared ahead, refrigerated and baked with dinner rolls for about 20 minutes before dinner. I save my big shells and they are ready to use whenever a bucket of clams hits our porch; baking is great for the toughies.

Smoked Clams

I have smoked small clams just as I smoke oysters, the one difference being that I steam the clams first, then dip them in oil and smoke in my popcorn popper or on a screening. Toasty and golden, these fully cooked smoked baby clams may be held in the icebox for several weeks if they are submerged in corn oil in a jar with a lid.

Terrapin or Turtle

Although terrapins and turtles hibernate in the winter, each summer they are addicted to snoozing in the sun and thus are easy to spot, catch and cook. Check game laws because many terrapins and snappers are protected. To clean, drop a live turtle into boiling water, snap on the pan lid and cook for 1 to 4 minutes. You have to be quick with the lid or it will jump out of the pan like frogs' legs. Remove from the water to a thick layer of newspapers, pry off the upper and lower shell, cut off the head and peel the skin which is easy if it's slit down the inside of each leg. Cut off the feet. To clean turtle pinch up the flesh of the underside and cut around the vent and discard, then slit the abdomen skin to the chest by inserting the knife, cutting edge up. Remove the innards, take the liver but be careful not to break the bile sac, a greenish pouch the size of a bean located at the base of the liver. The meat should now be put into cold water while you go bury the shell and innards 3 feet deep in your compost. Young turtle meat is excellent floured and fried. You may wish to make soup out of older turtle.

TERRAPIN SOUP

Preparation time: 30 minutes plus meat cooking. *Serves:* 4.

U.S. CUSTOMARY	METRIC

Each terrapin or turtle will have 4 chunks of meat, boil until tender in salted water seasoned with a stalk of chopped celery and a minced carrot; a bay leaf and a breath of basil, lemon thyme and marjoram. Drain and save liquid.

	U.S. CUSTOMARY	METRIC
In skillet melt and stir in	½ cup butter 2 tablespoons flour	125 ml butter 30 ml flour
Vigorously blend in	1 cup cooking liquid 3 cups milk salt, pepper to taste	250 ml liquid 750 ml milk salt, pepper
When scalded stir in	the terrapin meat, cubed the carrot and celery bits 2 teaspoons parsley, chopped 4 hard-boiled egg yolks, yolks should be whole 4 tablespoons lemon juice 1 cup thick cream	the terrapin meat carrot and celery 10 ml parsley 4 egg yolks, whole 60 ml lemon juice 250 ml cream

Heat over a low fire, do not boil, stir gently so as not to crush egg or meat. When piping hot, empty in a jigger or two of sherry and serve immediately, making sure that an egg yolk, simulating a turtle egg, is in each soup dish. Roughly cut French bread complements this tasty soup.

If your terrapin is a big one and there is too much meat and cooking liquid for a single soup, save part of the meat and liquid and make a casserole.

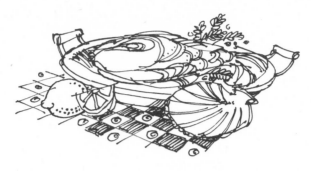

Fish

Midwest, Rockies, East Coast or West, the joy of catching fish is universal and so is the joy of eating it. I love to heat a pan of oil for a fish fry as much as I love to pull my rod from its hiding place and head for the river. Given the option, I prefer to clean and scale fish at the water's edge; that way I don't have to pick scales off the kitchen ceiling. If someone brings uncleaned fish to your kitchen however, don't turn them down. Scale the fish first, then clean them.

To Scale and Clean Fish

To scale, wet the fish in cold water and lay it on a board near the sink. Hold the fish firmly by the head. With the knife almost vertical, scrape off the scales, working from the tail to the head. With the point of your knife scratch out all the scales at the base of the fins and on the top of the head. Rinse the fish in cold water several times and run your fingers over the slick skin; it should feel as smooth as a freshly shaven cheek.

To clean or draw fish use a pointed knife and slit the entire length of the belly from the small opening or vent to the head. With your hand remove the entrails by working your fingers through the slit toward the head, around the lungs, along the back bone toward the tail and scoop out. Flush out with cold water. Cut out the belly fins. On small fish I leave the big back fin in place but if you wish to remove it, cut the flesh on each side, then give the fin a quick pull toward the head. Cut off the head by running your knife from the top toward the belly to include the head bone, collar bone, chin bone and the big pectoral fins on each side of the fishes' cheeks. If the fish is a citation size and the backbone is large, cut the flesh on either side of the head, then bend the fish over the edge of the sink and snap it. You can then cut the remaining flesh and remove the head. I have a friend who cooks fish heads for soup; I took one look at those heads all swimming around with tomatoes and mushrooms and could not taste it. I think the eyeballs discouraged me.

To Fillet Fish

Filleting fish is like wading a muddy creek in your bare feet, you have to inch along and feel the way as you go. With a sharp pointed knife cut through the flesh along the backbone and on one side of the dorsal fin, from tail to the head. Cut down to the backbone cleanly. Turn the knife flat and cut the flesh away from the sides of the backbone to the tail, feeling as you cut. Let the knife follow the bone and run over the outside surfaces of the rib bones. Ribs are left intact with the backbone. Lift the meat of the fish off in one piece, turn the one-sided fish over and repeat.

Lew's Fish Bone Soup

When filleting a large fish enough meat usually adheres to the bones to warrant making a soup and Lewis worked out this recipe. It's good and gets better as it is heated over.

Tie the bones of a filleted fish in a cheesecloth sack, put the sack in a pot, cover with boiling water, salt to taste and boil for 20 minutes. Remove the sacked fish from its broth and set it to cool while you peel, grind or finely chop, 4 or 5 medium potatoes. Put the potatoes into about 2 quarts (2 liters) of fish broth and boil. In a skillet saute ¼ pound (125 g) diced bacon and 3 finely chopped onions. When slightly brown drain and discard the excessive fat and add the bacon and onions to the fish broth. Season with a flurry of celery salt, cayenne and half a bay leaf, a mustard seed or two, a little cloves, mace, ginger and paprika. Reduce heat to simmer, pick fish from the bones, add to the soup together with 1 cup (250 ml) dry, powdered skim milk that has been mixed into 1 cup (250 ml) cold water. Stir, cover and cook very slowly for 1½ hours but do not allow it to boil. Serve as a hearty luncheon dish with celery and carrot sticks, caraway rye bread and a dish of anise-flavored pears.

Pan-Fried Fish

Using about ½ pound (225 g) of pan-dressed perch, bream, trout, herring or spot per person, salt the fish first because salt firms the flesh. In a skillet heat a skim of oil till it's hot but not smoking, dust each side of the fish in a mixture of cornmeal and flour half and half, and fry until brown. Turn once. Small fish take about 5 minutes on each side. When the fish flakes easily when tested with a fork, that is, the meat pulls apart, the fish is done. Serve immediately.

Fried Fish Steaks

If the fish is large, 7 inches (17 cm) across or more, it is generally cut crosswise into individual steaks. The backbone is usually left with the steak. To fry I melt about ¼ cup of oil in the skillet, drop in a salted steak, sprinkle with a touch of oregano and paprika, or with dill seed and fennel. I drizzle oil over each fish steak, cover the pan and cook for 10 minutes, then remove the lid, turn the fish and brown for about 5 minutes on the other side. Served with tufts of mayonnaise and parsley, lemon wedges on the side, fresh fried fish steaks are popular in our house.

Broiled Fish

Have supper completely ready and the table set. Preheat the broiler. Lay the whole fish, pieces or fillet on oiled foil in the broiler pan, skin side up. Brush with oil, salt and pepper. Place pan about 2 inches (5 cm) from the flame, broil for 5 to 8 minutes or until slightly brown, turn, baste top side with oil or daub with butter and cook 5 or 8 minutes more or until the fish flakes easily; that means when you insert a fork into the flesh, pieces of fish readily pull apart. Remove to a hot platter, squeeze half of lemon over it, garnish with finger-sized yellow hot peppers or a few onion and pepper rings and parsley. Serve at once.

Baked Fish

Rub the inner and outer surface of fish with salt, place fish on a greased or foil-lined baking pan, brush with oil and lay 3 slices of smoked bacon over the top. Bake at 350°F (175°C) about 45 minutes for a 3 or 4 pound (1.5 or 2 kg) fish. I usually grease and bake fist-sized potatoes in the same oven with fish, but some people parboil rice to about half done and stuff the fish belly with the half-cooked rice that has been mixed with salt, butter, lemon, thyme, minced basil and pepper. They sew or clamp the belly skin nearly closed but leave a steam hole. Stuffed or unstuffed, baste fish with its own buttery or smoky drippings 2 or 3 times and pour over a glass of sauterne or elder blow wine. As soon as the flesh flakes nicely when tested with a fork, serve on a hot platter garnished with lemon wedges and tufts of watercress.

Whether a juicy Rock Bass from the Chesapeake or a succulent salmon from Sitka Sound, I bake, broil, fry, or pie all kinds of fish in the same way.

Boiled Fish

This is a good way to prepare fish for people who are on fat-free diets. Cut the fish into serving portions, place in small, individual serving pie tins, salt if desired, and tie across with cheescloth. Lower the fish into salted water and simmer for 10 minutes. Do not boil. When fish flakes, drain, remove to individual dishes, garnish with lemon and serve. Vinegar or pickle juice added to the simmering water will reduce the fishy smell and lend flavor.

Oven Fried Fish

Medium-sized fish, 3 pounds (1.5 kg), may be oven fried by placing the oiled and salted fish that has been dressed with cracker crumbs or meal on a greased baking pan and baking it at 500°F (260°C) for 15 minutes. Test, and if the meat flakes cleanly, serve with a heaping platter of mashed potato balls and green bean casserole. Make the balls by mashing potatoes with egg, grated cheese and onion juice, rolling them into balls on a flour covered surface and bake the walnut-sized softies on a greased cookie tin at the same time as you cook the fish. You can get the most out of your oven by heating a casserole of precooked green beans mixed with creamed mushrooms and slivered almonds. Serve the fish and vegetables with a frilly Romaine lettuce salad garnished with dill pickle spears, black Italian olives and wedges of lemon.

Fish Salad

Most cooked or leftover fish makes a first class meal when folded with care into a salad. Combine bite-sized pieces of fish with chopped celery, onion, hard cooked eggs, boiled potatoes, a shred or two of cabbage, a nibble of green pepper, relish, a few green peas and mayonnaise.

Catfish

When I was not quite a teenager I went catfishing with my grandfather in a creek that ran into the Missouri. The day buzzed with insects, nervous greenery swished above and the air smelled of rain. We had no luck, not even a nibble, so while my grandfather took a walk to the river with a man who had wandered into our camp, I snoozed. There is nothing like a creek bank nap on a hot, early summer day for good dreams. Awakened suddenly by the sounds of the returning men, I searched for my rod that I had left with its line in the water at my feet. Panicked, I raced down stream, splashed in and caught it on a riffle just as my grandfather emerged from the underbrush. The line led to the far bank and was snagged there. None of the advice they hollered at me was to any avail, so the two men waded in, followed the line, reached under the bank and brought up a 22 inch (55 cm) hooked channel cat. Everyone bragged about "my fish" and I never had the courage to say that I had fallen asleep and had not been intimately acquainted with the big guy until he was in my mouth. I have caught and skinned catfish, though, and it is one of the few fish that I do not clean at the water's edge. To skin, tie a string around its neck, dip the fish in and out of boiling water, slit the neck around the head just skin deep, loop the string around a nail in a post and with pliers pull the skin off as you would a glove. Cut out around the dorsal fin but watch out, even stone cold dead, a catfish's big fin will sting. When the skin has been peeled back to the vent, place the fish on a board, slit the stomach with a forward movement to the chin and remove the entrails. If you wish to remove the big back fin do so with pliers and a quick pull toward the head. The only tricky part of skinning a catfish is starting to separate the skin from the flesh of the neck. Do this with a pointed knife, tenderly at first; once it is started it will peel with ease. Skinned, a catfish may be fried, broiled or prepared in the manner of other fish. Some people do not skin cats until they eat them; they simply scrub and clean them before cooking. The meat is moist and nearly boneless.

FISH PIE

A fancy way to stretch "a nubbin of fish."
Preparation time: 55 minutes. *Serves:* 5.

	U.S. CUSTOMARY	METRIC
Make pastry for a two crust pie.		
In a skillet melt,	2 tablespoons oil	30 ml oil
blend in and stir	2 tablespoons flour	30 ml flour
until thick	½ teaspoon salt	3 ml salt
	1½ cups milk	375 ml milk
Mix in, set aside	¼ cup dry wine	50 ml dry wine

Fit the bottom of a pie tin with pastry. Flake about a cup (250 ml) of cooked or canned fish into the pie. I use leftover fried perch or a small can of tuna.

Add to the pie	6 hard cooked eggs, sliced	6 hard eggs
	1 teaspoon dill seed	5 ml dill
	½ cup onions, finely chop.	125 ml onions
	¼ teaspoon black pepper	1 ml pepper
	½ teaspoon salt	3 ml salt

Pour the sauce over the filling and cover with the pastry top. Seal crust by fluting and pinching the moistened edge. Score top and bake at 450°F (230°C) for 35 minutes or until brown.

Outdoor Grilled Fish

How many gladsome eventides, as the sun was beginning to lower, we have beached our boat amid isolated rocks, climbed up to where screeching gulls whirled in protest, built a pit and grilled fresh-caught fish. Backyard grilled fish feasts bring back memories of earlier times and the taste is just the same. For the best flavor, fish must not be overcooked. Arrange salted and greased fish or fillets on a well greased grill and cook over medium coals. To turn fish I remove the grill and place the whole thing on a large skillet. The skillet serves as an emergency catcher; if a piece of fish falls through I can apprehend it and return it to the grill. After I have turned the fish I add a drop of oil and a scattering of garlic salt, soy and lemon juice to the cooked side and replace the grill over the coals. Depending upon the fish size and the heat, grilled fish take a total of between 15 and 20 minutes to cook. Supper should be pretty well on the table before starting the fish. Outdoor cooking is great fun; our Indian predecessors had a good thing which we are just learning to appreciate.

Pickled Fish

No ongoing stillroom would be complete without its crock of fish a-pickling in the corner; and although pickled fish is usually associated with herring, I have cured and pickled trout, mullet, salmon and any other finny friend that happened to swim by. Cooked fish or raw fish may be pickled.

Cooked Fish Pickle

Clean herring or alewives or any other diminutive edible fish, wrap them in a square of cheesecloth and cook them for about 15 minutes in boiling water to which you have added 1 tablespoon (15 ml) salt per quart liquid. If you prefer, the fish may be dusted with flour and fried in hot fat. When done, drain the fish, keep them intact, and layer them alternately with sliced raw onions in a crock. Cover with a pickle mixture. Weight the fish with a plate and rock to keep them under the liquid. Lid the crock and store in a cool place for at least a week before eating. These pickled fish may be kept for several months in the bottom of the refrigerator. They may be served cold as a relish, or drained and fried until heated through they make a tasty main dish. Cooked Fish Pickle are not firm fleshed, they tend to be soft and must be handled gently; even the small bones soften and become edible.

PICKLE MIXTURE

	U. S. CUSTOMARY	METRIC
Mix thoroughly,	6 cups vinegar	1.5 liters vinegar
boil for 15	6 cups water	1.5 liters water
minutes and cool	6 teaspoons salt	30 ml salt
before pouring	2 tablespoons pickling spice	30 ml pickling spice
over the layered	2 tablespoons sugar	30 ml sugar
cooked fish and	1 bay leaf	1 bay leaf
raw onion rings	1 red pepper pod	1 pepper pod

Baked Pickled Shad

Put a cleaned shad in a lidded baking pan and simmer in liquid to cover made of 6 parts water and 1 part vinegar. Cook for 15 minutes. Drain, leaving the fish in the pan. Add a sprinkle of salt, pepper, lemon juice and a dash of paprika. Cover tightly, weight the lid with a rock and bake at a low heat, 200°F (95°C) for 6 hours and serve with a light heart. Miraculously, the small bones disappear and the big ones are easy to spot. This is truly company fare.

Salt Fish

Most fish are salted in a crock before they are raw pickled, dried or smoked. You start with cleaned and scaled fish, either whole or filleted. Fill the bottom of the crock with plain salt and add a layer of fish. Continue layering salt and fish, skin side down if the fish are filleted, topping the crock with a layer of salt. Lay a plate on the top of the pack and weight it with a rock to keep the fish under brine. They will form their own liquid, so do not add water. If you plan to keep the salted fish longer than 6 weeks, rinse the fish in its old brine, throw the brine away and pack the fish in a new, lighter brine made of 2 cups (500 ml) plain salt dissolved in 1 gallon (4 liters) water. Cover and weight top to keep the fish submerged, put a lid on the crock and store in a cool place. Salt fish will keep indefinitely.

To Freshen Fish

Freshen salted fish by immersing them in running water, or soak, changing the water frequently, for 6 to 18 hours. Taste; if still salty, freshen longer.

PICKLED RAW FISH

Freshen salted fish to taste. If the skin is coarse, remove it. Cut fish into desired size for easy eating.

	U. S. CUSTOMARY	METRIC
For each 3 gallons (12 liters) of prepared fish:		
Mix, stir until dissolved	1 gallon cider vinegar	4 liters vinegar
	3 pounds brown sugar	1.5 kg brown sugar
	2 cups soy sauce	500 ml soy sauce
Mix separately	9 tablespoons pickling spice	135 pickling spice
	1 teaspoon dill seed	5 ml dill
	1 teaspoon caraway seed	5 ml caraway
	1 teaspoon celery seed	5 ml celery seed
	1 teaspoon mustard seed	5 ml mustard seed
	5 cloves garlic, sliced	5 garlic

Slice   1 lemon   1 lemon
                        6 large onions   6 onions

Layer the fish into six ½ gallon (2 liter) canning jars: fish, a pinch of spices, rings of onion, repeat. Place lemon rings against jar side so they will be seen. When jars are full, divide the vinegar mix into six parts and pour an equal amount into each jar of fish. If there is not enough liquid to cover the pack, fill jars with straight vinegar, leaving ½ inch (1 cm) head space. Rub the metal jar lids with paraffin to prevent rusting and tightly fasten onto each jar. Turn the jars upside down every few days, then back again. These pickled fish will be ready to eat in two weeks and will keep for months in a cool place.

Creamed Pickled Fish

Drain a jar of pickled fish and onions, combine with one quart (1 liter) of heavy sour cream and stir together gently. Garnish with a sprig of dill and watch your guests gather around the bowl.

Smoked Fish

All smoked fish must be presalted. The salt firms the meat and acts as a preservative too. To salt fresh fish for smoking, immerse scaled and cleaned fish in a brine made by dissolving 2 cups (500 ml) salt in 1 gallon (4 liters) of water for 4 hours. Drain, rinse in cold water and hang fish to dry at room temperature for about 4 hours or overnight. Cut the fish into strips or fillet, leaving the two sides of the boned fish connected by the tail. The process is the same if you use previously salted fish. Freshen it to taste as outlined above, cut into strips and hang to dry overnight.

Fish may be Hot Smoked or Cold Smoked for preservation. Cold Smoked fish may be eaten raw but it is usually coarse-grained, tough and chewy; in today's world it is most often cooked.

To Hot Smoke fish, hang freshened salt fish on wires or on a grate in a box over a heavy hickory or hardwood smudge, gradually raise the smoke temperature to 165°F (75°C) and hold the fish at that temperature for 4 hours. Cool, slice diagonally and serve plain as an hors d'oeuvre or chop the smoked fish finely and mix with mashed potatoes and egg to form fish cakes. Slivered, smoked fish is good in potato casseroles or tossed into green salads. Smoked fish shredded with chopped celery and onion in mayonnaise and relish is splendid as a sandwich spread. Minced into noodles layered with cottage cheese, sour cream and sauteed mushrooms and onions, it creates a smoky Romanoff. Hot Smoked fish requires refrigeration for safekeeping or the fish may be dipped in oil, wrapped securely in several layers of wax paper and frozen for a later day.

To Cold Smoke fish, hang the salted and freshened fish on wires over a light hardwood smudge, 90°F (32°C), for 3 to 5 days or until each fish or fish strip, if you have cut them into strips, is glossy and dry. Wrap the cured fish after it has cooled and store in a varmint and cat proof place. Cold Smoked fish may be sliced paper thin and eaten raw but it is not as moist as Hot Smoked fish. For cooking, soak Cold Smoked fish in fresh water for an hour, poach in a little water, then fry briefly in oil. Pre-soaked, Cold Smoked fish adds a zesty dash to macaroni salad with celery, relish, green pepper chips and shreds of cabbage; it makes a nice fish loaf or rice and white sauce with cheese casserole. In Alaska we used to put 2 or 3 strips of Cold Smoked salmon on dinner trays and the youngsters loved the fish and called their treat "Squaw candy." I must have a bit of squaw in me because I loved to nibble the dried fish, too.

SMOKED FISHERMAN'S STEW

This recipe was given to me by a restaurant proprietress. When I asked her about the name, she assured me that there was a "smoked fisherman." He did the smoking, she said, and he used any "kinda fish.... they is all the same once they got a little color on them."

	U.S. CUSTOMARY	METRIC
Soak a salted, freshened and smoked fish or two in water for an hour.		
In large skillet saute	3 tablespoons oil	45 ml oil
	1 onion, chopped	1 onion
	3 celery stalks, chopped	3 stalks celery
	1 clove garlic, minced	1 garlic
Add and simmer for 15 minutes	1 quart tomatoes	1 liter tomatoes
	1 teaspoon paprika	5 ml paprika
	½ teaspoon salt	2 ml salt
	1 teaspoon sugar	5 ml sugar
	½ teaspoon chili powder	2 ml chili powder
	¼ teaspoon each, pepper, basil and oregano	1 ml pepper, basil oregano
	the fish cut into servings	the fish

When sauce has cooked down and has become somewhat glossy, stir in a package, 7 oz. (210 g) of cooked spaghetti. Simmer for a few moments, pour into a serving bowl, shake a glug or two of catsup over it and serve with grated cheese.

Shrimp

Shrimp vary in size from 12 to the pound to more than 100 itsy bitsy Alaskan crustaceans to the same measure. The larger, Southern types are milder flavored but the tiny tidbits of taste that used to be served free at seaside taverns in the north rival any shrimp for flavor. We used to be able to enter a bar and with a scan tell who had been drinking the longest by his peelings pile.

To Cook Shrimp

Drop 1 pound (500 g) of shrimp into 1 quart (1 liter) boiling water in which 1 tablespoon (15 ml) salt has been dissolved. Boil for 15 minutes, drain them, cover them with a towel so that they will cool slowly and serve them in their shells to be peeled at the table or as pre-dinner nibbles. Shrimp turn bright coral colored when cooked and their flesh is firm. For raw shrimp dishes they must be washed well and stripped of their shells, a tedious task because shrimp don't undress with ease in public.

SHRIMP CREOLE

Preparation time: 1½ hours. *Serves:* 5.

	U.S. CUSTOMARY	METRIC
In a large skillet make a roux and stir in	1 tablespoon oil	15 ml oil
	1 tablespoon flour	15 ml flour
	2 onions, chopped	2 onions
	1 pepper, chopped	1 pepper
	1 clove garlic, crushed	1 garlic
	2 teaspoons parsley	10 ml parlsey
When onions soften, add	2½ cups stewed tomatoes	625 ml tomatoes
Season with	⅛ teaspoon red pepper	0.5 ml red pepper
	½ teaspoon salt	3 ml salt
	2 bay leaves	2 bay leaves
	¼ teaspoon celery seed	1 ml celery seed
	¼ teaspoon thyme	1 ml thyme

Stir well, bring to a boil and add 2 pounds (1 kg) raw, peeled shrimp. Cover tightly and cook slowly for 1 hour. Do not add more liquid. Serve with rice, a cooling salad, hot bread and a light dish of pears.

Chicken

"Every girl should learn to cook chicken," was my grandmother's pet phrase, and to her way of thinking, "cook chicken" started with the ax. It all began the evening before when we sneaked into the chicken house and selected our dinner, head under its wing, snoozing on a roost. If the hapless fowl was to be a fryer Grandma felt the breastbone to "feel for the meat" while thoughts of Hansel and Gretel danced in my head. For boiling or baking chicken she directed that I snatch a hen that she had noted to be a lax layer. We let our selection sleep overnight in a cage. The next morning we immobilized the poor chicken's head between two nails on the chopping block. One hand would hold the feet, and the other, the hatchet. The end was mercifully quick. The chicken was allowed to bleed, neck down for a minute while the wings were held to diminish the splatter. Picking the chicken or removing its feathers is a simple task if the bird is scalded, that is, dipped in and out of hot water, about 208°F (98°C). Hang the scalded chicken by one foot and pluck its feathers by pulling downward or toward the neck, taking little tufts or handfuls at a time. Start on the legs and pluck everything until you get to "the spot where the head ought to be." Dip the chicken in and out of the hot water if the feathers put up a fight. Rinse your hand from time to time, work fast and pull wing and pin feathers last using a dull knife. Singe the body hairs over a fire or candle, cut off the feet and you are ready to draw the bird. "Always kill and clean a chicken in one sitting," my grandmother advised. There is an awful temptation after the feathers are plucked to walk away and take a breather. Don't! It's much easier working with a warm and pliable bird that one that has turned cold and stiff.

To Clean Chicken

To draw a chicken, slit the skin from the breastbone to the vent, cutting around the vent. Insert your hand into the cavity along the inside of the rib cage. Follow the backbone toward the tail and scoop out. Remove the lungs that are located along each rib pocket, tuck your hand way into the bird and at the base of the neck feel the craw and on the far side, the windpipe. With your forefinger take a turn around the wind-pipe, and without squeezing the craw, pull the craw out together with the pipes. Rinse the cavity with cold water. Remove the gizzard, heart and liver, being careful to cut away the greenish gall sac intact. Let the chicken cool for 2 or 3 hours before cooking.

Of course chickens could be killed and eaten at any time during the year, but in stillroom times the meat calendar directed that July was for fryers and that March provided cull hens. "Crick fish" were sought as table food during the spring of the year and again during sultry August days. Game was hunted each fall and a pig provided meat during the winter.

Stewing Chicken

Cover whole bird with water, bring to a boil and cook gently for a few minutes. Skim. Add salt, chopped celery tops and onion. Cover the pan and cook slowly for about 3 hours or until done. Prick the meat with the tip of a knife, and if pink, clear juice runs out, the chicken is done. Remove the bird to a flat oven dish, pour over a glass of Madeira and dry, firming the meat in the oven 400°F (200°C) for 10 minutes. Serve whole on a platter garnished with cooked prunes that have been dried with a cloth, dipped in egg whites and in granulated sugar. Make a white sauce to which some chicken broth has been added together with preboiled, drained peas. Mashed potatoes, a salad of shaved carrots, shredded cabbage and sweet apples with nuts and a carrot spice cake complete this stillroom supper.

Baked Chicken

Pop the whole chicken into boiling water for 5 minutes to solidify its flesh. Remove, stuff with dressing if desired and place in a greased roasting pan. I have heard of shore cooks stuffing a baking hen with fresh raw oysters. Salt, pepper and butter liberally. Cover the breast with a cloth that has been dipped in the boiling juice, put the lid on the pan and bake at 325°F (160°C) for 3 hours or until the leg moves limply when touched. Baste regularly with the juices or with wine in which butter has been melted. When done remove the cloth carefully, moistening it if necessary, and return the bird to the oven 400°F (200°C) uncovered to brown for 15 minutes. Serve with boiled small potatoes, drained and briefly flipped into a skillet with diced crisp-fried bacon, and turnips, celery and carrots all cooked together, drained and with a spoonful or two of drippings from the roasting pan added at the last moment. A fresh cucumber sliced into sour cream, Corn Bubs and rice pudding complements this dinner.

CHICKEN CHOWDER

For leftover chicken try this all-in-one supper.

Preparation time: 30 minutes. *Serves:* 6.

	U.S. CUSTOMARY	METRIC
Chop, crisp fry	4 slices bacon	4 slices bacon
Add and fry until tender	½ cup onions, chopped	125 ml onions
	1 cup celery, chopped	250 ml celery
	2 cups cooked potato cubes	500 ml potatoes
	1 cup cooked chick, chop.	250 ml chicken
In large pan heat and add	2 cups chicken broth	500 ml chick. broth
	1 cup corn	250 ml corn
	2 tablespoons parsley, chop.	30 ml parsley
	the bacon and vegetables	bacon, vegetables
In the skillet blend	2 tablespoons oil	30 ml oil
	2 tablespoons flour	30 ml flour
Stir in briskly	1 cup milk	250 ml milk

Mix some of the soup liquid into the milk roux, stir to thicken and pour back into the soup, stirring all the while. Heat to scald but do not boil. Taste, add salt and pepper if needed and serve in a big tureen garnished prettily with yellow grated cheese.

Fried Chicken

Salt a cut-up chicken, dredge with flour and put into skillet with 4 tablespoons (60 ml) oil over a high heat for 10 minutes. Turn, reduce heat to very low, cover pan and cook on the second side for 45 minutes. Remove lid, raise heat, turn chicken to crisp the first side for 5 minutes and serve.

Chicken Ideas

Combine leftover cooked chicken with white sauce, breadcrumbs, parsley and an egg, form patties, dredge with flour, pepper, salt and fry in a little oil. Squeeze lemon over the croquettes when fried.

Fried chicken. In second skillet slice and fry 4 tomatoes in butter, flavor with garlic and a glass of wine. When chicken is done pour the sauce over it and serve.

Toss cubes of cooked chicken, half and half with smoked and cubed

ham in a buttered skillet, flavor with a touch of curry, mix in a cream
sauce and serve on toast.

Fry a chicken in one skillet. When almost done, fry a big skillet full of
sliced onions and pour over ¼ cup (50 ml) soy sauce. Transfer chicken to
a deep platter, smother with the onions.

Fry a chicken, remove to a deep dish and keep warm while you saute a
handful of mushrooms in the chicken skillet, add a glass of Rhine or
potato wine, fold in a cup (250 ml) sour cream, heat and pour over the
chicken.

Add a heavy dose of paprika, plus pepper to fried chicken coating, and
serve on a bed of briefly cooked, shredded cabbage.

Dip each piece of a fryer in orange juice, then into flour that has been
seasoned with ½ teaspoon (3 ml) ginger, pepper and salt before frying.

Eggs

Eggs fit into nearly every category of cooking from snacks to desserts
and they can be a main course, too. In stillroom times there was always
food on hand as long as the chickens produced. Keeping eggs fresh from
August until spring was done in several ways.

My grandmother preferred rubbing each egg with paraffin and laying
the eggs in a crock between layers of straw. I have heard of smearing the
shells with butter or lard and packing them in bran or sawdust. Some
farm wives used to put a basketful of fresh eggs into netting then dip
them in boiling water for half a minute before packing them in a crock
layered with sawdust. I have preserved eggs by packing them in a stone
jar with layers of salt between them and a thick layer of salt on top.

In each case the eggs were packed with the large end down, the container covered tightly and stored in a cool place such as on the floor of the stillroom.

From a neighbor I learned, "Take a piece of quicklime as large as a good-sized lemon, and two teacupfuls of salt; put it into a large vessel and slack it with a gallon of boiling water. It will boil and become thick as cream. Cool it, pour off the top which will be clear and cover your eggs with it and store your crock of eggs in a cool place. Eggs will keep 'till spring," she said.

Steamed Eggs

Heat a double boiler and rub butter around the inside of the top pan. In a bowl break 6 eggs and whisk with 1 tablespoon (15 ml) soy sauce and 1 tablespoon (15 ml) sherry. Empty into the top of the double boiler and cover the pan. While the eggs are cooking, saute a handful of sliced mushrooms in a skillet with a little butter. Add to the eggs as soon as they start to congeal. Replace the lid and finish cooking.

Sour Eggs

Melt 2 tablespoons (30 ml) butter in skillet, stir in 1 tablespoon (15 ml) flour and let brown. Thin with a scant ½ cup (115 ml) vinegar and ½ cup (125 ml) water, stir in 1 teaspoon (5 ml) salt, ½ teaspoon (2 ml) pepper and 1 teaspoon (5 ml) sugar. Let mixture boil up and break into it one at a time as many eggs as are needed. Baste the eggs with the sauce until they are cooked to taste. Remove with a slotted spoon and serve Sour Eggs over hot buttered toast. With fried potatoes, presoaked and poached salt herring and a tall glass of tomato juice, this makes a delightful late Sunday breakfast.

TSING TSING EGGS

A zesty culinary treat that can be served hot or cold, whole or sliced as an entree or with cocktails. Great for surplus Easter eggs.

Preparation time: 30 minutes.

	U.S. CUSTOMARY	METRIC
Hard-boil 6 eggs, peel.		
In skillet saute until brown	2 onions, chopped 1 tablespoon oil	2 onions 15 ml oil

Lower fire and	2 tablespoons soy sauce	30 ml soy sauce
add	2 tablespoons sugar	30 ml sugar
	¾ cup water	175 ml water

Cook until mixture comes to a boil, put in the hard-boiled eggs, roll each egg around so that it becomes thoroughly saturated with sauce; cook over a low fire, turning and moving the eggs from time to time until they become brown and the sauce is nearly evaporated. This takes about 20 minutes. Remove and serve whole on a bed of fried rice, or cool and use later.

Stuffed Eggs

This dish takes 1 pint (500 ml) sour cream.

Preparation time: 45 minutes.

Boil 10 eggs until hard. Peel, slice in half lengthwise and remove yolks. Mash the egg yolks with ½ cup (125 ml) sour cream, minced parsley, salt, pepper and ¼ cup (50 ml) soft breadcrumbs. Stuff the egg whites with the mixture and join two halves to form whole eggs. Butter a deep dish, sprinkle it with breadcrumbs, pour in ½ cup (125 ml) sour cream and place the stuffed eggs a single layer deep into the dish. Top with 1 cup (250 ml) sour cream, breadcrumbs, salt and pepper and brown in an oven, 350°F (175°C) for 7 to 10 minutes.

Deviled Eggs

For quick snacks that men love, cook eggs hard, cut in half lengthwise, remove yolks and mix them with finely chopped celery, pickle, a touch of onion and garlic, parsley, a drop of lemon juice and mash together with a tiny bit of prepared mustard, salt, paprika, plus 3 or 4 tablespoons (45 or 60 ml) mayonnaise. Heap the deviled mixture back into the salted egg whites and garnish the plate with greens and radish roses. I have included a platter of deviled eggs as hors d'oeuvres at nearly every party I have hosted and have never had one egg left over; they are likable, easygoing and friendly snacks. For variation: Add minced cooked chicken to the egg yolk mix, or ham nibbles or crisp fried bacon bits. For that special man, try mixing in a cup of crab meat; he will bow at your altar.

ANN'S EGG CAKE

Preparation time: 1 hour.

	U.S. CUSTOMARY	METRIC
In bowl beat and gradually add	4 eggs 2 cups sugar	4 eggs 500 ml sugar
While beating heat to lukewarm, mix with eggs	1 cup milk ½ cup butter, melt in milk 1 teaspoon vanilla	250 ml milk 125 ml butter 5 ml vanilla
In second bowl mix together	2 cups flour ½ teaspoon salt 2 teaspoons soda	500 ml flour 2 ml salt 10 ml soda

Fold dry ingredients into the egg and milk mixture, blend and pour into a greased square pan. Bake at 350°F (175°C) for 25 to 35 minutes. Remove from oven but do not take from pan.

TOPPING

	U.S. CUSTOMARY	METRIC
In bowl mix until creamy	¼ cup melted butter ½ cup brown sugar 2 tablespoons milk ½ cup grated coconut	50 ml butter 125 ml brown sugar 30 ml milk 125 ml coconut

Spread topping on the hot cake, place under the broiler for 2 or 3 minutes, remove cake from pan, cool and enjoy.

STRAWBERRY PIE

Preparation time: 40 minutes.

	U.S. CUSTOMARY	METRIC
Bake and cool	1 pie shell	1 pie shell, baked
In a bowl beat until stiff	3 egg whites	3 egg whites
Gradually add while beating constantly	½ cup sugar	125 ml sugar
Hull, wash and dry	2 cups strawberries	500 ml strawberries

Gently fold the strawberries into the egg white/sugar mixture, pour into the baked pie shell and bake in a hot oven, 425°F (220°C) for 10 minutes. Lower heat to 350°F (175°C) and bake for 10 or 15 minutes longer. When brown points show, remove, cool and serve.

LEMON CUSTARD OR PIE

Preparation time: 45 minutes.

	U.S. CUSTOMARY	METRIC
In bowl, combine	2 tablespoons flour	30 ml flour
	½ cup sugar	125 ml sugar
	¼ teaspoon salt	1 ml salt
Mix in, beat until	2 egg yolks	2 egg yolks
light and add	1 lemon, juice and grated rind	1 lemon j. & rind
Beat well and gradually stir in	1½ cups milk	375 ml milk
Beat stiff and fold in	2 egg whites	2 egg whites

Turn into a greased baking dish or into a baked pastry shell. Bake at 425°F (220°C) for 15 minutes, reduce heat to 350°F (175°C) and bake for 20 minutes longer or until a knife inserted into the custard comes out clean. Cool and serve.

A bachelor friend, a man of vast size with red hair flailing in the wind like the winter rye at his homestead, lived as he said, "from egg to mouth." A nervous, impatient kind of man, he beat a track from his cabin to the henhouse. So great was his hunger for eggs, he would even take them from under setting hens. "Never want anything that someone does not want to give to you," he once told me while wiping yolk from his beard. He admitted he was a compulsive egg eater, sometimes devouring eight a day. He never let one get cold, he boasted. I believed him but I often wondered why he did not keep more hens.

CHAPTER VIII
Garden Foods

Gardening gives man a faith that leaps into tomorrow, and the harmonies of a garden all come out together in soup.

Early day diets leaned heavily upon the use of garden produce in soups and upon foods devised to sop up the juice. The prolific family of 'Burgers as we know them, rarely visited stillroom tables; instead, the tough, stringy ends and pieces of meat were boiled into stock and soups over kitchen ranges. Bones are an important part of soup bases because the glutinous materials, gelatin and marrow, add strength and thickness; some mad, bony scientist once discovered that two ounces of soup bone contains as much gelatin as a pound of meat. Shinbone is considered the best soup meat but the "sticking piece," as a butcher I know calls the neck, makes good soup, too. A quart (liter) of water to a pound (500 g) soup bone and a teaspoon (5 ml) salt are simmered until everything falls apart, the stock is strained, any meat retrieved, marrow scraped out, and vegetables and seasoning are added.

Grated carrot gives an amber color to soup, pounded spinach adds green. Red you get by adding tomatoes, and brown coloring may be created from burnt sugar.

Flavorings of soups cover the horizon: parsley, thyme, summer savory, garlic, marjoram, red pepper pod, lemon peeling. I like a dash of allspice and a bay leaf; a friend spices her vegetable soup with cloves and browned onions.

Vegetables may be any combination of carrots, tomatoes, celery, peas, okra, corn, beans, rice, barley, parsnips, beets, turnips, onion or any other strays from the pantry.

Beef Soup

An old recipe dictates, "Select a small shin of beef and crack the bone." In Sitka, Alaska, I have watched ravens fly aloft carrying a shinbone that they had scrounged from the dump. Spying a hard looking rock they bombed the boulder with their bone, followed it down and with elegant aloofness, picked the marrow from their prize. When the rock trick did not work, these ingenious black birds dragged their shin dinners into the road and sat back to wait for a truck wheel to do the cracking.

After your shinbone has been cracked, and it often comes this way from the butcher, cover it with 6 quarts (6 liters) of cold water. Let it boil about 2 hours, and when it begins to break apart, season with a tablespoon (15 ml) salt, a teaspoon (5 ml) pepper and boil for an hour longer. Add to it a carrot, 2 turnips, a stalk of celery, all chopped, 2 tablespoons (30 ml) rice or barley, a teaspoon (5 ml) summer savory and 15 minutes before eating toss in 2 potatoes that have been chopped fine. The recipe went on to state that a fancy glass of brown sherry should be added just before serving.

If that soup had been mine, I would have done all that they said but I would have decreased the water by 2 quarts (2 liters) and added a quart (liter) of tomatoes, a handful of green beans, some corn, peas, an onion, chopped, slivered cabbage at the last moment, and I would not forget my allspice, ½ teaspoon (2 ml) and a bay leaf.

When your soup needs sweetening to cut the acid of tomatoes, use a spoonful of old jam drying up in the bottom of a jar in the icebox.

If you make homebrew and have a few bottles that are not up to par, a quart (liter) of it, mixed with tomatoes, makes a good soup base.

When time is short use pipe macaroni instead of barley or rice.

Wild foods such as sorrel for tartness, spicebush berry as a savory, peppergrass for bite, wild fennel for fragrance and any of the mustard family for heat, all give soup character.

Garden flowers such as chrysanthemum petals or marigolds add distinctive flavors, day lily flowers contribute glutinous textures, and dainty violets or rose petals sprinkled in at the last moment bring smiles to all who see them in soup.

Okra Soup

To beef or chicken stock add a quart (liter) tomatoes, fresh or canned, a quart (liter) of thinly sliced young okra, chopped parsley, a green pepper and an onion, both cleaned and chopped, plus 1 tablespoon (15 ml) chili powder, a teaspoon each (5 ml) celery seed, sugar and salt. Add water if necessary and simmer together for an hour, or until it is an "Amalgamated conglomerate" as my southern broker says. Serve hot with a side dish of fried oysters and new bread.

TAPIOCA CREAM SOUP

As a change of pace, try this with chicken broth base.

Preparation time: 1 hour. *Serves:* 5.

	U. S. CUSTOMARY	METRIC
In a large pan	4 cups chicken stock	1 liter stock
boil gently for	2 cups water	500 ml water
1 hour	⅓ cup tapioca	80 ml tapioca
	1 tablespoon butter	15 ml butter
	1 onion, chopped	1 onion
	2 stalks celery, chopped	2 celery
	small piece of mace	mace
	salt and pepper to taste	salt, pepper
Just before serving add	2 cups milk	500 ml milk

Heat to scalding and serve with dark bread and a bright cheese.

SPRING VEGETABLE SOUP

Preparation time: 20 minutes. *Serves:* 5.

	U.S. CUSTOMARY	METRIC
In a large pan heat to boiling	6 cups soup stock or bouillon	1.5 liters stock
	2 tablespoons butter	30 ml butter
Chop and add	2 handfuls of lettuce	2 handfuls lettuce
	2 handfuls young radish tops	2 handfuls radish
	1 spring onion, top included	1 onion
	1 bunch parsley	1 parsley
Mix in, stir, cook 10 minutes	1 cup new peas	250 ml peas
	salt and pepper to taste	salt, pepper
Beat in a bowl	3 egg yolks	3 egg yolks

Slowly pour some of the soup liquid into the yolks as you whip them with a fork. When lemon colored and quite liquid, pour the egg yolks back into the soup pan, stir around to thicken a minute and serve at once.

Pumpkin Soup

Preparation time: 20 minutes. *Serves:* 4.

Heat 1 quart (1 liter) milk to scald, do not boil; add 1½ cups (375 ml) cooked, mashed pumpkin; stir until dissolved and set on a low fire. In skillet saute 1 chopped onion in butter until clear, pour into the soup, add 1 teaspoon (5 ml) salt, pepper to taste and serve with a bowl of croutons flavored with a bit of garlic.

Sauerkraut Soup

Preparation time: about 2 hours. *Serves:* 4.

Cook a piece of meat, soup meat or smoked pork, in about 2 quarts (2 liters) water until almost done, add 1 onion chopped fine, 2 bay leaves, 1 teaspoon (5 ml) salt, ¼ teaspoon (1 ml) pepper and mix in 2 cups (500 ml) sauerkraut that has been squeezed out so that the soup will not be too sour. Boil, and about 15 minutes before supper add 2 large potatoes that have been cut into small cubes, cook until done. Taste for salt, and serve making sure that each bowl gets a piece of meat. My German grand-parents added a dollop of sour cream to each serving, but we enjoy Sauerkraut Soup plain.

Soup meat may be cooked in a pressure cooker for the required time, the pressure dropped naturally and vegetables added for a few minutes of tenderizing.

Lima Bean Soup

Soak lima beans overnight, boil in water to cover with ½ cup (125 ml) butter, a chopped onion, a teaspoon (5 ml) dill seed, pepper, salt and garlic powder. At the last moment add 2 tablespoons (30 ml) vinegar. Beans should be mushy with a few whole ones and the rest a blonde soup.

PIONEER SOUP WITH RIBBLES

Years ago people made soup from any meat that was leftover: a bone from a
lamb roast, turkey carcass or ribs.

Preparation time: 2 hours. *Serves:* 6.

	U. S. CUSTOMARY	METRIC
In a large pan	2 pounds pork spare ribs	1 kg pork ribs
gently boil	2 quarts water	2 liters water
When almost done	1 cup tomatoes	250 ml tomatoes
add and cook	3 onions, sliced thinly	3 onions
until tender	6 potatoes, diced	6 potatoes
	1 carrot, diced	1 carrot
	1 turnip, diced	1 turnip
	dried celery tops	celery
	salt and pepper to taste	salt, pepper

While cooking prepare the Ribbles which are made with an Egg Noodle
recipe.

Egg Noodles

Heap 2 cups (500 ml) flour on a board, mix in 1 teaspoon (5 ml) salt and
2 or 3 eggs, knead. Roll and pound, adding flour if needed until a pliable
dough is formed. Roll out thinly as for a pie crust, and using a straight
edged ruler and a pizza cutter, cut into strips. Flour the pizza cutter if the
dough sticks to it. Separate the noodles and let stand to dry for about 30
minutes and cook, covered for about 10 minutes in boiling soup. Egg
Noodles may be laid on wax paper in the sun to dry for 3 days. Bring into
the house each night and if the weather is muggy, heat in a very low
oven, 180°F (80°C) until dry. Wrap in wax paper and store covered in a
brown paper sack in a coffee tin and use as needed.

Ribbles

Instead of rolling the Egg Noodle dough as for a pie crust, roll out into
pencil-like strips between your palms; lay Ribbles on a floured board to
dry a few minutes while you put a colander into a large bowl and pour the
soup through it. Return the liquid to the pan, bring to a boil and drop
enough Ribbles into the soup broth to cover the surface. Cover the pan
and boil for about 7 minutes. Do not boil noodles too long or they will go
to pieces. While cooking, take the meat from the bones, chop, and when
the Ribbles are done or soft through, not hard-cored, mix in the vegeta-

bles and meat of the Pioneer Soup and serve hot. If there are too many Ribbles, flour them, roll them in wax paper, store in the icebox and use in a few days. I have made a welcome after-school treat for the children by frying leftover, uncooked Ribbles in butter and sprinkling them with cinnamon and sugar.

Lecki

These postage stamp sized noodles are nice in soup. If there are any leftovers, they can be reheated in butter, topped with crisp breadcrumbs and served as a potato substitute. Use the Egg Noodle recipe, add a little warm water if needed, and work dough on a floured board. Knead until you are able to roll very thinly. Let dry 30 minutes and flour the top of the rolled out dough. Cut into 1 inch wide (2.5 cm) strips, then cut across to make 1 inch (2.5 cm) squares. Cook rapidly in boiling, salted water for about 7 minutes or until the Lecki are soft and remain on the top of the water. Drain, rinse several times in cold water, daub with butter and serve separately for diners to spoon into soup. We enjoy Lecki with Lima Bean Soup.

If I am in a hurry I omit the 30 minute drying step in all of my noodle varieties. I find homemade noodles to be a convenience food as well as less expensive than store-bought kinds; they contain distinct personalities and noodle variations are almost endless.

Noodle Variations

Because there was usually flour in the stillroom flour bin and lots of vegetables in the garden or on the canned goods shelf, early-day cooks used oodles of noodles. They sometimes made a puree of spinach and added it, with eggs, to form green noodles; they cooked, mashed and added carrots for bright orange noodles; onions were minced and added with eggs for noodles to be boiled in chicken broth.

To fill noodles they are cut into 5 inch (12.5 cm) squares or rounds and moistened along the edges. A spoonful of vegetables blended with egg or meat and minced with onion and soy sauce is heaped on, and the filling is topped with a second noodle square or round. The edges are pressed down securely to seal and the filled noodles are boiled for 15 minutes in salted water. Serve filled noodles separately on a platter with a little browned butter or, if desired, a slightly browned, chopped onion in butter poured over the top of them.

Egg Balls for Soup

These are not noodles but we enjoy them for a change. Mash the yolks of 6 hard cooked eggs with 1 tablespoon (15 ml) flour, add the yolks of 2 raw eggs, a teaspoon (5 ml) salt, form into balls and drop into boiling soup for a few minutes of simmering.

Potatoes

Potatoes were the workhorses of stillroom menus. People ate them every day and in every way.

New potatoes are best for boiling. Cook for 15 minutes in salted water, drain, fluff in butter and garnish with parsley. The firmness of new potatoes lends itself to salads and fresh fried dishes.

Idaho type potatoes are best for baking: butter well washed potatoes, pop them into a hot, 400°F (200°C) oven and bake about 1 hour. We eat the skins after scooping out the mellow middles and love their brown crustiness oozing with butter. Many people slash an X on the potatoes to keep them from exploding in the oven. To puff potatoes, bake them, cut off their tops, spoon out the insides and mash the pulp with cheese, parsley, butter, pepper and salt. Return the cheesy pulp to the skins and bake for 10 more minutes.

Plain middle-aged potatoes are best in scalloped dishes. Slice the peeled, raw potatoes, alternate with layers of sliced bacon, onion and raw liver in a greased baking dish, salt, pepper, and lubricate with milk until the casserole is two-thirds full. Cover, bake in a 350°F (175°C) oven for 45 minutes. Omitting the liver, scalloped potatoes are excellent with cheese, or bacon, or with freshened, smoked herring.

French fried potatoes are cut into sticks, rinsed well in cold water, patted dry on a towel and fried in a basket immersed into oil heated to 375°F (190°C). Fill the basket no more than one-quarter full, lower into the hot oil and fry for about 5 minutes. Plain raw fried potatoes are sliced, cooked in a little oil in a covered pan for 15 minutes, turned once and browned, lid off, and salted. Add a little chopped onion shortly before serving if desired. Some people enjoy vinegar and sugar added to raw fried potatoes as a last minute seasoning and they garnish the dish with a bit of crisp fried bacon.

German Potato cakes are made by grinding 5 to 6 raw potatoes with an onion, mixing in a sprinkle of flour and a couple of eggs, pepper and salt. The potato cakes are fried by the spoonful in a lightly greased griddle.

Boiled dinners are a fine way in which to combine corned beef or bacon, carrots, onions, potatoes and at the last moment, coarsely chopped cabbage. Serve in soup bowls with lots of juice.

For mashed potatoes, first boil peeled potatoes in salted water until mealy, then drain. Mash and beat until free of lumps, add hot milk, butter and whip until light. Leftover mashed potatoes may be moistened with milk and an egg and spooned on top of a stew of leftover meat, gravy and vegetables. This is baked in a casserole dish at 350°F (175°C) for 45 minutes and called Cottage Pie. Leftover mashed potatoes, moistened with milk can also be used to stuff frankfurters or Polish sausage. Cut a slit into the side of the sausage, heap in the potatoes and bake at 350°F (175°C) for 20 to 30 minutes. In stillroom times fish cakes were made by adding leached and chopped salt fish together with an egg to leftover mashed potatoes. The mixture was formed into patties, dredged in flour and fried until brown.

Potato salads are perennial favorites. Soak cooked and diced potatoes in a sprinkle of vinegar for 30 minutes or overnight. Combine with chopped celery, onion, parsley, pickles, hard cooked eggs and mix with mayonnaise, salt and paprika. Additions include: shredded cabbage, chopped shrimp, diced beets, cheese cubes, tuna, cucumbers, crumbled bacon, dried beef, olives, chicken, or, for a far-out potato salad, chopped cashews.

Hot potato salad was a stillroom favorite. Dice, cook in salted water for 10 minutes 3 cups (750 ml) potatoes, drain and immediately add 6 slices of bacon that have been crisp fried and crumbled, 2 tablespoons (30 ml) minced onions and dress with ¼ cup (50 ml) vinegar into which a raw egg and 2 tablespoons sugar have been mixed. Garnish with chopped parsley and serve immediately.

Panning Vegetables

Panning is a quick steaming method which works well for tender cabbage, celery, green beans, young greens, young okra or carrots. For 5 servings heat 5 teaspoons (25 ml) water and 5 teaspoons (25 ml) oil in a heavy pan, add the finely chopped vegetable, cover tightly, lower the heat and cook until the vegetable begins to tenderize. Stir from time to time to prevent scorching. Panned vegetables should be crunchy and retain their color. Season lightly and serve at once.

Pan-Fried Vegetables

Summer squash, carrots, tomatoes, mushrooms, potatoes and egg-plant are all good when cooked with a small amount of oil. Heat the oil in a heavy skillet, add the sliced vegetables, cover and brown on one side. Turn, lower heat, cover and cook until tender. Remove cover when done, raise the heat and turn the vegetables to crisp them on the first side. Season and serve.

Broiled Vegetables

Onions, eggplant, halved tomatoes, summer squash or most leftover cooked vegetables may be broiled on a greased broiler rack. Brush them with butter, add seasoning and cook about 3 inches (7 cm) from the broiler. When the vegetable is tender and lightly brown, turn, brush with oil or butter and finish broiling.

Seasoning

In addition to butter and drippings try flavoring vegetables with salad oil and lemon juice, horseradish or a scattering of garlic powder. A squeeze of lemon juice, vinegar or herb vinegar is provocative on carrots, beets or turnips. Minced onion, green pepper, parsley, mint leaves or a small pinch of basil, dill or caraway seeds point up the flavor of cooked vegetables. Always go light on seasoning so as to not overshadow the delicate flavors of vegetables.

Vegetables

Vegetables usually arrived at the table via the stillroom where a bench and a pan of water were set near the window to "pick over" produce. Picking over meant examining every leaf, fruit and root for unwary insect friends. Vegetables were initially washed outside at the pump when they were brought from the garden, then bought to the stillroom for further cleaning, sorting and paring.

Garden Greens

To boil spinach or tender beet greens use only the water clinging to the leaves after washing. Put the greens into the pan, salt throughout, reduce heat after steam begins to escape from the lid and cook slowly for about 5 minutes. The first picking of kale, collards, mustard or turnip tops may be washed, chopped and boiled in water to cover for 8 to 10 minutes. I add salt at the rate of 1 teaspoon (5 ml) to the quart (liter) of water. Drain, dot with butter or garnish with hard-boiled egg slices or a crumble of crisp fried bacon. A Helennaise topping makes these plain-Jane dishes gourmet fare.

Helennaise

Melt ½ cup (125 ml) butter and cool to lukewarm. While cooling, beat 4 eggs, add the juice of 1 lemon, ½ teaspoon (3 ml) dry mustard, ¼ teaspoon (1 ml) each salt and pepper. Then slowly, very slowly at first, drizzle in the melted butter while beating a high speed. When thick, heat slightly over a low fire for 2 minutes, stir, and pour over well drained greens of the kale or collards variety. This sauce goes well over poke if you are lucky enough to live in poke country.

Wilted Greens

Wash and pick over garden lettuce, young beet greens, or young dandelion leaves, shred. For each 4 servings use about 1 pound (500 g) greens. Chop 3 slices bacon and fry crisp. While the bacon is frying chop 2 or 3 green onions and mix with the lettuce. When the bacon is done add ¼ cup (50 ml) vinegar and 1 teaspoon (5 ml) sugar to the skillet, swirl once or twice with a fork and pour hot over the shredded greens. Serve in bowls and eat at once.

Asparagus

Asparagus tips, steamed for 10 minutes then smothered in butter, have been a spring ritual since stillroom maids stepped outside their kitchen doors and cut the pale spears. Today every home with a spare 6 foot yard space should also grow asparagus. They are decorative and nearly carefree. If you ever have enough asparagus for experimenting, try them fried. Trim off tough bottoms, wash well, then cook for 10 minutes in salted water, 1 teaspoon (5 ml) salt to the quart (liter) of liquid. Drain carefully. Dip each asparagus in egg then into cornmeal and flour mixed half and half and fry in a lightly oiled skillet. If you enjoy cooked asparagus tips cold with a vinegar dressing, add a bit of grated orange peeling to the dressing.

Rhubarb

Though not a vegetable, rhubarb can be grown by the side of a house and will provide pie and sauce. Do not eat the leaves. Chop the stems coarsely, measure, add half as much sugar, a wineglass of water, a sprinkle of salt, cover and boil about 20 minutes. Dash in ½ teaspoon (2 ml) soda, cool and eat. For pie, blend sauce with 2 tablespoons (30 ml) minute tapioca and pour into an unbaked pie shell. Cover with pastry, seal edges with water, slit top for steam and bake 400°F (200°C) for 40 minutes.

BUTTER FRIED SHREDDED CARROTS

Preparation time: 30 minutes. *Makes:* 4 servings.

	U.S. CUSTOMARY	METRIC
Melt in skillet and add	3 tablespoons butter	45 ml butter
	3 cups shredded carrots (I shred with potato peeler or kraut cutter.)	750 ml carrots
Season with	1 teaspoon salt	5 ml salt
	¼ teaspoon pepper	1 ml pepper
	pinch of curry powder	pinch curry
	1 teaspoon lemon juice	5 ml lemon juice
Mix in	½ cup water	125 ml water

Cover and cook over low heat until tender, about 15 minutes. Remove cover and let the carrots nuzzle into their own golden butter. Serve hot.

French Peas

Simmer fresh green peas in salted water for 8 to 10 minutes, drain. Meanwhile in a buttered skillet saute a handful of sliced mushrooms and a small sliced onion. Add the peas to the skillet, swizzle them around for one minute and create an elegant dish.

The Germans prepare sweet young peas in the pod by covering tender pea pods, no bigger than 1½ inches (4 cm) long with water and boiling them about 15 minutes or until soft. They drain them, stir in a little butter with salt and a touch of lemon verbena.

Summer Squash

We enjoy tender-hearted and thin skinned summer squash sliced, salted and dredged in flour and fried until brown. Recently I tasted a superb dish in which sliced yellow squash were fried in butter with a bit of chopped parsley and dill. The dill herb made the difference; with salt, pepper, a breath of garlic and sweet basil, this golden dish was a delight.

PALESTINIAN VEGETABLES

I always feel luxuriantly wealthy when I cook a casserole of vegetables and this gorgeous dish makes me feel richer than ever.

Preparation time: 1 hour. *Serves:* 6.

	U.S. CUSTOMARY	METRIC
In large	1 large onion, sliced	1 onion
heavy cooker saute	4 tablespoons olive oil	60 ml olive oil
	garlic, minced	garlic
Season with	1 teaspoon salt	5 ml salt
	¼ teaspoon paprika	1 ml paprika
	¼ teaspoon ginger	1 ml ginger
	¼ teaspoon curry powder	1 ml curry
	¼ teaspoon pepper	1 ml pepper
Add, stir	4 large ripe tomatoes, cubed	4 tomatoes
briefly	1 yellow squash, sliced	1 yellow squash
	1 zucchini squash, sliced	1 zucchini squash
	1 small eggplant, peeled sliced	1 eggplant, sliced
	2 stalks celery, chopped	2 celery
	1 teaspoon salt on top	5 ml salt

Cover tightly and cook over a very low heat for about 40 minutes.

Clean, cut into strips and add	3 bell peppers	3 peppers

Simmer 5 or 6 minutes. Serve carefully so that the vegetables do not mash, swizzle over with olive oil and garnish with cured ripe olives.

I have used a pressure cooker for preparing mixed vegetable dishes and have found that it saves both time and cooking fuel. The small amount of water, usually ½ cup (125 ml), required by pressure cooking retains nutrients and I have discovered that tougher, less expensive meats may be used for flavoring. Manufacturer's instructions must be followed because cooking with steam pressure is different from ordinary stove top or stillroom cooking.

Baked Cucumbers

When stillrooms overflowed with cukes, many families relied upon an old Polish trick of baking the prolifigate cucumbers. Select long, straight cucumbers, one for each serving, wash, peel thinly, cut off the upper third lengthwise, keep the sliced off piece for use as the cuke lid. With a spoon scoop out all of the seedy innards and stuff the cucumber boat. Stuffing may be made by mincing 1½ cups (375 ml) cooked chicken, seasoning with salt and pepper, 2 tablespoons (30 ml) vinegar, 2 teaspoons (10 ml) onion juice and adding approximately ½ cup (125 ml) breadcrumbs. Mix well with 1 egg. Stuff lightly into 6 prepared cucumber shells, cover with cucumber lids and tie securely around each end. Bake in a generously buttered and covered baking dish, 400°F (200°C) for about 20 minutes or until cucumbers are soft when tested with a fork.

Cauliflower

To clean cauliflower and remove any insects that might be hidden in the head, immerse the large part of the head, top downward in a pan of cold salted water, 1 tablespoon (15 ml) salt to a quart (liter) water. When cleaned, drop the separated flower heads into boiling, salted water to which a slice of bread has been added, boil 10 minutes, drain and serve with melted butter, salt, pepper, grated nutmeg, chopped parsley and sprinkle with 1 teaspoon of vinegar or lemon juice. To fry cauliflower, boil until about half done, drain and dip each branch into Beer Batter. Fry in a little hot oil, salt and serve warm.

DRESSED ENDIVE

	U.S. CUSTOMARY	METRIC
Wash, shake out and cut endive into 1 inch (2.5 cm) lengths, salt to taste.		
In skillet heat	5 tablespoons butter ⅓ cup vinegar	75 ml butter 80 ml vinegar
Pour vinegar over	3 cups endive, cut up	750 ml endive
Blend in	½ cup hot riced potatoes or cooked in tiny cubes	125 ml potatoes
Garnish with	2 hard cooked eggs, sliced paprika and salt	2 hard eggs paprika, salt

Serve at once because the surprise element of warmth becomes this dish.

Indian Succotash

Boil 5 ears of corn for 10 minutes and in a separate pan boil 2 cups (500 ml) lima beans for 20 minutes, salt each. Cut corn from cob, combine with limas, add ½ cup (125 ml) cream, 1 tablespoon (15 ml) butter, paprika and a whisper of nutmeg. Steam in a double boiler for 15 minutes and serve.

Green Beans

One of the most prolific, versatile and best loved garden vegetables. First picking, there is no food more gracious than briefly boiled, 5 to 8 minutes, young snap beans, drained and doused with butter, pepper and salt.

Variations include: Cooked green beans mixed with tiny onions sauteed in butter and blended in mushroom sauce.

Cooked green beans baked with tomatoes, a mite of sugar, okra, summer squash and topped with cheese.

Cooked green beans sprinkled with brown sugar, Worcestershire sauce and drenched in sour cream.

Cooked green beans dressed with chopped onions that have been simmered in soy sauce. . . . A fat-free goodie.

Green Beans Creole, cooked in stewed tomatoes, okra, flavored with sauteed onions and green peppers and spiced with garlic, parsley, red pepper, a bay leaf, celery seeds, a touch of thyme, plus a handful of peeled, raw shrimp. Salt and pepper to taste, simmer slowly in covered pan for 1 hour.

Cooked green beans escalloped in butter sauce and flavored with bits of bacon, sauteed onions and topped with cheese and breadcrumbs before baking, 350°F (175°C) for 20 minutes.

Cooked cold green beans tossed with chopped celery, onion, hard-boiled eggs, pimiento strips and mayonnaise with lemon dressing.

Cooked green beans briefly sauteed in butter, a touch of curry powder and a handful of chopped salted peanuts.

Geriatric green beans cooked for an hour with the podded old-timers from the bean patch and seasoned with a square of smoked meat.

Green beans with baby onions, diced ham and cream sauce.

Sweet and sour cooked green beans, dressed with bacon that has been fried with onions and doused with vinegar, sugar and black pepper.

Cooked green beans dressed with minced onions, garlic, a drop of vinegar and a daub of sour cream.

Cooked green beans seasoned while hot with French dressing, a mite of sugar and garlic salt and parsley.... Any way you fix them green beans are great good food.

LIMA BEAN SALAD

Preparation time: 30 minutes to hull, 20 minutes to cook and 10 minutes to toss. *Serves:* 5.

	U.S. CUSTOMARY	METRIC
Cook green lima beans in salted water until tender, about 25 minutes.		
Drain and cool	2 cups lima beans	500 ml limas
Pour over and chill 1 hour	¼ cup French dressing	50 ml French dressing
	1 tablespoon vinegar	15 ml vinegar
Drain off excess dressing and combine beans with	¼ cup onion, chopped	50 ml onion
	½ cup cucumber, chopped	125 ml cucumber
	¼ cup pickle, chopped	50 ml pickle
	2 tablespoons mayonnaise	30 ml mayonnaise
	salt and pepper to taste	salt, pepper

Toss lightly, arrange on lettuce leaves in a bowl and garnish with chopped hard-boiled eggs and a sprinkle of paprika.

HOT BRUSSELS SPROUTS

Preparation time: 30 minutes. *Serves:* 5.

	U.S. CUSTOMARY	METRIC
Cook brussels sprouts in salted water until tender, about 15 minutes. Drain.		
In double boiler mix and cook over boiling water until thick	¼ cup vinegar	50 ml vinegar
	2 tablespoons oil	30 ml oil
	½ teaspoon dry mustard	2 ml mustard
	¾ teaspoon salt	3 ml salt
	1 teaspoon sugar	5 ml sugar
	¼ teaspoon paprika	1 ml paprika
	1 egg beaten	1 egg
When thickened add	1 tablespoon butter	15 ml butter
	½ teaspoon curry powder	2 ml curry
	1 teaspoon minced parsley	5 ml parsley
	1 teaspoon onion, grated	5 ml onion
Fold in	½ cup fresh or sour cream	125 ml cream

When blended and hot pour over 3 cups of hot, drained brussels sprouts.

Cabbage

When boiling cabbage cook it briefly, 4 to 8 minutes, for crunchy texture, better flavor and digestibility.

Red Cabbage Pickle

Cut a head of red cabbage into quarters. Boil for 8 minutes in slightly salted water. Drain, shake out and pour over a pickle mixture that has been boiled for 10 minutes. Pickle: 1 cup (250 ml) vinegar, 1 cup (250 ml) water, ¾ cup (175 ml) sugar, ¼ teaspoon (1 ml) salt and 12 whole cloves. Let the cabbage stand in pickle for 3 days and eat. I sliver this colorful pickled cabbage and serve it well drained as a complement to pork.

Pepper Cabbage Slaw

Shred cabbage together with red and green pepper, toss with salt, pepper, celery seed and a vinegar, water and sugar dressing.

Spiced Tomatoes

In a greased casserole dish layer thick slices of ripe tomatoes with toasted breadcubes: breadcubes on the bottom, tomatoes, a sprinkle of salt, sugar and a dash of cinnamon, breadcubes, tomatoes, etc.; top with tomatoes but poke breadcubes between them and daub with chunks of butter, salt, pepper and bake at 375°F (190°C) for 25 minutes.

Tomato Fritters

A speedy and simple supper. Mix 2 cups (500 ml) flour, 1 teaspoon (5 ml) baking soda, ½ teaspoon (3 ml) salt and 1 tablespoon (15 ml) sugar. Quickly stir in 1 cup (250 ml) tomatoes, drained if canned and cubed if fresh, plus 1 cup (250 ml) sour milk. Stir briskly and fry by spoonfuls in a lightly greased skillet. Dash with pepper and serve.

Celery Fritters

Wash, remove all good leaves from a celery, chop fine together with the tough, outside celery stalks. Cover with boiling water and cook until tender. Drain, shake out water. Beat 1 egg, add 4 tablespoons (60 ml) flour, salt and pepper to taste, stir in the drained celery and fry by spoonfuls in a lightly greased skillet. Very nice to serve with chicken.

Corn Casserole

In a buttered baking dish layer whole kernel corn, sliced onions, salt, pepper, breadcrumbs, top with stewed tomatoes or milk, daub with butter and bake at 400°F (200°C) for 30 minutes.

Harvard Beets

Precook, slip off skins, dice beets and set aside. In a pan mix ½ cup (125 ml) sugar, 2 tablespoons (30 ml) flour, ½ teaspoon (3 ml) salt, ½ cup (125 ml) vinegar, ¼ cup (50 ml) water and 2 tablespoons (30 ml) butter. Cook over a low heat, stirring continually until thick. Add the diced beets, reheat to boiling and serve.

Orange Sweet Potatoes

Boil peeled sweet potatoes in salted water to which 1 tablespoon (15 ml) sugar has been added. When tender, drain, mash with butter and mix in ½ cup (125 ml) moist raisins. Fill halved empty orange shells, sprinkle each smooth cone with chopped nuts and bake 20 minutes at 350°F (175°C). Serve hot. They make a pretty vegetable for the holidays.

Sweet 'Tater Treats

Try candied sweets topped with pineapple rings, or sweeten your sweets with a drizzle of maple syrup. Our family's favorite is sliced, raw, crisp fried sweet potatoes. Fry as you would raw white potatoes in a little oil. Eaten almost like potato chips, the clue is to salt them at the table so that they remain crunchy. Turn these sweets often because they love to trick you as soon as your back is turned and burn black. Boiled, cold sweet potatoes make a nice salad with celery, diced ham and chopped pecans. Dress with mayonnaise.

Eggplant

Peeled, sliced, soaked in a sprinkling of salt for an hour, then dredged in beaten egg and flour and fried, eggplant makes a fine supper.

BAKED EGGPLANT

Preparation time: 1 hour. *Serves:* 8.

	U. S. CUSTOMARY	METRIC
Peel, cube and boil 1 large eggplant in salted water until tender. Drain.		
In large skillet melt and stir in	2 tablespoons butter	30 ml butter
	2 tablespoons flour	30 ml flour
	1 cup milk	250 ml milk
When thick blend in	the cooked eggplant, mashed	the eggplant
	½ cup sharp cheese, cubed	125 ml cheese
	1 tablespoon catsup	15 ml catsup
	1 teaspoon onion, grated	5 ml onion
	2 eggs, beaten	2 eggs
	1 teaspoon salt	5 ml salt
	¼ teaspoon pepper	1 ml pepper

Pour into a greased baking dish. Brown in oven, 375°F (190°C), for 20 minutes. Serve hot or cold.

Turnip Puff

Boil and mash 2 cups (500 ml) each, turnips and potatoes. Combine with 4 tablespoons (60 ml) butter, 4 tablespoons (60 ml) cream, a well beaten egg, 1 teaspoon (5 ml) salt, pepper to taste, pour into a greased baking dish and bake for 20 minutes at 400°F (200°C). Serve this surprisingly mild and tasty dish on a windy night with breaded pork chops, fried apples and pumpkin pie. It's a cozy dish that harmonizes quietly while the elements rage outside.

Winter Squash

Halved and baked with butter, salt, pepper and a dash of nutmeg, winter squash was a signal to stillroom matrons that a bite of frost had touched the garden and that the harvest moon was riding high. Today we can purchase squash year-round but to my way of thinking they still echo frosty hoots of an owl, the crunch of dead leaves and the sounds of hurried steps as people crowd into the kitchen where everything is cozy warm. We like butterball-type squash baked with its cavity stuffed with sausage dressing; or with chopped apples, brown sugar, butter and a sprinkle of nuts in the middle. Winter squash, one of America's own foods, may be boiled or fried like potatoes, baked in cookies and custards, in soup, stewed with tomatoes or peeled, sliced lengthwise and broiled with meat. A versatile food and, like America, its potential is just beginning to be realized.

Parsnip Stew

An old-fashioned, one kettle supper was made by browning 2 pounds (1 kg) beef stew meat in 2 tablespoons (30 ml) oil and seasoning with salt and pepper to taste. Add 1 onion chopped small, water to cover the meat, cover and simmer for about 1½ hours. Add 6 large parsnips, pared and cut into pieces, simmer for a second 1½ hours or until the parsnips are tender. Stir in a little more water if necessary and add 6 potatoes which have been cut into serving pieces. Salt, cover and steam very slowly for 30 minutes. I cook Parsnip Stew over the fireplace and swing the big iron pot toward the front of the fire so that it will not cook too fast. If you like parsnips you will delight in this stew.

Storage of Garden Produce

The keeping qualities of garden vegetables and fruits stored for winter use can be maximized by control of temperature, light and humidity. Most stillrooms had slatted vegetable shelves or shallow bins built inside along the north wall that were used for keeping winter produce. I found out that some vegetable storage areas hold strange secrets. When the ancient, one-legged bootlegger did not return home after working ship-side on a boat bound for Hawaii, town officials boarded up his house and a few months later an awful odor hung over his alley. Everyone was apprehensive and called upon the local doctor to investigate. I was brought along to take notes. The old man must have had 15 bushels of turnips, all of them rotten, and while poking around, the doctor and I found 8 bottles of wine hand inscribed from Podensac, France. The wine was apparently a gift from the French town where the old boot-legger had fought during WW I. Looked upon as a ne'er-do-well by his townsmen, the old-timer had been honored as a hero during his youth; too late we learned about his valor.

Stillroom storage facilities should be ventilated with removable slatted flooring, bins and shelves should be kept clean and temperatures and humidity should be held as close to recommended conditions as possible. Handle fruits and vegetables carefully, bruised produce should not be stored with winter produce. If foods are harvested early in the morning when the weather is cool, and stored while they are cool, they will keep longer.

If garden seeds are saved for the following year, do not save hybrid seeds, and put regular seeds in marked containers and dust with insecticide to prevent weevil infestation. Store separately.

Recommended
Storage Conditions

Commodity	Place to store	Temperature °F	°C	Humidity	Length of storage
Dry beans	Cool dry place	32-40	(0-5)	Dry	As long as desired
Cabbage	Outdoor cellar	32	0	Moist	Through late fall
Endive	Roots in soil	32	0	Moist	6 to 8 weeks
Onions	Cool, dry place	32	0	Moist	Through late fall
Parsnips	Where they grew	32	0	Moist	Through winter
Potatoes	Dark, cool place	35-40	1-5	Moist	Through winter
Pumpkins	Warm, dry place	55	13	Dry	Through late fall
Squash	Warm, dry place	55	13	Dry	Through late fall
Roots	Cool, dark place	55	13	Moist	Through late fall
Sweet potato	Warm, dry place	55-60	13-15	Dry	4 to 6 weeks
Fruits					
Apples	Cool, moist in plastic	32	0	Moist	Through winter
Pears	Cool, moist place	32	0	Moist	4 to 6 weeks

Grains and corn should be stored in a cool, dry place free from weevil infestation.

Pudding

Because early day kitchens were heated by wood ranges, slow cooking puddings were convenient and popular. Rhubarb, raspberry, plum, sweet potato custards, corn and apple — there was no end to pudding ideas. Some were steamed; put into well floured cloths and tied to a stick that was then placed across the top of a kettle containing a little boiling water, not enough to touch the sacks. Some puddings were baked in greased pans, and some were poured into greased coffee tins, covered tightly with brown paper to allow steam to form and cooked in a low pan of water in the oven. Some puddings were poured into pastry shells and baked into pies.

BUTTERNUT SQUASH PUDDING OR PIE

Preparation time: 1 hour 15 minutes. *Makes:* 6 servings.

	U.S. CUSTOMARY	METRIC
In bowl mix	¾ cup sugar	175 ml sugar
	¼ teaspoon salt	1 ml salt
	1 tablespoon flour	15 ml flour
	1 teaspoon cinnamon	5 ml cinnamon
	½ teaspoon nutmeg	2 ml nutmeg
	½ teaspoon ginger	2 ml ginger
	¼ teaspoon mace	1 ml mace
Blend in	1½ cups cooked squash, mash.	375 ml squash
	2 eggs	2 eggs
	1½ cups milk, half evap.	375 ml milk
	2 tablespoons butter, melt	30 ml melted butter

Pour into a well buttered baking dish and bake at 450°F (230°C) for 15 minutes, then lower heat to 325°F (160°C) and bake for 40 minutes or until a knife inserted in the custard comes out clean. Or, pour the squash mixture into a single, unbaked pie shell and bake as for pudding. Pumpkin in the same amount may be substituted for squash in this recipe.

PERSIMMON PUDDING

This is a fine food when baked in 2 small loaves and eaten hot or cold, or when steamed into a ball and garnished with a sprig of holly for the holidays. Serve plain or with whipped cream.

Preparation time: 1 hour. *Makes:* 2 small loaves.

	U.S. CUSTOMARY	METRIC
In bowl mix	1 cup flour	250 ml flour
	1 tablespoon cinnamon	15 ml cinnamon
	2 teaspoons baking soda	10 ml baking soda

	½ teaspoon salt	3 ml salt
	1 cup sugar	250 ml sugar
Stir in, blend	1½ cups persimmon pulp	375 ml persimmon
and pour into	2 eggs	2 eggs
2 buttered loaf	2 tablespoons butter, melt.	30 ml butter
pans	½ cup milk	125 ml milk

Bake at 375°F (190°C) for 45 minutes, or until a deep mahogany glaze covers the pudding. Dates, raisins and nuts may be added to make this dessert more festive. Or try this as a pie!

Pie Crust Dough

In bowl mix 1½ cups (375 ml) flour with ¾ teaspoon (4 ml) salt, cut in or rub between your hands until pea-sized lumps are formed, 3 tablespoons (45 ml) solid shortening or lard. In bowl divide the dough into two parts. Make a pocket in one part and pour in 4 tablespoons (60 ml) cold water. Form into a dough and on a lightly floured surface quickly roll out thinly to form a bottom pastry crust. Repeat and form dough from the second part. In moving rolled out pie dough from the board to the pie pan, fold lightly in half, then unfold in the pan. If you prebake a pie shell without filling, poke all over with holes using the tines of a fork. This allows steam to escape from under the crust and it will lie flat. Bake pie crust in a quick oven, 400°F (200°C) and if there is any used dough, roll it thinly and cut into Cinnamonjigs for the children. Sprinkle the pie dough nibbles with cinnamon and sugar and bake 10 minutes.

GREEN TOMATO MINCEMEAT PIE

If all the harmonies of a garden come together in soup, then the orchard, garden and grove come into serene accord in mincemeat pie.

Preparation time: all day. *Makes:* 12 quarts (12 liters).

	U.S. CUSTOMARY	METRIC
Wash, core, chop and measure	1 gallon green tomatoes	4 liters green tomatoes
Mix in	2 tablespoons salt	30 ml salt

Let stand for 1 hour, drain and cover with boiling water. Let stand 5 minutes. Drain and squeeze. Using a medium grate, grind 1 gallon (4 liters) of washed, cored and coarsely chopped apples, 2 or more quarts (2 liters) of washed, peeled, cored and chopped pears, 1 quart (1 liter) of peeled, cored and chopped quince, if you have them, and three seeded oranges, skins included. Mix fruit with the drained tomatoes in a large kettle, heat.

Add, and boil	1 cup vinegar	250 ml vinegar
slowly, stirring	8 cups brown sugar	2 liters sugar
from time to	2 pounds raisins	1 kg raisins
time	1 tablespoon ground ginger	15 ml ginger
	2 teaspoons ground cloves	10 ml cloves
	3 tablespoons cinnamon	45 ml cinnamon
	2 teaspoons nutmeg	10 ml nutmeg
	1 teaspoon salt	5 ml salt

Cook, stirring often until the fruit is dark brown and mushy, about 3 hours. When all ingredients are cooked together to nearly the consistency of apple butter, pour boiling hot into hot, sterilized quart jars and seal at once. Do not forget to save out a quart or two for pies. Your whole neighborhood will smell the fragrance of your kettle and come knocking at your door.

Mincemeat is a salute to the triumph of nature and to man's ingenuity in bringing it all together in pie.

CHAPTER IX

Energy Savers and Dry Staples

The simplest method of saving food and energy is sun drying. Garden produce, just as meats and milk, play hosts to bacteria that spoil food; bacteria that require moisture, warmth, air, plus nutrients to survive. Precluding any of these factors preserves food. Sun drying is not only the easiest way to preserve foods, it is also the least expensive. True, dried fruits and vegetables lose much of their fresh flavor, but seasoned with ingenuity and herbs, dried foods can be a desirable addition to everyday meals. Some nutrients of fruits and vegetables are lost through drying but major portions of food values are only minimally affected.

Fruits and vegetables may be simply dried on racks in a sunny place; or fruits may be sulphured and vegetables steamed before being dried.

An old man who called himself a Russian General lived in a poverty-stricken abode on the shores of the Yukon. Visiting him one day when the riverboat on which I was traveling tied up to take on wood, I was surprised to see frame after frame of mushrooms drying in the sun. We talked and finally the old-timer confided, "She loved mushrooms and truffles." When I inquired, he hobbled into his house beckoning me to follow. On the wall stood a full-length portrait of a handsome dark-eyed woman in a flowered, low cut dress. Something intense and indomitable emanated from her face; from the arch of her brows to her thin nose and expressive lips the woman dominated as she stared coldly from her portrait. The General, silently grinning like a schoolboy stood staring at the picture as if in a trance. Embarrassed, I asked him how he dried his mushrooms. Suddenly startled by my presence, the old man glowered and stormed from the room muttering, "Sun." Alone with the imperious woman and tablefuls of curing mushrooms, I knew that he was right. To dry mushrooms you simply set them in the sun for a few days then bring them inside until they are shriveled and tough as the cartilage of your ear.

211

Sun Drying

For sun drying, gather firm, ripe produce, wash, peel and cut if necessary and layer one layer thick on clean, dry trays. Trays may be made by stretching cheesecloth or netting over frames, tacking or sewing a drawstring hem, so that the cloth can be tightened; or they may be made of lathing or mats. Cover with netting to keep insects and dust from the food and place the trays in the direct sunlight, such as on the roof of a shed. Turn two or three times a day, take trays in at night. When the fruit is two-thirds dry, or when a handful is squeezed you feel no moisture and the food springs apart when you open your hand complete the drying indoors. Put the partially dried food into large containers set in a dry warm spot and stir 2 or 3 times a day for about a week. Pack and store in clean, moisture, insect and dirt-free containers and just before winter, heat produce in the oven 180°F (80°C) for 10 minutes. This kills lurking larvae. I use brown paper sacks inserted into coffee cans with a lid to store my dried produce; do not use plastic.

To Sulphur Fruit

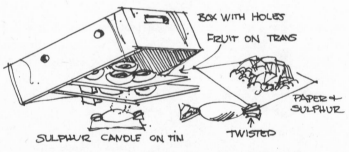

SULPHURING FRUIT BEFORE DRYING

Fruits may be sulphured to prevent insect attacks before being sun dried. To sulphur fruit place prepared fruit on nonmetal slotted or coarsely woven trays one layer deep. Out of doors, in a protected spot, put the bottom tray on bricks and stack the other trays one on top of the other about 1½ inches (4 cm) apart separated with bricks. Fumes must be able to circulate around the fruit. Prepare a sulphur candle by sprinkling 1 teaspoon (5 ml) powdered sulphur on a 6 inch (15 cm) square of newspaper, wrap as you would a cigar, twist ends, and place on a disposable pie tin. Get a box to cover the trays for sulphuring ready by poking 2 holes in the top and quickly set fire to the twist of paper, push the sulphur tin under the side of the tray stack and cover the stack with the box. Make sure that the flame is out but that the sulphur is smoldering before you turn your attention from the area. On a T.V. demonstration I sulphured apples, turned to talk with the show host, heard sirens from the sound effects man and looking back, saw my whole demonstration ablaze. During sulphuring, smoky fumes will filter around the trays and weep out of the holes in the top of the box. After the prescribed time in sulphur is completed—and you may have to relight your twist of paper several times—fruits should be sun dried as previously described.

To Steam Vegetables

Vegetables may be steamed to help retain food value and color before drying. To steam vegetables in preparation for sun drying them, shell, hull, peel or slice as required and suspend the prepared and loosely held food in steam above boiling water. The produce may be put into a basket and inserted into a larger pan containing about 1 inch (2.5 cm) water and a rack to keep the vegetable container out of the water. Or the vegetables may be tied loosely in a cloth and held above the water by connecting the sack to a stick laid across the top of a large kettle. Cover the kettle to keep in the steam. Vegetables should not touch water, they should be heated through, wilted, but not completely cooked. After the prescribed time in steam is completed—and you may have to add more water to the kettle—vegetables should be sun dried as previously described.

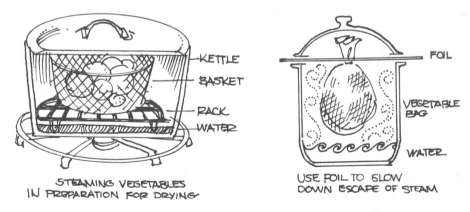

STEAMING VEGETABLES
IN PREPARATION FOR DRYING

USE FOIL TO SLOW
DOWN ESCAPE OF STEAM

Steam and sulphur times vary. A chart showing prescribed times as well as suggested treatment methods before sun drying fruit, follows.

CONDENSED DIRECTIONS FOR PREPARING AND SUN DRYING SOME FRUITS AND VEGETABLES

ITEM	Selection and Preparation	Treatment before Drying Method	Time in minutes	Tests for Dryness
FRUITS:				
Apples	Peel and core. Cut into slices or rings about ⅛ inch thick.	Sulphur	60	leathery; glove-like; section cut in half, no moist area in center
Pears	Peel, cut in half lengthwise and core. Section or cut into slices about ⅛ inch thick.	Sulphur	(60, sliced) (120, quartered)	springy feel
Large stone fruits	Peel and slice peaches. Cut in half and pit apricots, nectarines and large plums and prunes. Fruits dry more rapidly if cut in quarters or sliced.	Sulphur	(60, sliced) (120, quartered)	pliable; leathery; a handful of prunes properly dried will fall apart after squeezing
Berries (except strawberries)	Pick over, remove defective, wash.	Steam	½ to 1	hard; no visible moisture when crushed
Cherries	Pick over, remove defective, wash, pit.	No further treatment		leathery but sticky
Figs	If figs are small or have partly dried on the tree, they may be dried whole without blanching. Otherwise, cut in half.	Steam	20	leathery; flesh pliable; slightly sticky
Grapes	Only seedless varieties should be dried. Pick over, remove defective.	No further treatment		pliable; leathery

VEGETABLES:				
Asparagus	Cut tender green tips only.	Steam	4-5	brittle; greenish black
Beans — green snap	Remove defective pods. Wash and remove strings from string varieties. Split pods lengthwise to hasten drying.	Steam	15-20	brittle
Beets	Select small, tender beets of good color and flavor, free from woodiness; wash; trim the tops but leave the crowns; steam for 30-45 mins. until cooked through. Cool, trim off the roots and crowns, peel. Cut slices about ⅛" thick.	No further treatment		tough, leathery
Broccoli	Trim and cut as for serving. Wash. Quarter stalks lengthwise.	Steam	8-10	brittle
Cabbage	Remove outer leaves, quarter, and core. Cut into shreads about ⅛" thick.	Steam	5-6 wilt	tough to brittle
Green chili or Peppers	Use full grown pod, bright green. Peel and slit pod; remove seeds and dry.	No treatment		crisp; brittle; medium green
Red chili or peppers	Use mature pod, dark red. String and hang in sun.	No treatment		shrunken pod; flexible; dark red
Carrots, turnips, rutabagas	Select crisp, tender, free from woodiness. Wash. Trim off roots and tops. Peel thin. Cut into slices or strips about ⅛" thick.	Steam	8-10	tough, leathery
Corn, cut	Select tender sweet corn. Husk. Steam 10-15 min., or until milk is set. Cut from cob.	No further treatment		dry; brittle
Leaves for seasoning; celery; parsley	Wash.	No treatment		brittle

		No treatment		brittle; light colored
Onions, garlic	Remove outer discolored layers. Slice.			
Peas	Select young, tender peas of a sweet variety. Shell.	Steam immediately	10	hard; wrinkled; shatter when hit with a hammer
Potatoes	Peel, cut into shoestring strips 3/16″ in cross section, or cut into slices about 1/8″ thick.	Rinse in cold water steam	4-6	brittle
Spinach and other greens	Select young, tender leaves. Wash. See that leaves are not wadded when placed on trays. Cut large leaves crosswise into several pieces to facilitate drying.	Steam	4, or until thoroughly wilted	brittle
Squash	Wash, peel and slice in strips 1/4″ thick.	Steam	6	tough to brittle
Squash (Hubbard) Pumpkin, yellow	Cut into strips about 1″ wide. Peel off the rind. Scrape off the fiber and seeds. Cut peeled strips crosswise into pieces about 1/8″ thick.	Steam	Until tender	tough to brittle
Sweet potatoes	Wash, peel, trim and cut into 1/4″ slices (alternate method — steam before peeling).	Steam	Until tender	tough to brittle
Tomatoes for stewing	Select tomatoes of good color. Steam or dip in boiling water to loosen skins. Chill in cold water. Peel. Cut into sections, not over 3/4″ wide. Cut small pear or plum tomatoes in half.	No further treatment or may sulphur	10-20	leathery

This chart was compiled by Helen Strow, Extension Educationist with technical assistance of Dr. Evelyn Spindler, Federal Extension Service, for the U. S. Department of Agriculture pamphlet, *Sun Dry Your Fruits and Vegetables*.

Oven Dehydration

If the weather does not cooperate and it is impossible to sun dry fruits and vegetables, ovens may be used. In addition, I usually store my sun drying foods in the oven when I bring them in at night. There are hazards in using the oven for drying. One morning I snapped on the heat for biscuits and melted my favorite plastic drying racks. I had forgotten the fruits and when I smelled the awful odor, it was too late, plastic had dripped all over the oven racks and my plastic coated peaches did not look healthy either. Temperatures must be watched carefully in oven drying. Prepare, sulphur or steam fruits or vegetables as you would for sun drying. Work with small quantities and make trays that will fit in the oven. If a wood range is used, very little fuel is needed, the heat should not rise above 160°F (70°C). Gas and electric ovens should be preheated and set as low as they will go. The top element should be removed from an electric oven before preheating. Spread the prepared food evenly but sparingly over the trays. A lady wrote me saying that her dried apples had hatched tiny two-winged butterflies before springtime and she wanted to know what went wrong. Upon investigation we discovered that she had heaped a half bushel of sliced apples on a tray and oven dried them. No wonder when she opened her storage container a swarm of butterflies flew away. Her second mistake was in using a plastic canister; foods stored in plastic sweat, mold and hatch. Lightly loaded trays will dry faster and the trays should be stacked so that heat can circulate around them. Put a thermometer on the top tray and keep it as close to 160°F (70°C) as possible. Prop open the door of an electric oven about ½ inch (1 cm), gas and wood ranges may need to be opened farther to control temperatures and to let moisture out.

Commercial or homemade drying units using small fans and electric bulbs for heat are excellent if you live in a wet climate. Local Agriculture Department Extension services usually have plans and can supply data.

After fruits and vegetables have been treated with sulphur or steam and oven dried, store in containers that are moisture proof and that will keep wildlife out. Brown paper sacks and metal canisters are great.

I cannot think of food in a brown paper sack without remembering some crisp smoked herring eggs that a shy Indian maid brought to me in my Alaskan classroom. Later when I had a chance to thank her and her father, she told me this story: Long ago when the Russians owned Alaska, a soldier accused one of her relatives of stealing a sack of herring eggs. With abusive howls the Russian berated the Indian who steadfastly denied that he would steal. At length he was dragged before a tribunal. The judge listened to the complaint and asked the petrified Indian what he had to say. Showing his teeth as though laughing, the Indian did not reply. The judge ordered, "Shoot him," and dismissed court. Suddenly the accuser sobbed, "Mistake! There was no sack. I found the herring eggs. Everything is in error!" The soldier even knelt before the Indian begging forgiveness, but to no avail. Military discipline swept my narrator's kinsman to the execution. "God knows I do not steal," said the Indian quietly, adding, "Tell the Russian that I have already forgiven him." My student squeezed out a tear as she told me that she was glad that I had enjoyed the sack of herring eggs.

To Reconstitute Dried Food

To restore dried foods, cover with a small amount of cold water and soak in a covered pan until tender, from ½ to 6 hours. Cook the food in its soaking water, boil, saute or mix into stews or soups. A little sugar and a bit of lemon juice added to reconstituted fruit restores part of the fresh food flavor.

Peanuts

Peanuts, a nearly 25% protein food, are easy to grow if your garden is sandy and does not support woodchucks on welfare. Gather peanuts when mature, spread on trays in the sun and when dry, store in a cool, dry place. To roast peanuts place dried, unshelled nuts, one layer deep, in a flat pan and heat to about 300°F (150°C) for from 10 to 20 minutes. Test when cool and if still green flavored, return to the oven. Freshen stale peanuts the same way.

Peanut Butter Recipe

Shell roasted peanuts, remove skins and pass through a meat grinder several times. To every 3 cups (750 ml) of ground peanuts add ½ teaspoon (2 ml) salt and 2 tablespoons (30 ml) sugar. Grind several more times, pack into sterilized jars and seal. Peanut butter will keep well in the icebox; however, it will separate and must be stirred before use.

PEANUT BUTTER CUSTARD

Preparation time: 45 minutes. *Makes:* 4 servings, about 2 cups.

	U. S. CUSTOMARY	METRIC
In bowl beat	2 eggs	2 eggs
and stir in	1/3 cup peanut butter	80 ml peanut butter
When blended	1 1/3 cups skim or whole milk	330 ml milk
add and stir	3 tablespoons honey	45 ml honey
to mix	¾ teaspoon salt	3 ml salt

Pour into a small greased baking dish, set the dish in a pan of hot water and bake at 325°F (160°C) for about 30 minutes or until a knife inserted into the custard comes out clean. These small servings of custard are tasty with plain vanilla cookies.

PEANUT BUTTER PATTIES

A meat substitute dish, coarse ground nuts add texture.

Preparation time: 20 minutes. *Serves:* 5.

	U. S. CUSTOMARY	METRIC
Spread on bread	½ cup peanut butter	125 ml peanut butter
and cut into cubes	6 slices old bread	6 slices bread
Pour bread into	2 tablespoons onion, grated	30 ml onion
bowl and mix well	1 cup rice, cooked	250 ml rice, cooked
with	2 eggs	2 eggs
	1 teaspoon salt	5 ml salt
	1 teaspoon Worcestershire	5 ml Worcester-shire
	1 tablespoon catsup	15 ml catsup
	½ teaspoon paprika	2 ml paprika
	2 teaspoons parsley, chopped	10 ml parsley
	¼ cup water (approx.)	50 ml water
When blended	2 tablespoons flour	30 ml flour
sprinkle with		

Mix well, form into patties, add more water if necessary, dredge in flour and fry in oil until brown.

NUT CASSEROLE

Each fall when I am nut rich I substitute walnuts for part of the meat called for in casseroles.

	U.S. CUSTOMARY	METRIC
In skillet saute	1 onion, chopped	1 onion
	½ cup celery, chopped	125 ml celery
	1 tablespoon green pepper, chopped	15 ml green pepper
Add and cook slightly	1 cup hamburger or pork sausage	250 ml hamburger or sausage
	½ teaspoon powdered sage	3 ml sage
	¼ teaspoon black pepper	1 ml pepper
	1 teaspoon salt	5 ml salt
Mix in and stir vigorously	1 tablespoon flour	15 ml flour
	½ cup water	125 ml water
Blend with	1½ cups cooked rice	375 ml cooked rice
	½ cup chopped nuts or peanuts	125 ml chopped nuts

Pour into a greased casserole, top with a squiggle of catsup and bake at 350°F (175°C) for about 30 minutes.

All kinds of nuts may be used interchangeably, native nuts, commercial nuts or your old favorite nut and they all stretch the meat dollar, especially if your children gather or grow them for you. Nuts are best stored in the shell in a cool, squirrel-proof place because those little bushy tails are smarter than most Homo sapiens when it comes to nut stealing; they are expert thieves.

Dried Beans and Peas

Beans and peas, including soy beans may be dried and kept for home use in several ways: pick the pods as soon as they are mature and spread them in a warm, dry place until they are thoroughly dry; or pull the bean plants after most of the pods are ripe and pile or hang in a warm, dry place.

After drying, shell beans and peas and treat them to destroy weevils. They may be heated in the oven at 180°F (80°C) for 10 minutes or frozen at 0°F (minus 18°C) for 3 or 4 days.

Plain Cooked Beans

Soak overnight, drain, cover with water, bring to a boil and for every 2 cups (500 ml) beans add 1 teaspoon (5 ml) salt. Season with ½ pound (225

g) smoked corned beef or bacon and a chopped onion. When the beans are soft and you blow on a few in the spoon and their skins peel, remove from heat, taste, add pepper and more salt if needed. My family enjoys a soup bowl of beans with bean juice and thickly cut fresh bread and butter.

BLACK BEAN SOUP

Preparation time: Overnight plus 4 hours. *Serves:* 10.

U.S. CUSTOMARY	METRIC

Soak 2 cups (500 ml) dried black beans overnight, drain, cover with water.

	U.S. CUSTOMARY	METRIC
In skillet saute and add to beans	1 onion, chopped	1 onion
	1 stalk celery, chopped	1 celery
	3 tablespoons butter	45 ml butter
	¼ teaspoon dry mustard	1 ml dry mustard

Bring beans to a boil, salt and cayenne to taste, cover and simmer for 3 hours, or until beans are soft and soup is thick. Rub through a sieve (optional), reheat and serve garnished with chopped hard-boiled eggs and a slice of lemon on each plate.

BEAN NUT CHOWDER

Preparation time: Overnight plus 4 hours. *Serves:* 12.

U.S. CUSTOMARY	METRIC

Soak 2 cups (500 ml) dried lima beans overnight, drain, cover with water. Season with 2 teaspoons (10 ml) salt, lid and boil gently for 1 hour. Pour off water and save.

	U.S. CUSTOMARY	METRIC
In large pan arrange	half of the beans	half of the beans
	2 cups potatoes, sliced raw	500 ml potatoes
	1 cup onions, sliced	250 ml onions
	½ cup carrots, diced	125 ml carrots
	the remaining beans	the remaining beans

Sprinkle each layer with salt and pepper, return the bean liquid and simmer gently until all of the vegetables are done.

	U.S. CUSTOMARY	METRIC
Scald	1 quart milk	1 liter milk
In bowl mix with a little hot milk to form a paste	1 cup peanut butter	250 ml peanut butter

Add the paste to the simmering vegetables with the remaining hot milk, blend and serve. The secret to this mellow chowder is slow, gentle cooking.

DUTCH PEA SOUP

Preparation time: Overnight plus 4 hours. *Serves:* 10.

U.S. CUSTOMARY	METRIC

Soak 1 pound (500 g) dried split green peas overnight, drain, cover with water.

Add and boil	2 pig hocks or a shank	2 hocks
slowly for 1 hour	2 teaspoons salt	10 ml salt
Stir in	3 potatoes, raw, diced	3 potatoes
	6 onions, chopped	6 onions
	2 carrots, diced	2 carrots

Boil slowly until mushy, about 1 hour, put through sieve if desired, or serve immediately. We like pea soup with a spoonful of sauerkraut in the center of each bowl.

BEANS AND WIENERS

Preparation time: Overnight plus 3 hours. *Serves:* 10.

U.S. CUSTOMARY	METRIC

Soak 1 pound (500 g) dried beans overnight, drain, cover with water, add 2 teaspoons (10 ml) salt, put the lid on the pan and boil for 2 hours with a ham bone or a handful of bacon.

In a large, deep	6 cups cooked beans	1.5 liters beans
greased baking	3 tablespoons brown sugar	45 ml br. sugar
dish mix together	2 teaspoons prepared mustard	10 ml mustard
	1½ cups catsup	375 ml catsup
	½ teaspoon pepper	2 ml pepper
	salt if needed	salt

Add a little bean juice if the dish is too dry and top with 1 cup (250 ml) chopped onions. Poke wieners vertically into the beans, up and down so that only the top half shows. Bake at 325°F (160°C) for about 30 minutes until the wieners have split and the beans are bubbly red.

When I went to school, I soaked beans overnight, cooked them the next morning until I raced for the bus, let them stand, covered on the stove, fire off, until evening when I baked them with wieners for supper. The crown of meat, cockily poking from the baked beans makes a good-natured dish.

CHICK PEAS GARBANZOS

Preparation time: Overnight plus 4 hours. *Serves:* 4-5.

Soak 2 cups (500 ml) garbanzos overnight, drain, put into a loose cheesecloth sack and boil slowly in unsalted water for 3 hours. Remove from sack, salt to taste and serve with a Spanish sauce.

	U.S. CUSTOMARY	METRIC
In skillet saute until tender	1 large onion, chopped fine	1 onion
	3 cloves garlic, minced	3 garlic
	1 green pepper, chopped	1 pepper
	3 tablespoons olive oil	45 ml olive oil
Add and simmer for 30 minutes	2 cups tomatoes	500 ml tomatoes
	1 tablespoon chili powder	15 ml chili powder
	dash of thyme, rosemary and a few grains of cumin	seasoning

Pour sauce over about 2 cups (500 ml) of the cooked garbanzos, simmer briefly and serve with a huge roughly torn green salad topped with anchovies and wedges of cheese. Dress the salad with a flurry of garlic powder, olive oil and vinegar. Refrigerate the remaining garbanzos for a tart Four Bean Salad another day.

Lima Beans

Spread lima beans to dry in their shells when gathered green as for summer use. When the weather is damp they may be dried indoors but generally limas are dried outside under a tree on a table or box; direct sunlight will bleach and harden limas. Take your beans inside if it looks like rain; one year I had popped limas all over the yard as the dried shells curled and opened in a downpour. Dried lima beans should be soaked overnight, drained, covered with salted water, 1½ teaspoons (8 ml) to the quart, and simmered for 2 or 3 hours. My family likes me to hide browned pork chops in a casserole of partly cooked limas, dress the dish with ½ cup (125 ml) catsup, ⅓ cup (80 ml) molasses, salt and pepper, and bake the beans and pork chops for 1½ hours. I use part of the juice from the boiled limas when I mix in the catsup, the rest is saved to moisten the casserole if needed as it bakes, uncovered in a 350°F (175°C) oven.

To Cook Rice

Rice was as versatile a staple in the stillrooms of last century as it is in today's kitchen. To cook rice, wash it in warm water, then in cold and sprinkle the rice into salted boiling water. Boil steadily without a lid for

20 minutes. Drain, shake well and pour back into the saucepan. With the pan lid partly off, set the rice where it will keep warm but not cook. Allow the rice to dry for about 5 minutes; the moisture will evaporate and the grains of rice will be separated. Save cooking water for soup or breadmaking.

Fried Rice

Fry minced pieces of leftover pork or bacon in a skillet. When it starts to brown, add a finely chopped onion and saute. When the onion is clear add cooked, drained and salted rice, fluff with fork, season with 3 or 4 dashes of soy sauce, pepper and serve immediately.

RICE PUDDING

Preparation time: 1 hour. *Makes:* 4 cups.

	U.S. CUSTOMARY	METRIC
In a large bowl mix	3 cups cooked rice, drained	750 ml cooked rice
	3 tablespoons butter	45 ml butter
	1 cup sugar	250 ml sugar
	1 teaspoon cinnamon	5 ml cinnamon
	½ teaspoon salt	3 ml salt
	1 teaspoon grated nutmeg	5 ml nutmeg
Beat separately	4 eggs	4 eggs
Mix in and beat together	1 quart milk or lt. cream	1 liter milk
	1 teaspoon vanilla	5 ml vanilla
Combine rice, milk mix and add	½ cup raisins or dried elderberries	125 ml raisins

Pour into a buttered baking dish and bake at 350°F (175°C) for 45 minutes or until well set and brown on top. Oh so good!

RICE MEAT BALLS

Preparation time: 30 minutes. *Makes:* 50 meatballs.

	U.S. CUSTOMARY	METRIC
In large bowl combine and knead with hands	3 cups rice, cold, cooked	750 ml rice
	1 pound ground meat	500 g ground meat
	1 onion, chopped	1 onion
	1 garlic clove, minced	1 garlic
	4 teaspoons Worcestershire	20 ml Worcestershire
	½ teaspoon oregano	2 ml oregano
	¼ teaspoon pepper	1 ml pepper

	1 teaspoon caraway seed	5 ml caraway seed
	salt to taste	salt
When blended add	2 eggs	2 eggs
	4 tablespoons flour	60 ml flour

Sprinkle the flour into the meat while stirring. Press into meatballs and brown the balls in a lightly greased skillet. Cover with your favorite tomato or barbecue sauce and simmer on a low fire for 20 minutes. I have cooked half of this recipe as meat balls and baked half in a meat loaf. Very nice.

Rice Salad

Combine 3 cups (750 ml) cooked rice with chopped onion, celery, pickle, hard-boiled eggs, mayonnaise and press down firmly into custard cups. Unmold on lettuce and garnish with tomato wedges and sour cream dressed with chopped chives.

Rice Cakes

If you are out of bread and have leftover cooked rice in the icebox bake Rice Cakes for supper. Mix until well blended 2 cups (500 ml) boiled rice, 1 cup (250 ml) milk or water, 1 tablespoon (15 ml) melted butter or oil, 1 teaspoon (5 ml) salt and about ¾ cup (175 ml) flour. Using a tablespoon, spoon onto a well greased cookie tin and bake at 425°F (220°C) for 10 to 15 minutes.

Cornmeal Dishes

Cereal grain foods were a staple of the stillroom and quick breads always go well with supper.

MEAL BREAD

My neighbor baked this cornmeal bread in a skillet.

Preparation time: 1 hour.

	U.S. CUSTOMARY	METRIC
In a bowl mix	2 cups cornmeal	500 ml cornmeal
	1 teaspoon baking soda	5 ml baking soda
	½ cup flour	125 ml flour
	1 teaspoon salt	5 ml salt

Stir in quickly,	2 cups sour milk	500 ml sour milk
waste no time	2 eggs beaten	2 eggs
pouring into a	2 tablespoons oil	30 ml oil
greased skillet	¼ cup molasses or sugar	50 ml molasses

Bake at 375°F (190°C) for about 50 minutes.

CUSH

Leftover cornbread soup that is thick and warming on a winter night.

Preparation time: 10 minutes. *Serves:* 4.

	U.S. CUSTOMARY	METRIC
In skillet saute	1 onion, minced	1 onion
	3 tablespoons bacon drip.	45 ml drippings
Mix in, lower heat and brown	2 cups crumbled cornbread	500 ml cornbread
Blend in	2 cups milk	500 ml milk
	salt and pepper to taste	salt, pepper

Scald but do not boil, stir so that the cush will not scorch and serve hot with a pat of butter on top.

Tamale Pie

Preparation time: 1¼ hours. *Serves:* 6.

Make a cornmeal mush by blending 1 cup (250 ml) cornmeal into 1½ cups (375 ml) cold water and stirring the mixture into 1½ cups boiling water. Add 1½ teaspoons (8 ml) salt. Mix cornmeal in cold water so that it will not cook prematurely and lump. Stir the mush continually until it comes to a boil, lower heat because it will send out little spurts of mush, burn you and dirty the stove. Cook for 3 minutes, remove from heat and stir in ½ teaspoon (3 ml) garlic powder, 4 teaspoons (20 ml) chili powder and ⅛ teaspoon (0.5 ml) cumin. Taste. Season more highly if desired. Pour half of the seasoned mush into a well greased baking pan, add the filling, cover with the rest of the cornmeal mush, top with cheese if you wish and bake at 350°F (175°C) for 30 minutes.

CHILI FILLING

	U.S. CUSTOMARY	METRIC
In skillet, chop and brown	½ pound ground beef	225 g ground beef
	1 onion, large	1 onion
	½ green pepper	½ green pepper
	1 clove garlic	1 clove garlic

Season with	2 tablespoons chili powder	30 ml chili powder
	¼ teaspoon cumin	1 ml cumin
	salt and pepper to taste	salt, pepper
Mix in and	2 cups corn, drained	500 ml corn
simmer for 30	2 cups tomatoes	500 ml tomatoes
minutes	¼ cup catsup	50 ml catsup
	2 cups kidney beans, cook	500 ml cooked beans

Pour into the cornmeal mush-lined pan, cover with the seasoned mush, bake.

I have substituted chicken broth for the liquid in the mush, seasoned it with celery salt and black pepper and made a filling with bits of cooked chicken, peas, chopped celery and briefly sauteed onion. Topped with the chicken broth mush, this makes a mild mannered meal.

Sometimes I season the cornmeal mush with 1 teaspoon (5 ml) sage and black pepper and make the Tamale Pie filling of scraps of cooked pork, a cup (250 ml) of sauteed onions and season with pepper, salt and sage. Topped with a layer of sagey mush this tastes like scrapple.

CHILI STACKS

Preparation time: 40 minutes. *Serves:* 6.

Make corn patty Stacks by frying batter into cakes 6 inches (15 cm) across.

	U.S. CUSTOMARY	METRIC
In large bowl,	1 cup flour	250 ml flour
mix and add	2 teaspoons baking powder	10 ml baking
milk or water		powder
to make a	3 cups cornmeal	750 ml cornmeal
medium thin	1 teaspoon salt	5 ml salt
batter	4 tablespoons oil	50 ml oil
	2 eggs	2 eggs

Keep hot by putting the Stack in a warm oven.

STACK SAUCE

In skillet chop	1 pound hamburger	500 g hamburger
and brown	1 onion, large	1 onion
	1 green pepper, cleaned	1 green pepper
Season with	1 clove garlic, minced	1 garlic
	1½ teaspoons salt	8 ml salt
	2 tablespoons chili powder	30 ml chili powder
	½ teaspoon cumin	3 ml cumin
	2 teaspoons sugar	10 ml sugar
	¼ teaspoon black pepper	1 ml pepper
Mix in, boil	1 quart tomatoes	1 liter tomatoes

In cup blend	½ cup water	125 ml water
and add to	1 teaspoon soy sauce	5 ml soy sauce
the briskly	2 tablespoons flour or	30 ml flour, tapioca
cooking sauce	instant tapioca	

Cook until thickened and serve by stacking 3 patties alternately with a little sauce, pancake fashion on each plate and top with a big spoonful of sauce. Chili Stacks make a welcome supper for a gang of teenagers who possess a gang of hollow legs. They love them.

Biscuits

I grew up thinking that girls just naturally knew how to make biscuits, as boys knew how to fix bikes, until my daughter asked me how to make them.

Sweet and Sour Milk Substitution

Sweet milk may be substituted for recipes calling for sour milk by adding 1½ tablespoons (25 ml) vinegar to each cup (250 ml) milk. Sour milk may be substituted for recipes calling for sweet milk by adding ½ teaspoon (2 ml) baking soda to each cup of sour milk.

LIGHT'NING BISCUITS

The key to making good biscuits is to work fast.
Preparation time: 25 minutes. *Makes:* 24 biscuits.

	U.S. CUSTOMARY	METRIC
In bowl mix	2 cups flour	500 ml flour
thoroughly	2 teaspoons baking powder	10 ml baking powder
	1 tablespoon sugar	15 ml sugar
	¾ teaspoon salt	4 ml salt
Add, rub with hands to form little peas	⅓ cup solid shortening	80 ml shortening
Quickly stir in	¾ cup milk, approx.	175 ml milk

Add just enough milk to make a soft, but not sticky dough. Drop by spoonfuls onto a greased cookie tin or roll quickly to about ½ inch (1 cm) thick, cut into circles and place on a baking sheet. Bake at 450°F (230°C) for 10 to 15 minutes.

Biscuit Variations

If you wish a quickie shortcake to serve under fresh fruits, use the Light'ning Biscuit recipe but substitute ½ cup (125 ml) solid shortening for the given amount and add 2 tablespoons (30 ml) more sugar.

Cheese Biscuits are made by adding 1 cup (250 ml) grated cheese to the dry ingredients in the above recipe. Serve under creamed mushrooms.

Peanut Butter Biscuits may be baked by adding 4 tablespoons (60 ml) peanut butter to the shortening, then blending into the dry ingredients in the above recipe.

SCOTCH OATCAKES

As a hungry 'teen, my daughter used to barge into the house after school, whip up a batch of Oatcakes and sit munching a half dozen of them as she reviewed her day in the outside world.

Preparation time: 25 minutes. *Makes:* 2 dozen.

	U.S. CUSTOMARY	METRIC
In bowl mix	1 cup flour	250 ml flour
	1 tablespoon sugar	15 ml sugar
	1 teaspoon baking powder	5 ml baking powder
	½ teaspoon salt	3 ml salt
	2 cups quick oats	500 ml quick oats
	½ cup melted butter	125 ml butter, melted
Blend in	½ cup milk, approx.	125 ml milk

When well mixed, divide dough into 6 parts. Roll each part into a 5 inch (12 cm) circle. Cut each circle into 4 pie-slice sections or triangles with one rounded side. Bake at 450°F (230°C) on a greased pan for 15 minutes.

OATMEAL CASSEROLE

If you do not care for meat, this dish is flavorful and nutritious.

Preparation time: 45 minutes. *Serves:* 4.

	U.S. CUSTOMARY	METRIC
Chop and saute	1 onion	1 onion
	¼ cup mushrooms	50 ml mushrooms
	¼ cup butter	50 ml butter
In bowl mix	1 cup toasted bread cubes	250 ml bread cubes
	½ cup milk	125 ml milk
	3 eggs, well beaten	3 eggs
	1 cup oatmeal, cooked	250 ml oatmeal
	1 cup chopped nuts	250 ml nuts

½ teaspoon salt	3 ml salt
3 tablespoons parsley, minced	45 ml parsley
¼ teaspoon sage	1 ml sage
¼ teaspoon black pepper	1 ml pepper
3 tablespoons catsup	45 ml catsup
the sauteed onions and mushrooms	onions and mushrooms

Blend well, add more milk if needed to moisten, pour into a greased casserole and bake at 350°F (175°C) for 30 minutes or until the peaks of toasted bread are brown.

To Steam Wheat

Early day cooks steamed whole grain wheat by putting 1 cup (250 ml) wheat into a casserole pan together with 2 cups (500 ml) water or stock, 1 teaspoon (5 ml) salt, and they placed the uncovered casserole on a rack in a large steamer kettle. They put an inch or so of water in the kettle, covered the steam kettle tightly, brought it to a boil and steamed the wheat for about an hour. Fire off, they let the wheat set in its unlidded casserole in the covered kettle until morning. If the wheat had not absorbed all of its water they steamed it for about 30 minutes before seasoning it with cream and honey. If the steamed wheat was to be used as a potato substitute it was flavored with minced parsley and butter. Steamed whole grain wheat was often used in pilaf or in chicken casseroles. Chewy and satisfying, steamed wheat has a nut-like flavor. Whole grain rye was often steamed in the same manner.

Double Boiler Steamed Grains

Using the ratio of 4 cups (1 liter) water, 1 teaspoon (5 ml) salt to 1 cup (250 ml) whole grain or coarsely cracked oats, corn or wheat, bring the salted water to a rapid boil, sprinkle in the grain and cook for 5 minutes, stirring constantly. Put the pan of boiling grain over boiling water in a double boiler, cover and steam or simmer 4 hours or overnight if you have a cook stove.

Bulgur Wheat

Bulgur wheat, a partially cooked and toasted cereal, was made by steaming wheat, thinly spreading the swollen grains on a cookie tin and drying the wheat in a low oven, 200°F (95°C) for 2 to 3 hours, or until it was very dry and could be easily cracked, like toasted old maids in a batch of pop corn. Some people dried bulgur wheat by placing the cookie trays in the sun and it took 3 or 4 days. Wheat chaff was removed by slightly wetting the surface of the grain and rubbing the kernels between the palms of the hands as if praying. I have done this in my youth and it is fun to blow the chaff on your companion. Bulgur wheat was usually cracked using a medium blade on the grinder and grain was stored in dry crocks under a tin lid. Used in meat dishes, chili, chicken and Middle East recipes, bulgur adds a delicious flavor and texture.

Sprouted Wheat

Wash 1 cup (250 ml) of long grain wheat in several waters and divide it into two quart jars. Cover each portion with 1 cup (250 ml) of room temperature water. After tying a nylon stocking over the bottle opening soak the wheat overnight. Drain and shake the jar to remove excess moisture. Set the jar upside down against the edge of a saucer to allow for drainage and air and cover the whole contraption with a brown paper sack. Sprouts are like some people, they like a dark, warm and misty moisty place. Rinse the sprouting wheat with fresh, room temperature water each morning and night and return the jars to their upside down position under the sack on the kitchen counter. Wheat begins to sprout in about 4 days and it is best eaten when the growth is as long as the grain. Store extra sprouts in the refrigerator for not more than a week and eat them fresh in salads, baked into rolls, cooked into meatballs or briefly sauteed in Chinese food.

Soybeans

Soybeans outrank all legumes in protein content — 38% — and they rank high in other nutrients too; no wonder they are looked upon as a future meat substitute in many diets. Soybeans do not sprout as readily as wheat, but they use the same process and scientists tell us that if you can get them to sprout, they sprout into a very rich source of vitamin C. Use the current year's crop, Illini, Richland or Chief varieties, and drain them extra carefully for best results. Eaten raw, in soups, sandwiches or in casseroles they remind me of fresh peanuts.

To Cook Soybeans

Many people suggest that soybeans should be washed, soaked overnight in the refrigerator, drained and ground through the medium blade of the food chopper before being simmered in water to cover. Salt soybeans, 1 teaspoon (5 ml) salt per quart (liter) of water and cook the presoaked and ground beans for about 2 hours. Of course this does not produce whole beany beans but it makes soybeans more digestible. Presoaked beans may be simply covered with water, daubed with butter, salted and simmered until tender but it is a lengthy process and soybeans have a tendency to resent long hot sessions and they stick. Cooked in a pressure cooker, using the manufacturer's directions, soybeans become tender hearted in about an hour. Cooked soybeans, either ground or whole may be used interchangeably in most bean recipes and they are especially interesting in meatloaf.

SOY MEATLOAF

A fine way to stretch a pittance of meat and I have used other beans than soybeans with good results, too.

Preparation time: 1 hour. *Serves:* 5.

	U.S. CUSTOMARY	METRIC
In a large bowl combine	½ pound ground meat	225 g ground meat
	2 cups cooked soybeans	500 ml soybeans
	1 cup soft breadcrumbs	250 ml breadcrumbs
	1 onion, chopped fine	1 onion
	2 eggs	2 eggs
	3 tablespoons oil	45 ml oil
	2 tablespoons catsup	30 ml catsup
	1 tablespoon soy sauce	15 ml soy sauce
	1 teaspoon Worcestershire	5 ml Worcestershire
	2 tablespoons parsley, chop.	30 ml parsley
	1 teaspoon salt	5 ml salt
	¼ teaspoon pepper	1 ml pepper
	¼ teaspoon celery salt	1 ml celery salt

Mix with a spoon, later with your hands until everything is well blended. Add bean juice if you have it, skim milk or water, about ½ cup (125 ml) to lubricate the ingredients and meld them all together. Place 2 hard-boiled eggs in the center and form the meat mixture around the eggs. Transfer to a greased loaf pan, top with a squiggle of catsup and bake at 350°F (175°C) for about 45 minutes. Serve with baked winter squash such as butternut that has been halved, seeds removed and dressed with butter, honey, a sprinkle of sesame seeds and a flurry of mace. A shredded cabbage and carrot salad with French dressing, hot, dark bread and strawberry pie completes this good meal.

Tea — A Toast to the Health of the Earth

Although teas from the East Indies were popular during stillroom days the handpicked, rolled and roasted leaves were basically a rich man's drink. Ordinary people foraged for New Jersey Tea, *Ceanothus Americanus*, Sweet Goldenrod, *Solidago odora*, and Linden flowers. On a bright day, tea branches were snapped off just before the plants came into flower or while they were blooming, tied loosely into bunches, and dried by hanging from stillroom rafters. Being tall, I can remember catching my hair in the tea and I often wondered how much of my hair was later, unknowingly, brewed.

When the native tea leaves dried to crispness they were picked from the stalk and roasted on sieves in the oven, 160°F (70°C) for about 10 minutes; the leaves were then stored in brown paper bags, labeled and shoved into tightly lidded jars.

One of my favorite teas is a blend of strawberry leaves and rose petals. And though I have been brewing various things since I was very young, a neighbor recently instructed me on the art of brewing tea. A good cup of tea, she emphasized, starts with properly boiled water. Do not boil water longer than 4 minutes because it becomes 'dead'. In brewing beverage teas, 1 teaspoon (5 ml) of tea is allowed per cup (250 ml). Boiling water is poured over the leaves and allowed to steep for 4 minutes before being served piping hot.

Some wild teas are so volatile that their essence escapes into the air simply by infusing them in boiling water. Distillation would capture the elixir, but short of distilling tea, if you place a saucer over the cup immediately after covering the tea leaves with water, the essence will drip back into the cup.

As a reference I have listed common medicinal teas as well as native beverage herbs that were grown in kitchen gardens or found in fields. The preparation of medicine from foraged or home grown herbs was an accepted stillroom chore. Many teas were reduced by distillation and the elixir was bottled for later use. The caution with regard to use of native teas and herbals is to IDENTIFY FIRST. Discovery is a fascinating and thrilling experience but it can also reduce the unwary to violent stomach cramps or worse if they don't know what they are brewing.

As Schiller might have written:

Would man purge his heart of tiredness
    And achieve his own true worth,
He must pause and sip with gladness
    Tea, a hearty toast to the health of the earth.

Native Teas: Beverage and Medicinal

Common Name.	Botanical Name.	Part Used.	Used For.
APPLE	*Malus* species	Dried peelings	Beverage
BALM	*Melissa officinalis*	Dried leaves	Cooling drink
BASIL	*Ocimum basilicum*	Fresh leaves	Nervous headache
BIRCH, Sweet	*Betula lenta*	New leaves, buds	Beverage
BONESET	*Eupatorium perfoliatum*	Leaves	Mild laxative
BORAGE	*Borago officinalis*	Leaves and stalks	Sore throat
CATNIP	*Nepeta cataria*	Leaves	Sedative
CELERY	*Apium graveolens*	Leaves	Rheumatism
CLOVER	*Trifolium*	Flowers	Beverage
COMFREY	*Symphytum officinalis*	Root and leaves	Cold, bronchitis
COWSLIP	*Primula veris*	Dried flowers	Sedative
DANDELION	*Taraxacum officinalis*	Roots	Laxative, tonic
ELDER	*Sambucus nigra*	Flowers	Cold, bronchitis
EYEBRIGHT	*Euphrasia officinalis*	Herb	Hay fever
HEMLOCK TREE	*Tsuga canadensis*	Young twigs	Vitamin C
LABRADOR TEA	*Ledum palustre*	Leaves	Beverage
LETTUCE	*Lactuca*	Leaves	Sedative
MALLOW, Dwarf	*Malva*	Seeds	Cough and throat
MULLEIN	*Verbascum thapsus*	Leaves	Colds
NETTLE	*Urtica dioica*	Leaves	Beverage and tonic
PARSLEY	*Petroselinum*	Herb	Beverage and tonic
PERSIMMON	*Diospyros Virginiana*	Leaves	Vitamin C
PLANTAIN	*Plantago lanceolate*	Seeds, leaves	Laxative, tonic
ROSEMARY	*Rosmarinus officinalis*	Leaves, flowers	Tonic
SAGE	*Salvia officinalis*	Leaves	Calmative
SPEEDWELL	*Veronica officinalis*	Leaves	Beverage
STRAWBERRY	*Fragaria Virginiana*	Leaves	Beverage
SUNFLOWER	*Helianthus*	Leaves	Beverage
TARRAGON	*Artemisia Dracunculus*	Leaves	Cough, throat
THISTLE	*Centaurea benedicta*	Herb	Tonic
THYME	*Thymus vulgaris*	Herb	Hangover
VERVAIN	*Verbena officinalis*	Leaves	Calmative beverage
WORMWOOD	*Artemisia absinthium*	Herb	Worms and moths
YAM	*Dioscorea villos*	Root	Sedative
YARROW	*Achillea Millefolium*	Herb	Stimulant
YELLOW DOCK	*Rumex crispus*	Root	Mild laxative
YERBA SANTA	*Monarda didyma*	Herb	Soothing beverage

X

Preserving Stillroom Produce

R itual is necessary to open and close doors in our lives but most ritual seems to be not so much for the benefit of participants as it is for the peripheral people. The ritual of preserving produce is no exception. A cucumber sees little significance in the ritual of graduating into picklehood; but to the pickler, the pickle eater and the crocked pickle society, proper graduation is important. It saves the cucumber from spoiling.

Fermented and Salted Food

Fermenting and salting vegetables to keep them from spoiling was a routine chore in stillroom days. When surplus food could not be preserved by drying or canning, many pioneer families immersed vegetables in brine similar to that used in making sauerkraut. Salt firms and preserves produce by drawing out juices, and when working with vegetables, the sugary juices serve as food for lactic acid bacteria which convert the sugars into acid. Brine cured vegetables change color and taste just as cabbage changes into sauerkraut. The idea is to maintain a brine strong enough to retard spoilage and weak enough to permit fermentation.

Equipment needed for brining and pickling are: jars, crocks or plastic buckets, cloths, paraffin and canning jars. Ingredients are: plain salt, vinegar, sugar and spices. Pickling or fermenting vegetables requires three steps: 1. The vegetables are put down in salt which may be added over a period of time in order to permit fermentation. If salt is added all at once, fermentation does not take place and vegetables are salty and in time will mush and spoil. 2. The salt fermented vegetables are leached of part of their salt so that they may be flavored differently, or in some cases, cooked. 3. The fermented product, its preserving salt removed, must be sealed in either paraffin or by canning. Pickles are usually flavored with vineagar and spices after the salt has been leached and they are then sealed.

Fermenting Pickles

To ferment pickles, pack 10 pounds (5 kg) cucumbers in a nonmetal container such as a crock or plastic bucket and cover with a brine made by dissolving 2.8 cups (700 ml) salt in 6 quarts (6 liters) water. Cover the cucumbers to keep them submerged by using an upside down plate that will fit inside the bucket and weighting the plate with a rock. The following day add plain salt to the brine by piling it on the covering plate at the rate of 2 cups (500 ml) salt to every 10 pounds cucumbers. The salt will weep into the liquid through the space around the plate and will maintain the strength of the brine. One week later, and at the end of each succeeding week for 5 weeks, add ½ cup (125 ml) salt to the plate. Always place the salt on the pickle covering so that it will slowly weep into the brine. Ferment at 85°F (30°C) and skim regularly. At the end of 5 weeks if you wish to hold the salted cucumbers in brine, cover the area between the plate and the side of the bucket or container with melted paraffin. Pour on a second layer after the first has hardened to insure a seal and keep the salted cucumbers in a cool place.

Leaching Pickles

After salting or curing in brine has been completed pickles must be leached of salt, or processed in water to remove excess salt to make them edible. Do this by covering them with water, heating the water to about 120°F (50°C), hot to the touch and uncomfortable to keep your hand in, and hold the leaching pickles at that temperature overnight. Repeat the process until the pickles are only slightly salty. They may be eaten as plain salted pickles that taste somewhat like green olives, or they may be sealed into jars. Leached pickles may be further processed into sour, sweet pickles or relish.

Sour Pickles

Sour pickles are made by covering the drained leached pickles with 45 to 50 grain strength vinegar, held a few days and eaten or sealed. If kept, the vinegar must be renewed by throwing off the diluted liquid and adding fresh. This is necessary because unsealed pickles are in a constant state of change, withdrawing and excreting liquid. These sour pickles tweak bland meals like an enthusiastic person spirits a lethargic gathering. Covered with vinegar of the proper strength, sour pickles keep well.

Sweet Pickles

After being leached of excessive salt, pickles are immersed in vinegar, 45 to 50 grain strength, for 1 week. Discard the diluted vinegar and cover the pickles with a sweet liquid. Heat 1 gallon (4 liters) vinegar and add 8 cups (2 liters) sugar and 4 tablespoons (60 ml) mixed pickling spices that have been tied in a bag. Do not boil but keep the liquid just under simmer for 10 minutes. Allow the sweetened vinegar to cool before covering the pickles. Seal into jars or after a few days these sweet pickles may be eaten straight from the bucket. Children love them.

Dill Pickles: Cucumbers, Green Bean or Green Tomato Dills

Dill pickles are generally not made from the leached fermented pickles because the delicate flavor of dill does not stand up well with them. Green or dried dill, the herb or seeds may be used for flavoring dill pickles, and because of the weaker brine, the vegetables must be sealed with paraffin or by canning when fermentation is complete. In the bottom of a bucket or a crock place a layer of grape leaves, a layer of dill and 2 tablespoons (30 ml) mixed pickling spices. Fill container with briefly washed cucumbers, do not let them stand in water. The container may be filled with washed and stemmed whole green beans or with washed green tomatoes. After every 4 inches (10 cm) of vegetables, repeat layers of dill, spices and grape leaves; top the crock with a layer of dill and spices and a heavy layer of grape leaves. Make a brine by dissolving 2 cups (500 ml) salt in 2 gallons (8 liters) water and 2 cups (500 ml) vinegar and pour it over the layered vegetables and spices. Cover with an upside down dinner plate and a rock to hold the pickles under brine. Ferment at 86°F (30°C) for about 2 weeks. Watch carefully after the 10th day. If no bubbles or other signs of action are present seal the pickles by pouring paraffin around the exposed edges of the covering, or seal them in hot, sterilized jars or set the crock in the middle of a neighborhood picnic gathering and eat them. I seal jars of pickles with a couple of layers of melted paraffin and they keep nicely in a cool place. For a more permanent seal bring pickle juice to a boil, cool to about 160°F (70°C), pack the pickles into hot, sterilized jars and cover with their own hot pickle juice to within ½ inch (1 cm) of the top. Dill and spices may be added to each jar before it is sealed. The important step is to catch your pickles just as they graduate into picklehood, which you discover by nibbling an end or two, and to transfer them into their new life in jars at the right moment.

I have heard of people pickling immature corn on the cob, small okra, baby eggplant, burr gherkins and thrice-boiled young milkweed pods in the same way in which dills are fermented. I am tender on motherhood and cannot bring myself to incarcerating babies; pods or cobs.

Peppers and cauliflower may be fermented as described in Fermenting Pickles, but the peppers should be cleaned of seeds and halved first, and the cauliflower heads separated. After leaching peppers and cauliflower in the manner described they may be used as you would fresh produce, or preserved in a brine made by dissolving 4⅓ cups (1 liter, generous) salt in 6 quarts (6 liters) water. Cover the vegetables and keep under brine with a plate and rock, and leach before use.

In extreme emergencies vegetables and fruits may be simply salted by mixing them with ¼ their weight in salt and if they do not make enough brine to cover, add brine by dissolving 2 cups (500 ml) salt in 2 quarts (2 liters) water. Leach before use as described. Corn may be straight salted in this manner, but unless you wish to end up with awfully salty moonshine makings, "set the milk" first by boiling the corn on the cob for 10 minutes before cutting the corn from the cob and mixing the kernels with ¼ of their weight in salt.

Sauerkraut

Because I had dozens of cabbages and dozens of eager students I put them together one year and made sauerkraut. Every passerby, from tramps along the railroad to the school superintendent, stopped to inquire about the smell. One bewhiskered prospector volunteered to take any excess sauerkraut juice off my hands. "Best thing in the world for a hangover," he told me. My students made about 20 gallons, sold it at 25¢ a quart and had enough money for a basketball loop which the boys constructed.

Select sound heads of cabbage, quarter, and using the core as a handle, shred to desired fineness. Weigh the cabbage. In a dishpan mix 3¼ tablespoons (50 ml) salt to every 5 pounds (2.5 kg) cabbage. Pack firmly, but not too tightly, in a stone jar or plastic bucket. Cover the surface with cheesecloth, an upside down plate which fits inside the container, and weight with a rock. Throw a towel over the whole thing and set at room temperature for 10 to 12 days. Skim if necessary. When fermentation is complete, keep in a cool place that is free from varmints (I have heard of a mouse that was addicted to kraut), and eat your proud product as needed. You may wish to seal the top by pouring melted paraffin around the edge of the plate. For a more complete seal and handier packaging, simmer the finished kraut for 10 minutes, pack into hot, sterilized canning jars, fill to within ½ inch (1 cm) of the top with brine and can. If there is not enough brine to fill the jars properly make brine by diluting 2 tablespoons (30 ml) salt in 1 quart (1 liter) water, and adding it to the top of each jar. If preferred, process the quarts in a Boiling Water Bath for 10 minutes and store the sealed jars in a cool, dark place.

I have 'krauted' carrots by using the same recipe. Carrots should be slivered or shredded with a potato peeler or a kraut cutter and processed in the same manner as cabbage. Eaten raw as relish, or heated, carrot kraut is a nice change.

If any of your kraut turns out to be too salty, empty it in a colander and run cold water over it for a minute.

SQUASH PICKLE

Select summer squash: zucchini, yellow crookneck or patty pan that are tender, that is, their skins can be easily pierced with the fingernail, cut in half, scoop out the pulp, cut into 1 inch (2.5 cm) pieces, boil about 5 minutes and drain. Make a pickling solution at the ratio of 1 pint (500 ml) juice for every quart (liter) pickles.

	U.S. CUSTOMARY	METRIC
In pan bring to boil	1 quart vinegar	1 liter vinegar
	3 tablespoons salt	45 ml salt
	3 cups sugar	750 ml sugar
Add and cook 5 minutes	the squash	squash

Pack the squash cubes into pint jars, add ½ teaspoon (2 ml) pickling spice, ½ teaspoon (2 ml) lemon juice and a pinch of alum to each jar. Fill jars to within ½ inch (1 cm) of the top with boiling pickle solution, wipe rim with a sterile cloth — dip it in gin or in boiling water — and seal. Process pints for 10 minutes in a Boiling Water Bath and store in a cool, dark place.

PICKLED PEARS

U.S. CUSTOMARY	METRIC

Make a pickle solution at the ratio of 1 pint (500 ml) juice for every quart (liter) pears.

In large pan boil	1 quart vinegar	1 liter vinegar
	½ cup water	125 ml water
	2 cups sugar	500 ml sugar
	4 tablespoons pickling	60 ml pickling spice
	spice tied in bag	
	1 lemon peeling slivered	1 lemon peel

Peel pears or do not peel, as you wish; process whole with stems or halved. Boil 5 minutes and let stand in the pickle solution overnight. The next morning remove pears, and if whole, prick skins. Boil the syrup for 10 minutes, add the pears and boil until tender, about 30 minutes. Let stand in pickle solution overnight the second time. The next morning remove the spice bag, squeeze. Heat syrup and the pears to boiling, pack pears into hot, sterilized jars, poke 1 inch (2.5 cm) of cinnamon stick and 2 whole cloves into each jar and fill to within ½ inch (1 cm) of the top with boiling syrup, wipe rim and seal at once.

Pickled Peaches

Clingstone peaches may be pickled in the same way as pears except that the amount of sugar is halved and the cooking time is 15 minutes. Slip off peach skins by immersing them in boiling water and then into cold.

Tom's Hot Pepper Rings

Slice cherry peppers into rings, place into pint jars, and fill with boiling vinegar and water, half and half. Add ½ teaspoon (3 ml) salt to each pint jar, cover at once and allow your pickled peppers to seal.

Canning

Canned goods are a woman's pride; many ladies have shown me fruit that they have "put up" and the bright jars marching prettily along the inside wall of the stillroom seemed to represent an extension of self. More than security, canning garden produce fulfills a need for recognition, response and something 'new'; all very important needs of the individual in today's helter-skelter world.

The canning process was invented by a French pickler who, before

Pasteur's discoveries, sealed boiled produce in corked and tarred or waxed jars and collected Napoleon's reward for contribution to the military effort. John Mason of New Jersey invented a glass jar with a threaded top and zinc lid for household use in canning, and though his discovery and his name became well-known, the poor chap died in poverty.

For a family of 5, I put up about 50 quarts each of peaches, applesauce and green beans, 100 quarts of tomatoes, a few pears, beets, berries, pickles, sauerkraut and anything else that stumbles into my kitchen. I combine tomatoes with several low acid vegetables such as okra or squash, and I leap upon any oddball produce available to give variety. I do not can greens, corn or peas any more, they are less troublesome and better when frozen, but I used to can them using an acid solution made by mixing 2 quarts (2 liters) water, 1½ cups (375 ml) vinegar and a tablespoon (15 ml) salt. About 1½ cups (375 ml) of the solution are needed for each quart of produce. To remove acid flavor for serving, drain, rinse with cold water and soak for 2 or 3 minutes in water to cover in which ¼ teaspoon (1 ml) baking soda has been dissolved. Drain, rinse and cook the vegetables in the regular manner.

Canning garden produce, or the process of heating and subsequently sealing fruits and vegetables in jars to kill harmful bacteria such as the deadly CLOSTRIDIUM BOTULINUM which is killed above 230°F (110°C), may be done in several ways. 1. Boiling Water Bath method, which may be cold pack, that is, packing raw, cold produce into jars and then processing the jars in boiling water; or hot pack, the packing of cooked hot produce into jars before processing the jars in boiling water. 2. Canning in a pressure cooker, in which steam creates temperatures higher than boiling water, is used for processing jars of meats, poultry, fish and low acid foods. Generally speaking, the first method, the Boiling Water Bath, is used for canning high acid foods and the boiling time is for a period of from 30 minutes to 3 hours. Some extremely acid foods such as sauerkraut and tomato juice may be simply packed boiling hot into hot, sterilized jars and sealed at once.

Fundamental rules of canning apply to both Boiling Water Bath method and to pressure cooker canning. The jars and lids must be without chips or dents, and completely sterilized before using. I boil all jars and lids, keep them in simmering water until used and process the jars immediately after packing. Select sound food and after washing, peeling or precooking as directed, pack solidly, but not packed smash-tight, into hot, sterilized jars, cover with boiling liquid to within ½ inch (1 cm) of the top, work out air bubbles with a knife blade and as a general rule, add 1 teaspoon (5 ml) salt to each quart. Wipe jar lip clean with boiling water or alcohol and tighten self-sealing caps before processing. Old Mason caps should not be tightened securely until after processing. I knew this, yet carelessly tightened some zinc caps last summer and lost 3 quarts, all of them oldies. Within an hour after my jars had popped in the canner a friend stopped by and nearly blew a gasket when he saw that I had foolishly destroyed a lavender treasure that, as an old jar collector, he had been searching for. I had found the bottle on the dump, thought it pretty with its curious bubbles, used it as a flower holder for years until I needed it when the jar lid pinch was on. Tighten Mason jar lids, zinc and glass types, after the filled jars have been processed in a Boiling Water Bath.

Boiling Water Bath

This method of canning was used extensively during stillroom times and is still the simplest, most inexpensive way in which to can. For the Boiling Water Bath method, the hot, filled and lidded jars are placed on a rack in a little hot water in the canner and more hot water is poured into the canner to cover the jars. It is important to see that the water temperature and the jar temperatures are nearly the same. Cover the canner, heat and start counting time when the boiling begins. After processing for the time indicated, remove jars, check the seal, screw the old zincies tight, cool and store in an area with constant temperatures. Do not taste home canned goods to determine whether or not they are spoiled. Discard any off-colored, or unnatural smelling food and boil all canned goods that are not high acid for 10 minutes before tasting. Remember that Botulism poisoning is generally fatal.

In canning fruits, prepare a syrup in advance and heat it to boiling so that it is ready to pour over fruit that has been packed into jars.

Standard Syrup Proportions

Thin: 1 part sugar to 3 parts fruit liquid or water.
Medium: 1 part sugar to 2 parts fruit liquid or water.
Heavy: 1 part sugar to 1 part fruit liquid or water.

My favorite syrup is thinner than thin; 1 part sugar to 9 parts liquid and I substitute honey when I have it on hand, using it in the same proportion as sugar.

Boiling Water Bath Method — Fruits

Fruit	Style of pack	Processing time in Boiling Water Bath — 212°F (100°C) Quarts and Pints	Syrup
Apples	Pack in boiling syrup or water	15 minutes	Thin
Applesauce	Cook ahead, pack hot	15 minutes	None
Apricots	Heat to boiling, pack	25 minutes	Medium
Blackberries	Heat to boiling, pack	20 minutes	Medium
Blueberries	Precook, pack hot	5 minutes	Medium
Cherries	Heat to boiling, pack	25 minutes	Thick
Peaches	Heat to boiling, pack	15 minutes	Medium
Pears	Precook, pack hot	20 minutes	Medium
Plums	Precook, pack hot	20 minutes	Medium
Rhubarb	Precook, pack hot	5 minutes	Heavy
Strawberries	Precook, pack hot	5 minutes	Medium
Tomatoes	Precook, pack hot	35 minutes	None
	or cold pack	45 minutes	None
Tomato Juice	Pack hot	seal at once	None

Low acid fruits such as banana or May apple should be treated with lemon juice, ½ cup (125 ml) per quart (liter) before being processed using the Boiling Water Bath method.

Boiling Water Bath Method — Vegetables

Vegetable	Preparation before canning	Precooking time	Processing time in Boiling Water Bath 212°F (100°C)
Beans, Green	Wash, snap, string	Boil 5 minutes	3 hours at rolling boil
Beets	Wash, retain short stems	Boil 15 minutes until skin slips	3 hours if plain 1 hour if pickled
Corn	Precook, cut from cob	Boil 5 minutes	3 hours at rolling boil
Greens	Wash, pick over	Steam 15 minutes	3 hours at rolling boil
Peas	Shell	Boil 5 minutes	3 hours at rolling boil

Low acid vegetables canned in pint jars permit a greater heat penetration. Add ½ teaspoon (3 ml) salt to pints and 1 teaspoon (5 ml) salt to quarts if canned without the acid solution. Modern food processors do not recommend that low acid vegetables be canned using the Boiling Water Bath method. To insure killing bacteria these foods should be processed by the pressure cooker method of canning. Stillroom tech-

niques utilized the above processing times and I have used this method
with good results but awareness of the danger involved and caution when
using these foods is extremely important.

Pressure Cooker Method of Canning

Canning with a pressure cooker is quicker and, with low acid foods,
safer than Boiling Water Bath. Manufacturer's instructions and cautions
must be followed explicitly for safety in handling the cooker as well as for
timing and steam pressure recommendations because cookers vary in
heat and pressure. Temperatures range higher than with the Boiling
Water Bath method thus the time in process is shorter. Family sized
cookers hold only 3 quart (liter) canning jars or 4 pint (500 ml) jars but
food may be prepared and cold packed at the same time that a batch of
jars are being processed in the pressure cooker. When canning several
batches of produce, the time works out to be less with the Boiling Water
Bath. Make sure that the pressure cooker is adjusted and that the gauge
is working. Use a suitable rack and sufficient water. Exhaust the filled
jars and the cooker as directed and when the time in steam is up, release
the pressure gradually.

Pressure canning is hazardous, but if care is taken, this method saves
fuel, time and it is ideally suited for people with small gardens. If you
stagger garden plantings in order to have fresh produce throughout the
summer, the pressure cooker method facilitates canning of small
amounts of surplus food. Times under pressure vary from a few minutes
for pints of acid foods to about an hour for corn, peas and low acid
produce.

Several communities that I know sponsor federal government canning
projects that are run as cooperatives. Participants bring in their produce,
process it in the U.S. government owned pressure canners and pay their
portion of costs. People have reported that government and community
sponsored canning projects are excellent. If you are interested contact
your local or county agricultural extension service for information.

Preserving Sweets

Next to canning up a storm, my greatest summertime pleasure is
making jelly, jams and preserves. Sugar preservation of fruits has been
known since man first found out about honey, and it didn't take women
long to find out that honey or tender, quivering, translucent jelly can

steal a man's heart away. Credibility is essential in making jelly; it should look and taste like the fruit from which it came. Disillusionment correlates positively with bitterness.

The combination of heat, sugar and acid deters bacteria that enjoy fermenting and spoiling fruits. Some stillroom cooks put down preserves in stone crocks with beeswax around the lid, others wet paper with egg white and pasted it across jelly glass tops; neither method allowed jams to spoil because of the high concentration of sugars, but the sweets suffered from drying or surface molds. Today airtight containers insure success. In making jams and jellies, color, flavor, pectin and acid, plus sugar are desired, but prolonged exposure to heat alters these components: reds turn brown, volatile oils are driven off, pectin deteriorates and acids sharpen. The clue is speed; do not dawdle when making jelly. Fruits, usually made up of flavoring juices and a coloring cellulose framework, absorb little sugar when raw. Cooking changes the cell walls allowing sugar to penetrate but it is a slow process; that is why many old recipes advise that fruits be allowed to stand overnight in syrup after the preserves have been heated.

Pectin, with the right proportion of sugar and acid, forms jelly, and is found more abundantly in underripe fruit, especially in tart apples, blackberries, cranberries, grapes and quinces. To extract pectin it is necessary to boil fruit until soft as rapidly as possible, prolonged cooking destroys its jellying power, so use only enough water to cook the fruit, then strain the juice through cloths. The little flowering crab apples are an excellent source of pectin.

Acid in fruit makes jelly form but as fruits ripen acid decreases, thus a combination of ripe and partly ripe fruits is recommended.

Sugars used in proper balance with pectin and acid produce jelly but if too little sugar is used the jelly is tough, too much sugar makes it syrupy.

Equipment for jelly and jam making includes large heavy pans, a colander, a long handled spoon and a jelly bag or a square of strong muslin. Low, broad jelly glasses are best for storage and a large flat pan is needed for sterilizing the jars. Tongs for lifting hot glasses are helpful and paraffin in a can for heating is necessary unless jelly is to be vacuum sealed.

Jelly

The primary rule in jelly making is to work with small quantities. Jellies boil up to over four times their initial volume and there is nothing more frustrating than to know that you should boil jelly quickly and not be able to bring your jelly to a full rolling boil. Jelly will prove to you that it likes to be handled with individualized attention when it either boils itself over or burns its bottom. First rule: work with small lots at a time.

The first step in jelly making is to find and wash the jelly glasses and boil them in a little water for sterilizing. Next prepare the fruit by washing and sorting, cube if needed, but do not throw away the greenies or cores, they contain some pectin and acid. Of course any little squigglies in the fruit will not help. To extract juice for jelly making, boil fruit in a broad pan, crush soft fruits and stir from time to time. Berries and grapes require 5 to 10 minutes to cook and apples take about 25 minutes. Water necessary is generally 1 cup (250 ml) per pound (500 g) of apples and wild grapes, and about ¼ cup (50 ml) per pound (500 g) of berries or Concord grapes. After the fruit has boiled soft, pour into a jelling cloth that has been draped over the colander placed in a large pan in the sink. Do not forget the pan under the colander, I become very distressed when I see my juice run down the drain. It is possible to boil strong grapes or crab apples twice, then combine the 1st and 2nd juices for more jelly.

Some recipes suggest cup for cup, juice to sugar for jelly; I make jelly by mixing 4 cups juice to 3 cups sugar, stir until dissolved then boil rapidly until the jellying stage is reached. I use a heavy pan with a wide mouth so that evaporation is accelerated.

The Jellying Point

To test for the jellying point, dip a large spoon into the boiling syrup, lift the spoon so that the syrup runs off the side. When the syrup separates into two distinct droplets, watch the jelly carefully, the jellying point is getting close. When the two droplets flake or run together and sort of slither off the spoon together, which is called sheeting, remove the jelly from the heat.

Take the glasses from their boiling water, skim any foam from the jelly and pour the clear liquid into the hot, sterilized jelly glasses. As soon as the jelly is firm and well set, wipe the inside rims of the glasses with a cloth dipped in a little whiskey or boiling water to clean jelly drops and insure a better seal. Melt paraffin in a can placed in a saucepan containing water and pour hot paraffin on top of each glass. Rotate the glass before the paraffin hardens, label, date and store in a cool, dry, ant-free place. Neat rows of ants parading up the wall, across the pipe and dive-bombing your jelly shelf is disconcerting. If you discover the invasion, sprinkle the area with red pepper, clean and re-paraffin the damaged jars.

Jams

Jams are made from crushed fruit, mixed well with sugar and cooked until homogenized and thick. The standard proportion is 1 part prepared fruit to ¾ parts sugar. In boiling down small batches, use 4 cups (1 liter) prepared fruit to 3 cups (750 ml) sugar. I have found that you can expect as much jam as the amount of sugar used, thus with the above ratio your finished product would be 3 cups jam.

The first step in making jams or any preserves is to wash and sterilize jars; the second step is to find a large, heavy pan.

Blackberry Jam

Wash and pick over berries, scoop out fruit from the wash water with outstretched palms, do not drain through the colander or you will get all the little things in the bottom. Measure 4 cups (1 liter) fruit, put into the large heavy pan and add 3 cups (750 ml) sugar. Stir and mash. Usually the water clinging to the berries is sufficient to start juicing the sugar, if not, add a bit of water. Bring to a boil, stir from time to time and when thick and glassy looking, about 20 minutes, pour into hot, sterilized jars, clean lips, seal or pour over melted paraffin. Dewberries, loganberries and raspberries may be made into jam in the same manner. It generally takes 1 hour to pick a quart (liter) and 30 minutes to make 3 cups (750 ml) of jam.

Strawberry Jam

This recipe was given to me by a Florida lady who was strawberry rich; what a wonderful way in which to be wealthy!

Use 2½ cups (625 ml) sugar for each 5 cups (1.25 liters) of washed and stemmed strawberries. Place layer of berries in a bowl, cover with part of the sugar, alternate layers of sugar and berries. Allow the mixture to stand overnight. In the morning bring mixture to a simmer and cook for about 20 minutes. Do not boil hard. Remove from stove and allow mixture to stand overnight. The following day bring the jam to the simmering point for 10 minutes. Pour into hot, sterilized jars, clean the jar lips and seal or use paraffin.

Apricot or Peach Jam

Wash and dip fruit into boiling water for 3 minutes, plunge into cold water and slip off the skins. Pit and cube. To each 4 cups (1 liter) fruit add 3 cups (750 ml) sugar. Mash, let stand for 4 hours and then slowly bring to a boil. Stir and cook until fruit is clear and jam is thick, about 30 minutes. Pour boiling jam into hot, sterilized jars, wipe jar lips clean, seal at once or cover with melted paraffin. If the jam is somewhat juicy, wait until the paraffin has hardened and pour over a second layer, rotating the jar so that it will form a good seal.

FRAN'S HOT PEPPER JAM

This sparkling pepper jam was created by a sparkling young neighbor when her garden overflowed with hot peppers. A true complement to cheese and a tribute to the ingenuity of our country's young gardeners.

Preparation time: Overnight plus 6 hours. *Makes:* 3 pints (1.5 liters).

	U.S. CUSTOMARY	METRIC

Remove the stems and seeds from 4 cups (1 liter) hot red cherry peppers and chop medium fine. Cover peppers with boiling water, let stand 5 minutes. Drain and repeat. Drain well.

	U.S. CUSTOMARY	METRIC
In a large pan, boil for 30 minutes	the scalded peppers	peppers
	2 cups onions, chopped	500 ml onions
	2 cups white vinegar	500 ml vinegar
	3 cups honey	750 ml honey
	4 teaspoons salt	20 ml salt
Tie spices in a cloth bag	1 lemon, sliced thin	1 lemon
	½ teaspoon ground ginger	3 ml ginger
	4 teaspoons whole allspice	20 ml allspice

Stir from time to time while boiling. After 30 minutes, remove from heat and let stand overnight. The next day, bring the jam to a boil, stir, and reduce to the desired consistency. Pour into hot sterilized jars and seal immediately.

Fruit Butter

These old-fashioned spreads made from boiled down fruit pulp with a minimum of sugar usually require the ripest fruit and are cooked slowly for a long time.

TOMATO BUTTER

Preparation time: About 4 hours. *Makes:* 8 pints (4 liters).

	U.S. CUSTOMARY	METRIC
Scald, peel and cut up	10 pounds ripe tomatoes	5 kg tomatoes
Put into a large heavy pan and bring to boil with	2 pounds brown sugar	1 kg br. sugar
	1 quart vinegar	1 liter vinegar
	1 tablespoon salt	15 ml salt
	12 apples, peeled, cored and chopped	12 apples
	½ teaspoon cayenne pepper	2 ml cayenne
Tie in bag and add	1 tablespoon whole cloves	15 ml cloves
	2 tablespoons cinnamon bark	30 ml cinnamon
	1 tablespoon whole allspice	15 ml allspice

Boil slowly for about 3 hours or until thick, stir frequently because butters tend to sulk in the bottom of the pan and burn. When the surface swells and little puffs of steam escape like miniature volcanoes erupting, remove from the heat, fill hot, sterilized pint jars and seal immediately.

Apple Butter

Cook about 2 dozen washed, peeled, quartered and cored apples in about 2 quarts (2 liters) apple cider, juice or wine. When the pulp is thick enough to round up in a spoon, stir regularly and lower the fire. As the sauce thickens add 3 cups (750 ml) sugar, stir frequently, flavor with 1½ teaspoons (8 ml) cinnamon and ½ teaspoon (2 ml) ground cloves. The kettle will labor to puff up and boil as the butter starts to turn and when the apple butter hangs onto a tilted spoon, you know that it is done. Pour boiling hot into hot, sterilized jars to within ½ inch (1 cm) of the top, wipe jar lips with boiling water or gin and seal. If the jars do not seal, process in a Boiling Water Bath for 10 minutes. Corn bread, apple butter and milk is just about the best Sunday night supper I can imagine.

Cantalopes, grapes and peaches all make delicious and colorful butters when boiled with ⅕ their weight in sugar, a little salt and spices tied neatly in a sack. My neighbor used to boil butters in a low oven overnight and said that she had no sticking problem.

Conserves

Conserves occupied a special place on stillroom 'company' shelves, and though made similarly to jam, they usually included a mixture of fruit, raisins, oranges, plus nuts.

Rhubarb Conserve

Wash, drain and chop young rhubarb stalks, do not peel. Weigh. For each pound (500 g) rhubarb allow 4 cups (1 liter) sugar. Remove the peeling from 1 orange and 2 lemons, parboil skins for 5 minutes and drain. Discard seeds from orange and lemons and chop the pulp and skins fine. Combine with rhubarb and sugar and heat slowly until the sugar is dissolved, then heat rapidly, stirring from time to time and boiling the conserve until it is somewhat thick, about 35 minutes. While boiling, chop 1 cup (250 ml) nuts and add just before removing from the fire. Pour at once into hot, sterilized jars, wipe lips with alcohol and seal or cover with paraffin. You may wish to re-paraffin this conserve because it will not stand firm like jam, but it is great on fresh bread or for an after-the-movie snack.

Marmalade

A jellied sweet which holds suspended fruit and peel.

As students, nearly penniless, my girlfriend and I kidded an old bachelor friend along for months by nodding 'yes' when he repeatedly told us that he was going to drive us to Yosemite after Labor Day. On the first Tuesday in September our friend arrived at the dorm and neither Edith nor I had courage to tell him that we had been joking; that we possessed $2.68 between us, and that even if we wished to go with him we could not afford it. Subdued by shame we went to the Park and for 5 days and 6 nights Edith and I lived on soda crackers, Merced River water and marmalade. Pride is a wondrous and terrible thing.

Amber Marmalade

Select thickskinned citrus, equal amounts of grapefruit, oranges, and lemons, peel them, slice the peeling very thin, add cold water to cover and boil for 5 minutes. Drain. Repeat 5 minute boilings of the peelings with fresh water 3 times. Drain. Cut the fruit pulp into thin slices, remove seeds and rags, combine with the parboiled peelings and to each pressed measure of citrus add twice the quantity of water and boil rapidly for 40 minutes. Measure this mixture and add an equal measure of sugar. Add ¼ teaspoon (1 ml) salt for each 2 cups (500 ml) of the marmalade mix. Boil rapidly for 30 minutes or until it thickens and turns amber. Stir as the mixture boils down to keep it from burning. When thick and the pulp is clear and glassy remove from the fire. Pour into hot, sterilized jars making sure that each jar contains solids as well as transparent jelly. When the jars of marmalade are slightly cool stir each jar with a teaspoon to distribute the floating citrus throughout the jelly. Wipe the jar lips with alcohol and seal with paraffin. . . . If you ever go to Yosemite, take along crackers to go with a jar of your marmalade, it's a wondrous adventure.

Preserves

A fruit product made with whole small fruits that are cooked in a syrup until clear: cherry, peach, ginger pear and my favorite, damson. The standard ratio of 1 part fruit to ¾ part sugar is generally recommended and for tender fruits such as strawberries, bring the fruit to a boil in syrup, let them stand overnight and the following day boil to thicken. Firmer fruits can simply be boiled until thick.

Damson Preserves

Wash, drain, pit plums and for each 4 cups (1 liter) of damsons add 3 cups (750 ml) sugar and ½ cup (125 ml) water. Dissolve sugar in the water and bring to a boil, add the plums and boil gently at first but harder when the fruit takes on a glassy look. Stir and test and when droplets of the liquid run together and slither or sheet from the spoon, remove from the fire, pour into hot, sterilized jars, wipe the jar lips and seal or cover with paraffin.

Preserving produce, whether by fermentation or by other methods, unites man with the underlying order and harmony and meaning of life. The act of saving becomes a sign of hope and a symbol of tomorrow. Why save if there will be no tomorrow? Excessive reliance upon fast foods, the instant satisfaction of desires, distorts mans' faith in the future. Instead of gaining freedom with fingertip convenience men sink into materialistic slavery; dissension, isolation and bondage to self follows as all life becomes dry and flat.

The concept of Stillroom Cookery is more than living in harmony and in faithfulness to the earth, it embraces thoughts of not wasting even the littlest element of earthly energy or goods. It is living with, and for, and as a guardian of, the earth.

Appendixes

CHAPTER I. DOORWAYS TO THE STILLROOM

GUIDE TO BASIC FOOD EQUIVALENTS

Discrepancies in conversions are due to rounding off measurement figures in order to avoid cumbersome fractions.

Natural products often vary in size and dryness, thus measurements are approximate.

	WEIGHT (Mass)		VOLUME	
FOOD	U. S. CUSTOMARY	METRIC	U. S. CUSTOMARY	METRIC
Beans, dry	1 pound	500 g	2 cups	500 ml
Butter	1 stick	125 g	½ cup	125 ml
	9 ounces	250 g	1 cup	250 ml
	1 pound	500 g	2 cups	500 ml
Cheese, cottage	1 pound	500 g	2 cups	500 ml
fresh grated	3⅓ ounces	100 g	1 cup	250 ml
Coffee, ground	2⅘ ounces	85 g	1 cup	250 ml
	1 pound	500 g	6 cups (scant)	1.5 liters
Cornstarch	⅓ ounce	10 g	1 tablespoon	15 ml
Eggs, medium	1 dozen	725 g	2 cups	500 ml
Flour, all-purpose	1 pound	500 g	4 cups (scant)	1 liter
Fruit, dried	1 pound	500 g	2 cups	500 ml
Ground spices	¹⁄₁₂ ounce	2.5 g	1 teaspoon	5 ml
	½ ounce	15 g	2 tablespoons	30 ml
Lemon, 1 juiced			3 tablespoons	45 ml
Macaroni	1 pound	500 g	3 cups	750 ml
Meat, chopped	½ pound	225 g	1 cup	250 ml
	1 pound	500 g	2 cups	500 ml
Nuts, shelled almonds & English walnuts	¼ pound	125 g	1 cup	250 ml
Peanuts, chopped	½ pound	225 g	1 cup	250 ml
Raisins	1 pound	500 g	2 cups (generous)	530 ml
Rice	9 ounces	250 g	1 cup (generous)	275 ml
Salt	⅙ ounce	5 g	1 teaspoon	5 ml
	½ ounce	15 g	1 tablespoon	15 ml
	8 ounces	225 g	1 cup	250 ml
	1 pound	500 g	2 cups	500 ml
Sugar	1 pound	500 g	2 cups	500 ml

BRIEF GUIDE TO METRIC MEASUREMENTS IN COOKING

Volume.

To simplify conversion, the different dry and liquid measurements of volume will be abandoned and the liter and quart measure will be adopted. The customary cup will be replaced by the metric cup in which there will be no difference between dry and liquid measure. The metric cup will be ¼ of a liter. There are 1000 milliliters (1000 ml) in a liter and 250 milliliters (250 ml) in a metric cup. A milliliter (ml) holds about ⅕ of a teaspoon but for ease in converting from customary measures a milliliter will hold ¼ teaspoon.

Volume:

¼ teaspoon	1 ml	¾ cup	175 ml
½ teaspoon	2 ml	1 cup	250 ml
1 teaspoon	5 ml	1 pint	500 ml
1 tablespoon	15 ml	1 quart	1 liter
⅛ cup	25 ml	1 gallon	4 liters
¼ cup	50 ml	10 gallons	40 liters
½ cup	125 ml		

The metric system has only one unit for the unit of capacity or volume: the liter, and decimal fractions thereof are called milliliter (ml).

Weight.

To avoid the need for using household metric scales and weighing ingredients, the use of volume metric measures, those that measure capacity as listed above, will be adopted whenever possible. However, we will be buying meat by the kilogram (kg) instead of by the pound and cheese by the gram (g) instead of by the ounce.

Weight:

	½ ounce	15 g
	1 ounce	30 g
	3 ounces	100 g
¼ pound	4 ounces	125 g
½ pound	8 ounces	225 g
	9 ounces	250 g
1 pound	16 ounces	500 g
2 pounds	32 ounces	1000 g or 1 kilogram (kg)

The principal unit of weight in the metric system is the gram (g), a little more than the weight of a paper clip. A kilogram is about 2.2 pounds.

Length.

Measurement of baking pan sizes and the dimensions of a casserole or sausage will be a decimal fraction of a meter (m) which is a little longer than a yard. A centimeter (cm) is 0.01 meter (m) about the width of a paper clip.

Size in length:

½ inch	1 cm
1 inch	2.5 cm
2 inches	5 cm

STILLROOM COOKERY TEMPERATURES

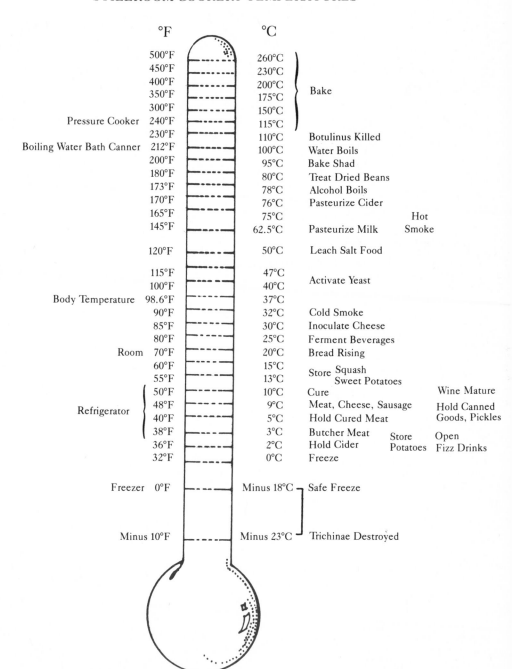

°F		°C	
	500°F	260°C	⎫
	450°F	230°C	⎪
	400°F	200°C	⎬ Bake
	350°F	175°C	⎪
	300°F	150°C	⎪
Pressure Cooker	240°F	115°C	⎭
	230°F	110°C	Botulinus Killed
Boiling Water Bath Canner	212°F	100°C	Water Boils
	200°F	95°C	Bake Shad
	180°F	80°C	Treat Dried Beans
	173°F	78°C	Alcohol Boils
	170°F	76°C	Pasteurize Cider
	165°F	75°C	Hot
	145°F	62.5°C	Pasteurize Milk Smoke
	120°F	50°C	Leach Salt Food
	115°F	47°C	Activate Yeast
	100°F	40°C	
Body Temperature	98.6°F	37°C	
	90°F	32°C	Cold Smoke
	85°F	30°C	Inoculate Cheese
	80°F	25°C	Ferment Beverages
Room	70°F	20°C	Bread Rising
	60°F	15°C	Store Squash
	55°F	13°C	Sweet Potatoes
	50°F	10°C	Cure Wine Mature
Refrigerator	48°F	9°C	Meat, Cheese, Sausage Hold Canned
	40°F	5°C	Hold Cured Meat Goods, Pickles
	38°F	3°C	Butcher Meat Store Open
	36°F	2°C	Hold Cider Potatoes Fizz Drinks
	32°F	0°C	Freeze
Freezer	0°F	Minus 18°C	Safe Freeze
	Minus 10°F	Minus 23°C	Trichinae Destroyed

STILLROOM SUGGESTIONS

Salt proportions, rule of thumb:

1 teaspoon (5 ml) salt to 1 quart (1 liter) soup.

1 teaspoon (5 ml) salt to 2 cups (500 ml) hot cereal.

1 teaspoon (5 ml) salt to 1 pound (500 g) fresh meat.

1 teaspoon (5 ml) salt to 4 cups (1 liter) flour in dough.

1 teaspoon (5 ml) salt to 1 pound (500 g) cottage cheese.

8 pounds (4 kg) salt to 100 pounds (50 kg) cured meat.

1 teaspoon (5 ml) salt to 1 quart (1 liter) canned vegetables.

1 pound (500 g) salt to 4½ quarts (4.5 liters) water for a 10% pickling brine.

Substitutes:

⅞ cup (220 ml) oil or shortening plus ½ teaspoon (2 ml) salt for 1 cup (250 ml) butter.

3 tablespoons (45 ml) cocoa plus ½ tablespoon (7 ml) oil for 1 square (30 g) chocolate.

4 tablespoons (60 ml) nonfat dry milk plus 2 teaspoons (10 ml) oil and 1 cup (250 ml) water for 1 cup (250 ml) whole milk.

Hints:

To flavor fried sweets or doughnuts, add a few whole cloves to the frying oil.

To bake potatoes quickly heat them in boiling water before baking.

If pie juice runs into the oven, shake salt over the spill to reduce the scorched smell.

To retard egg white from leaking when boiling cracked eggs, add vinegar to the water.

Place a bar of milk chocolate on top of the cake as soon as it is taken from the oven, spread as it melts for a smooth icing.

Helpful References:

Armbruster, Dr. Gertrude, (ed.) *Metric Measurement of Foods*. Division of Nutritional Sciences. Ithaca, N.Y.: Cornell U. 1975.

U.S. Department of Commerce. *What About Metric?* National Bureau of Standards. Washington; G.P.O., 1974. $1.10. Address: Washington, D.C. 20402.

Metric information available through:
National Bureau of Standards
Washington, D.C. 20234

American National Metric Council
1625 Massachusetts Ave., N.W.
Washington, D.C. 20036

American National Standards
1430 Broadway
New York, N.Y. 10018

American Society for Testing
1916 Race Street
Philadelphia, Pa. 19103

TEMPERATURE CONVERSION TABLE: FAHRENHEIT TO CELSIUS

To Convert °F	To °C	°F	°C	°F	°C	°F	°C
−10	−23.33	30	−1.11	70	21.11	110	43.33
−9	−22.78	31	−0.56	71	21.67	111	43.89
−8	−22.22	32	0	72	22.22	112	44.44
−7	−21.67	33	.56	73	22.78	113	45
−6	−21.11	34	1.11	74	23.33	114	45.56
−5	−20.56	35	1.67	75	23.89	115	46.11
−4	−20	36	2.22	76	24.44	116	46.67
−3	−19.44	37	2.78	77	25	117	47.22
−2	−18.89	38	3.33	78	25.56	118	47.78
−1	−18.33	39	3.89	79	26.11	119	48.33
0	−17.78	40	4.44	80	26.67	120	48.89
1	−17.22	41	5	81	27.22	121	49.44
2	−16.67	42	5.56	82	27.78	122	50
3	−16.11	43	6.11	83	28.33	123	50.56
4	−15.56	44	6.67	84	28.89	124	51.11
5	−15	45	7.22	85	29.44	125	51.67
6	−14.44	46	7.78	86	30	126	52.22
7	−13.89	47	8.33	87	30.56	127	52.78
8	−13.33	48	8.89	88	31.11	128	53.33
9	−12.78	49	9.44	89	31.67	129	53.89
10	−12.22	50	10	90	32.22	130	54.44
11	−11.67	51	10.56	91	32.78	131	55
12	−11.11	52	11.11	92	33.33	132	55.56
13	−10.56	53	11.67	93	33.89	133	56.11
14	−10	54	12.22	94	34.44	134	56.67
15	−9.44	55	12.78	95	35	135	57.22
16	−8.89	56	13.33	96	35.56	136	57.78
17	−8.33	57	13.89	97	36.11	137	58.33
18	−7.78	58	14.44	98	36.67	138	58.89
19	−7.22	59	15	99	37.22	139	59.44
20	−6.67	60	15.56	100	37.78	140	60
21	−6.11	61	16.11	101	38.33	141	60.56
22	−5.56	62	16.67	102	38.89	142	61.11
23	−5	63	17.22	103	39.44	143	61.67
24	−4.44	64	17.78	104	40	144	62.22
25	−3.89	65	18.33	105	40.56	145	62.78
26	−3.33	66	18.89	106	41.11	146	63.33
27	−2.78	67	19.44	107	41.67	147	63.89
28	−2.22	68	20	108	42.22	148	64.44
29	−1.67	69	20.56	109	42.78	149	65

150	65.56	195	90.56	240	115.56	285	140.56
151	66.11	196	91.11	241	116.11	286	141.11
152	66.67	197	91.67	242	116.67	287	141.67
153	67.22	198	92.22	243	117.22	288	142.22
154	67.78	199	92.78	244	117.78	289	142.78
155	68.33	200	93.33	245	118.33	290	143.33
156	68.89	201	93.89	246	118.89	291	143.89
157	69.44	202	94.44	247	119.44	292	144.44
158	70	203	95	248	120	293	145
159	70.56	204	95.56	249	120.56	294	145.56
160	71.11	205	96.11	250	121.11	295	146.11
161	71.67	206	96.67	251	121.67	296	146.67
162	72.22	207	97.22	252	122.22	297	147.22
163	72.78	208	97.78	253	122.78	298	147.78
164	73.33	209	98.33	254	123.33	299	148.33
165	73.89	210	98.89	255	123.89	300	148.89
166	74.44	211	99.44	256	124.44	301	149.44
167	75	212	100	257	125	302	150
168	75.56	213	100.56	258	125.56	303	150.56
169	76.11	214	101.11	259	126.11	304	151.11
170	76.67	215	101.67	260	126.67	305	151.67
171	77.22	216	102.22	261	127.22	306	152.22
172	77.78	217	102.78	262	127.78	307	152.78
173	78.33	218	103.33	263	128.33	308	153.33
174	78.89	219	103.89	264	128.89	309	153.89
175	79.44	220	104.44	265	129.44	310	154.44
176	80	221	105	266	130	311	155
177	80.56	222	105.56	267	130.56	312	155.56
178	81.11	223	106.11	268	131.11	313	156.11
179	81.67	224	106.67	269	131.67	314	156.67
180	82.22	225	107.22	270	132.22	315	157.22
181	82.78	226	107.78	271	132.78	316	157.78
182	83.33	227	108.33	272	133.33	317	158.33
183	83.89	228	108.89	273	133.89	318	158.89
184	84.44	229	109.44	274	134.44	319	159.44
185	85	230	110	275	135	320	160
186	85.56	231	110.56	276	135.56	321	160.56
187	86.11	232	111.11	277	136.11	322	161.11
188	86.67	233	111.67	278	136.67	323	161.67
189	87.22	234	112.22	279	137.22	324	162.22
190	87.78	235	112.78	280	137.78	325	162.78
191	88.33	236	113.33	281	138.33	326	163.33
192	88.89	237	113.89	282	138.89	327	163.89
193	89.44	238	114.44	283	139.44	328	164.44
194	90	239	115	284	140	329	165

330	165.56	375	190.56	420	215.56	465	240.56
331	166.11	376	191.11	421	216.11	466	241.11
332	166.67	377	191.67	422	216.67	467	241.67
333	167.22	378	192.22	423	217.22	468	242.22
334	167.78	379	192.78	424	217.78	469	242.78
335	168.33	380	193.33	425	218.33	470	243.33
336	168.89	381	193.89	426	218.89	471	243.89
337	169.44	382	194.44	427	219.44	472	244.44
338	170	383	195	428	220	473	245
339	170.56	384	195.56	429	220.56	474	245.56
340	171.11	385	196.11	430	221.11	475	246.11
341	171.67	386	196.67	431	221.67	476	246.67
342	172.22	387	197.22	432	222.22	477	247.22
343	172.78	388	197.78	433	222.78	478	247.78
344	173.33	389	198.33	434	223.33	479	248.33
345	173.89	390	198.89	435	223.89	480	248.89
346	174.44	391	199.44	436	224.44	481	249.44
347	175	392	200	437	225	482	250
348	175.56	393	200.56	438	225.56	483	250.56
349	176.11	394	201.11	439	226.11	484	251.11
350	176.67	395	201.67	440	226.67	485	251.67
351	177.22	396	202.22	441	227.22	486	252.22
352	177.78	397	202.78	442	227.78	487	252.78
353	178.33	398	203.33	443	228.33	488	253.33
354	178.89	399	203.89	444	228.89	489	253.89
355	179.44	400	204.44	445	229.44	490	254.44
356	180	401	205	446	230	491	255
357	180.56	402	205.56	447	230.56	492	255.56
358	181.11	403	206.11	448	231.11	493	256.11
359	181.67	404	206.67	449	231.67	494	256.67
360	182.22	405	207.22	450	232.22	495	257.22
361	182.78	406	207.78	451	232.78	496	257.78
362	183.33	407	208.33	452	233.33	497	258.33
363	183.89	408	208.89	453	233.89	498	258.89
364	184.44	409	209.44	454	234.44	499	259.44
365	185	410	210	455	235	500	260
366	185.56	411	210.56	456	235.56		
367	186.11	412	211.11	457	236.11		
368	186.67	413	211.67	458	236.67		
369	187.22	414	212.22	459	237.22		
370	187.78	415	212.78	460	237.78		
371	188.33	416	213.33	461	238.33		
372	188.89	417	213.89	462	238.89		
373	189.44	418	214.44	463	239.44		
374	190	419	215	464	240		

CHAPTER II. CHEESE AND SAVORY STILLROOM MILK PRODUCTS

Native milk coagulation plants:

Cleavers, *Galium aparine*
Nettles, *Urtica dioica*
Jerusalem artichoke flowers, *Helianthus tuberosus*

Where to purchase rennet:

CHR. HANSEN's LABORATORY, INC.
9015 W. Maple
Milwaukee, Wisconsin 53214

Canada:
HORAN-LALLY CO. LTD.
Rexdale, Ontario

Cheesecloth may be purchased in grocery markets under cleaning materials.

A dairy-type thermometer that measures temperatures between 70°F (20°C) and 173°F (78°C) may be purchased at hardware stores.

Where to purchase cheesemaking materials, presses and kits:

HOMECRAFTS
111 Stratford Road
Winston-Salem, N.C. 27104

Helpful References:

Flake, Lue Dean Jr. *Kitchen Cheesemaking.* Harrisburg, Pa. 17105: Stackpole Books, 1975.

Ehle, John. *The Cheeses and Wines of England and France with Notes on Irish Whiskey.* New York: Harper and Row, 1968.

U.S. Department of Agriculture. *Making Cottage Cheese at Home.* Home and Garden Bulletin No. 129. Washington: G.P.O., 1967.

U.S. Department of Agriculture. *Cheese Varieties.* Agriculture Handbook No. 54. Washington: G.P.O., 1953.

U.S. Department of Agriculture. *A Soft Cheese of the Bel Paese Type.* Agriculture Circular No. 522. Washington: G.P.O., 1939.

U.S. Department of Agriculture. *Making American Cheddar Cheese.* Agriculture Circular No. 880. Washington: G.P.O., 1951.

U.S. Department of Agriculture. *The Manufacture of Camembert Cheese.* Agriculture Bulletin No. 1171. Washington: G.P.O., 1924.

If the Government Printing Office cannot supply the Agriculture Department material, write to the U.S. Department of Agriculture, National Agricultural Library, Photoduplication Section, Beltsville, Maryland 20705 and ask for copying charges for the periodical desired.

CHAPTER III. RAISED DOUGHS AND YEASTY TREATS

Whole and cracked grain flours can be purchased at most natural food stores.

Where to purchase stonegrinding mills:

LEE MILLS
2023 West Wisconsin Avenue
Milwaukee, Wisconsin

ALL-GRAIN COMPANY
425 West Main
Tremonton, Utah

Bakers' yeast may be purchased in bulk at bakers' supply companies, usually listed in the phone book. The Instant Blend or Active Dry Yeasts that are sold in quarter ounce packages in grocery stores are suitable for baking.

Problem breads:

Large air holes are usually caused by not kneading all of the gas bubbles out of the dough before putting it into the pan. Knead gently but thoroughly each time.

Limp crusts may be caused by underbaking. Bake at a higher temperature for a longer time.

Crumbling is often caused by bread being allowed to rise too long. Room temperature and humidity affect rising time. Judge by the size of the dough.

Mold spores, usually airborne, are killed by heating suspect or infected bread in the oven. Wash and air bread box after infection.

Bread will not rise properly if ingredients in the dough are too hot, over 120°F (50°C) or if temperatures of ingredients are too cold, 55°F (13°C) or under.

Ropiness in bread, a soft, uncooked streak in the center may be caused by bacteria that infects flour, yeast or the liquid. Boil utensils and rinse in a 3 part water to 1 part vinegar mix. Sticky middle can also be caused by oven temperature, so make sure the oven bakes evenly.

Sourness in bread is caused by the excessive growth of lactic acid bacteria. Shorten the bread rising period.

Heaviness may be caused by inadequate gluten in the flour used, mix non-wheat flours with all-purpose wheat flour.

Helpful References:

Rosenvall, Vernice G. et al. *Wheat for Man.* Salt Lake City: Bookcraft, 1975.

U.S. Department of Agriculture. *Homemade Bread.* Farmers' Bulletin No. 1775. Washington: G.P.O., 1942.

CHAPTER IV. BEVERAGES: SOFT SPURIOUS AND STRONG

Where to buy apple and grape presses:

HOMECRAFTS
111 Stratford Road
Winston-Salem, N.C. 27104

Where to buy brewers' yeast, malt, beermaking supplies:

AMERICAN HOME BREWS, Inc.
Rochester, New York 14615

HERTER's INC.
Waseca, Minnesota 56093

Where to buy winemaking equipment and supplies:

VINO CORP.
80 Commerce Drive
Rochester, New York 14623

E.S. KRAUS
307 East Cherry Street
P.O. Box 451
Nevada, Missouri 64772

Where to buy flavorings and extracts:

NICHOLS GARDEN NURSERY
1190 N. Pacific Hwy.
Albany, Oregon 97321

Malt extract in 3 pound (1.5 kg) cans may be purchased at many supermarkets, and is priced considerably lower than in specialty shops.

Siphon hoses, crocks, corks, caps, capper and the makings for fermentation locks may be purchased at rural hardware stores.

Wine permit:

Form 1541
Registration for Production of Wine for Family Use.
Department of the Treasury
Bureau of Alcohol, Tobacco and Firearms
2 Penn Center Plaza
Philadelphia, Pa. 19102

or write to your Regional Commissioner, Alcohol and Tobacco Tax.

Helpful References:

U.S. Department of Agriculture. *Cidermaking.* Farmers' Bulletin No. 2125. Washington: G.P.O., 1970.

Bravery, H.E. *Home Brewing.* N.Y.: Gramercy Publishing, 1966.

Eckhardt, Fred. *A Treatise on Lager Beers.* Portland Oregon: Hobby Winemaker, 2758 N.E. Broadway, 1975.

Turner, B.C.A., Berry, C.J.J., Marshal, A.I. *The Winemaker's Companion,* Toronto: Mills & Boon, 101 Duncan Mill Road, Don Mills, Canada, 1972.

CHAPTER V. VINAIGRES BONS AND SAUCY SECRETS

Good, clear vinegar of 40 to 60 grain strength, 4 to 6% acetic acid may be purchased at most grocery stores.

HERB LADY:

Florence Williamson
Oak Forest
Woodville, Virginia 22749

Spices and herbs may be purchased through local coffee, tea and spice companies and many supermarkets, or:

WASHINGTON CATHEDRAL HERB SHOP
Wisconsin and Massachusetts Avenue
Washington, D.C.

As a reference, less common spices, flavorings and herbs are listed:

Name	Part used and description	Preparation
Angelica	Crystallized stalks. Fragrant and sweet.	Cream cheese dressing, cake icing.
Arrowroot	Root. Glutinous, flavorless.	Thickening.
Burnet	Herb. Cucumber flavored.	Salad dressings, drinks.
Cardamon	Seeds. Aromatic, peppery.	Tomato sauces, sausage.
Chervil	Leaves. Mildly parsley-like.	Meat sauces, soups, salads, omelettes.
Coriander	Seeds. Semi-sweet, citrus.	Pickles, sausages.
Cumin	Fruits. Pungent, gingery.	Chili sauce, tomatoes, salad dressings.
Curry Powder	Spice mixture. Warm, heavy.	Sauces of Africa/India.
Fennel	Seeds. Licorice flavored.	Fish dressings.
Leeks	Tuber. Onion-like.	Salads and soups.
Mace	Outer coat of nutmeg. Mild spice, nut-like flavor.	Meat sauces.
Mallow	Root. Mild, mucilaginous.	Thickening.
Paprika	Seeds of sweet pepper.	Goulash, dressings.
Saffron	Flowers. Yellow, pungent.	Sauce coloring, rice.
Turmeric	Root. Spicy as ginger.	Sauces for lamb.

Helpful References:

David, Elizabeth. *Spices, Salt and Aromatics in the English Kitchen.* Middlesex, England: Penguin Books, Ltd., 1970.

Crowhurst, Adrienne. *The Flower Cookbook.* New York, New York: Lancer Books, Inc., 1973.

CHAPTER VI. CURED MEATS

Buy dry sugar cure or smoked sugar cure products for preserving meat at rural grocery stores, hardware stores or write to:

MORTON SALT COMPANY
110 N. Wacker Drive
Chicago, Illinois 60606

Saltpeter can be bought in the drug store.

Commercial sausage casings may be purchased from butcher shops and meat processing plants. Some Independent Grocers' Association stores, IGA, handle sausage casings for retail trade.

Sausage grinders and stuffers may be bought in hardware stores and in the houseware sections of department stores or write to:

UNION MANUFACTURING CO.
New Britain, Connecticut

Commercial smokers may be purchased from houseware sections of large department stores or write to:

LUHR JENSEN AND SONS, INC.
Hood River, Oregon

Helpful references:
Government publications may be ordered through the Superintendent of Documents, G.P.O., Washington, D.C. 20402.

McKensie, Donald S. *Prepared Meat Product Manufacturing.* For information write to the American Meat Institute, 1600 Wilson Blvd., Arlington, Virginia.

U.S. Department of Agriculture. *Beef and Lamb in Family Meals.* Home and Garden Bulletin No. 118. Washington: G.P.O., 1967. 15¢.

U.S. Department of Agriculture. *Freezing Meat and Poultry for Home Use.* Home and Garden Bulletin No. 15. Washington: G.P.O., 1954. 15¢.

U.S. Department of Agriculture. *Home Canning of Meat and Poultry.* Home and Garden Bulletin No. 106, Washington: G.P.O., 1969. 15¢.

U.S. Department of Agriculture. *Meat for Thrifty Meals.* Home and Garden Bulletin No. 27. Washington: G.P.O., 1953. 20¢.

U.S. Department of Agriculture. *Protecting Home-Cured Meat from Insects.* Home and Garden Bulletin No. 109. Washington: G.P.O., 1970. 10¢.

U.S. Department of Agriculture. *Slaughtering, Cutting and Processing Beef on the Farm.* Farmers' Bulletin 2209; *Lamb.* Bulletin 2152; *Pork,* Farmers' Bulletin No. 2138. All three published in Washington: G.P.O., 20¢.

CHAPTER VII. FISH AND FOWL

An oyster knife with which to open live oysters may be purchased at most coastal hardware stores.

Fish scalers may be bought at most hardware stores.

Quicklime may be purchased at hardware and rural building supply stores.

Helpful References:

Pamphlets published by Seafood Marketing Authority, Dept. of Economic Development, 2525 Reva Road, Annapolis, Md. 21401.

Day, Bunny. *Hook 'em Cook 'em.* New York: Funk and Wagnalls, 1968.

U.S. Department of Agriculture. *Poultry in Family Meals.* Home and Garden Bulletin No. 110. Washington: G.P.O., 1967. 15¢.

U.S. Department of Agriculture. *Eggs in Family Meals.* Home and Garden Bulletin No. 103. Washington: G.P.O., 1968. 15¢.

CHAPTER VIII. GARDEN FOODS

STILLROOM GARDEN PLANTING CHART — FAMILY OF 5

VEGETABLE	Amount of Seed or Plants for 50 foot row		*May be planted	Days to Harvest after Seeding or planting
	Approximate		Approximate	Approximate
Bean, Lima bush	6 oz.	(180 g)	May 10	65 to 75
				48 to 54
Bean, Snap bush	8 oz.	(225 g)	May 1	48 to 54
				48 to 54
Bean, Snap pole	5 oz.	(150 g)	May 15	60 to 64
Beet	½ oz.	(15 g)	April 15	58 to 68
Broccoli	25 plants		April 1	60 to 80
Brussels Sprouts	25 plants		April 1	90
				90
Cabbage	50 plants		March 25	68 to 95
				68 to 95
Cabbage, Chinese	¼ oz.	(8 g)	April 1	80
Carrot	¼ oz.	(8 g)	April 1	70 to 75
				70 to 75
Chard	½ oz.	(15 g)	April 15	60
Corn	2 oz.	(60 g)	May 1	65 to 95
				65 to 95
Cucumber	¼ oz.	(8 g)	May 10	62 to 68
Eggplant	25 plants		May 10	80 to 100
Endive	½ oz.	(15 g)	April 1	85 to 90
Kale	¼ oz.	(8 g)	March 25	55
				55
Lettuce	¼ oz.	(8 g)	April 15	47 to 86
				47
Melon	½ oz.	(8 g)	May 10	84 to 90
Okra	1 oz.	(30 g)	May 10	56 to 58
				56 to 58
Onion sets	1 lb.	(500 g)	April 1	70 to 80
Parsley	⅛ oz.	(4 g)	April 1	70
Parsnip	¼ oz.	(8 g)	April 1	100 to 120
Pea	8 oz.	(225 g)	April 1	60 to 75
Pepper	25 plants		May 10	65 to 70
Potatoes	40 lbs. in 12 rows	(20 kg)	March 25	100 to 120

VEGETABLE	Amount of Seed or Plants for 50 foot row		*May be planted	Days to Harvest after Seeding or planting
	Approximate		Approximate	Approximate
Pumpkin	¼ oz.	(8 g)	May 10	106 to 112
Radish	¼ oz.	(8 g)	April 1	22 to 28
Spinach	½ oz.	(15 g)	April 1	46 to 48
				46 to 48
Squash, Summer	¼ oz.	(8 g)	May 10	48 to 50
Squash, Winter	¼ oz.	(8 g)	May 10	80 to 105
Sweet Potato	50 plants		May 10	120
Tomato	100 plants in 4 rows		May 10	70 to 90
Turnip	½ oz.	(15 g)	March 25	50 to 55
				50 to 55

*For temperate zone, areas having about 160 to 200 growing days.

Helpful References:

U.S. Department of Agriculture. *Green Vegetables for Good Eating.* Home and Garden Bulletin No. 41. Washington: G.P.O., 1964.

U.S. Department of Agriculture. *Root Vegetables in Everyday Meals.* Home and Garden Bulletin No. 33. Washington: G.P.O., 1963.

U.S. Department of Agriculture. *Potatoes in Popular Ways.* Home and Garden Bulletin No. 55. Washington: G.P.O., 1962.

U.S. Department of Agriculture. *Storing Vegetables and Fruits.* Home and Garden Bulletin No. 119. Washington: G.P.O., 1970. 15¢.

Unusual Seeds available through:

NICHOLS GARDEN NURSERY
1190 North Pacific Hwy.
Albany, Oregon 97321

THOMPSON AND MORGAN
Ipswich, England

CHAPTER IX. DRY STAPLES AND ENERGY SAVERS

Drying frames for vegetables and fruits may be made from discarded wooden storm windows.

A yellow powdered sulphur sometimes called Flowers of Sulphur or flour sulphur may be purchased at most drug stores.

Steamers, large pans with a rack and a tight lid, are available at household goods sections of many large department stores.

Cracked grain mills may be purchased from:
LEE ENGINEERING COMPANY
2023 West Wisconsin Avenue
Milwaukee, Wisconsin

Hand mills from:
QUAKER CITY MILLS
4059 Ridge Avenue
Philadelphia, Pa.

Seed sprouters are available at some natural food stores.

Herb dealers:
To buy herbs and teas:
INDIANA BOTANIC GARDENS
P.O. Box 5
Hammond, Indiana 46325

Where to sell roots, herbs and pollen:
GREER LABORATORY, INC.
P.O. Box 800
Lenoir, North Carolina 28645

Helpful References:

U.S. Department of Agriculture. *Sun Dry Your Fruits and Vegetables.* Federal Extension Service. Compiled by Helen Strow with technical assistance of Dr. Evelyn Spindler for the Home Economics Extension Worker. Issued July, 1958.

U.S. Department of Agriculture. *Dry Beans, Peas, Lentils.* Leaflet No. 326. Washington: G.P.O.

Fernald, Merrit L., Kinsey, A.C. and Rollins, Reed C. *Edible Wild Plants of Eastern North America.* New York: Harper and Row, 1958.

Gibbons, Euell. *Stalking the Healthful Herb.* New York: David McKay, 1970.

CHAPTER X. PRESERVING STILLROOM PRODUCE

Salt to be used in pickling should be plain, not iodized or flavored, purchased at most grocery stores.

A Salinometer, an instrument for measuring the salt strength of a brine, is useful and available at chemical apparatus suppliers.

To make a brine, salt is dissolved in a small volume of water and water is added to make the required solution. 2 cups (500 ml) salt dissolved in 9 pints (4.5 liters) water makes approximately a 10% brine that is strong enough to float a fresh egg. Fermentation proceeds slowly in 10% brine, pickles will not spoil in a brine maintained at this strength. 1 cup (250 ml) salt dissolved in 9 pints (4.5 liters) water makes approximately a 5% brine which permits rapid fermentation. Vegetables kept in 5% brine will spoil within a few weeks if air is not excluded. Fermentation stops in a 20% brine. The volume of brine necessary to cover vegetables is about half the volume of the material to be fermented: if you have 2 gallons (8 liters) of pickles to be fermented, 1 gallon (4 liters) of brine is required.

TROUBLED PICKLES

Difficulty	Causes	Remedy
Dull color	Poor quality produce or pickles not well cured.	Get good product. Keep brine strong enough and leave pickles in brine until all bubbles disappear.
Whitish or opaque spots	Pickles not well cured.	Keep pickles covered with brine of the right strength until fermentation stops.
Dark	Too much spice, cooked too long or too much spice in jar when packed.	Use whole spices in a loose bag and have good proportions.
Blackening of pickles	Hard water or iron in water.	Use soft water for brine.
Strong bitter taste	Cooked vinegar too long with spices.	Do not boil spices with vinegar more than 30 minutes.
Slippery pickles	Bacteria; brine too weak or did not cover pickles. Sometimes vinegar is too weak or pickles overcooked in vinegar.	Once soft, cannot be made firm. Keep brine strong by adding extra salt. Do not stir pickles while curing. Have the right strength vinegar.
Scum on pickles	Wild yeasts on surface of brine may destroy acidity of brine.	Skim often.

| Shriveled pickles | Placing too quickly in brine, sugar solution or vinegar, not allowing fruit to plump. | Use weaker solutions at first. Heat slowly. Plump in syrup overnight. |

Boiling Water Bath Canner with rack and lid available at most hardware and department stores.

Canner should be deep enough to have 1 inch (2 cm) of water over the tops of the jars.

Steam Pressure Canners are available in houseware departments of large stores.

Follow the manufacturers' directions, overcooking will cause mushy produce.

YIELD OF CANNED FRUIT FROM FRESH

		Canned:
Apples	1 bushel, 48 pounds about 3 pounds	16 to 20 quarts 1 quart
Berries	1 crate, 24 quarts 5 to 8 cups	12 to 18 quarts 1 quart
Cherries	1 bushel, 56 pounds 6 to 8 cups	22 to 32 quarts 1 quart
Peaches	1 bushel, 48 pounds 2 pounds	18 to 24 quarts 1 quart
Pears	1 bushel, 50 pounds 2 pounds	20 to 25 quarts 1 quart
Plums	1 bushel, 56 pounds 2 pounds	24 to 30 quarts 1 quart
Tomatoes	1 bushel, 53 pounds about 3 pounds	15 to 20 quarts 1 quart

VEGETABLES

Corn in husk Peas in pod Limas in pod	1 bushel, 32 pounds	6 to 8 quarts
Snap beans	1 bushel, 30 pounds	15 to 20 quarts
Beets	1 bushel, 52 pounds	17 to 20 quarts

Helpful References:

Single copies of the following are available free by writing U.S. Department of Agriculture, Washington, D. C. 20250.

Home Canning of Fruits and Vegetables, Home and Garden Bulletin 8.
Home Freezing of Fruits and Vegetables, Home and Garden Bulletin 10.
Making Pickles and Relishes at Home, Home and Garden Bulletin 92.
How to Make Jellies, Jams and Preserves, Home and Garden Bulletin 56.

Index

275